To Ken Thompson
with gratitude,
Tony Pearce

Democratic Ideals and Reality

DEMOCRATIC IDEALS
AND REALITY

HALFORD J. MACKINDER

With additional papers

Edited and with an introduction by

Anthony J. Pearce

*Assistant Professor of Government
New York University*

The Norton Library

W · W · NORTON & COMPANY · INC

NEW YORK

PREFACE

THIS book, whatever its value, is the outcome of more than the merely feverous thought of war time; the ideas upon which it is based were published in outline a good dozen years ago. In 1904, in a paper on "The Geographical Pivot of History," read before the Royal Geographical Society, I sketched the World-Island and the Heartland; and in 1905 I wrote in the *National Review* on the subject of "Man-Power as a Measure of National and Imperial Strength," an article which I believe first gave vogue to the term Man-Power. In that term is implicit not only the idea of fighting strength but also that of productivity, rather than wealth, as the focus of economic reasoning. If I now venture to write on these themes at somewhat greater length, it is because I feel that the war has established, and not shaken, my former points of view.

H. J. M.

1st February, 1919.

CONTENTS

INTRODUCTION

HALFORD J. MACKINDER'S *Democratic Ideals and Reality* is a masterly analysis of the permanent strategic factors which have governed all struggles for world empire. First published in 1919 as a warning to the peacemakers at Versailles, the book was largely ignored in the West until the Second World War. Mackinder must have anticipated this neglect; for, echoing Pericles, he knew that "Democracy refuses to think strategically unless and until compelled to do so for purposes of defense."[1] The enemies of democracy were not so reluctant to seize upon the British geographer's ideas, twisting them from the frame of peace into the guidelines of conquest. Karl Haushofer—founder of the German school of geopolitics, counsellor to the Japanese militarists, one-time adviser to Stalin, and the "geographical conscience" of Adolf Hitler—took his fundamental conceptions from Mackinder, considering him the author of "the greatest of all geographical world views."[2] But England and America refused to think strategically until forced to do so by German vengeance and Japanese ambition. A few months after Pearl Harbor *Democratic Ideals and Reality* was reissued in America, where it immediately assumed its rightful place as the most authoritative exposition of world strategy in the English language. The present edition of this book makes available to a new gen-

[1] H. J. Mackinder, *Democratic Ideals and Reality*, p. 23.
[2] Quoted in E. W. Gilbert's introduction to Sir Halford J. Mackinder, *The Scope and Methods of Geography and The Geographical Pivot of History* (London, 1951).

eration a classic analysis of international relations, which provides remarkable insights into the global struggle between the Western democracies and Asian communism.

Writing when the European sea-empires were at the climax of their power, Mackinder's greatest single accomplishment was to fix in Western minds the unity and potential of the land mass of Asia, particularly its most prominent natural feature, that huge northern region in which the rivers run into the ice-locked Arctic or into the land-locked Caspian and Aral Seas. It was for this region, impenetrable to the fleets of Western sea power, that Mackinder coined the famous name, "Heartland." From East to West the Heartland is traversed by a continuous lowland plain; and through this great corridor waves of mobile horsemen had ridden for centuries, robbing and conquering the settled lands of Europe, Arabia, India and China. Viewed from within the Heartland, all these settled, historic lands appear to be only so many peninsulas of a great "World Island." Previous conquerors issuing from the Heartland had failed to conquer the entire World Island, because the limited natural fertility of the Siberian steppes could not support a sufficient mass of man-power. But the Cossack explorers of Siberia had been followed by Russian plowmen and, eventually, by a net of railroads. As early as 1904, Mackinder warned that a great power in full command of the Heartland might presage the empire of the world. For a great Heartland power—an industrialized Russia, or Germany or China in control of Russia—could press simultaneously and by internal lines of communication upon all the peninsulas of the World Island. If the World Island were ever conquered from within, Mackinder believed that although the surviving democracies would "fight with all the heroism begotten of their histories, . . . the end would be fated."[3]

3 *Democratic Ideals and Reality*, p. 70.

In 1890, Alfred Thayer Mahan had proclaimed the strategic pre-eminence of great navies which could range over the oceans covering three quarters of the globe. To extend this great but partial truth, Mackinder offered his conception of the unity of the World Island, warning that sea bases are often vulnerable to land attack. (In the 1920's Haushofer noted that the guns of Singapore pointed "the wrong way"—out to sea instead of against the mainland— an observation for which the Japanese became duly grateful.) But as the perfection of steam navigation had prompted Mahan's theories and the completion of the Trans-Siberian railroad triggered Mackinder's basic conception, so the invention of long-range rockets has forced us to consider the strategic importance of the ocean of air, the only element through which uninterrupted passage can be made from any point on the globe to any other point. At first thought, Mackinder's work might seem to be superseded, just as developments in continental communication enabled Mackinder to supersede Mahan. But since the American and Soviet governments have committed themselves—by action and by words—to an indefinite stalemate in strategic air weapons, the direct conflicts in the Cold War have been waged by carefully limited land, sea, and air forces in the peninsulas of the World Island. Far from being outdated, *Democratic Ideals and Reality* appears to be more relevant than ever.

By the end of the Second World War the United States had won unprecedented mastery over all the world's oceans, while the Soviet Union had amassed the greatest land power ever known. For the containment of communist land power, American command of the seas is vital to the maintenance of American forces in Europe, to the defense of Japan, Taiwan and the Philippines, and to the reinforcement of Viet Nam and Thailand, hard-pressed from land-locked Laos. Mackinder foresaw, almost sixty years ago, that Korea would become one of "so many bridge heads where outside navies would support armies,"[4] thus compelling the land powers to disperse their strength. In 1919 he judged that "the possession of Greece by a great Heartland power would probably carry with it the control of the World Island."[5] According to Milovan Djilas, Stalin moved to halt the Greek civil war because he understood that America and England would never tolerate a Communist Greece athwart their Mediterranean lifeline.[6]

Almost all the criticism of Mackinder's political writings has centered upon his judgment of the relative strategic importance of the Heartland, the marginal peninsulas, and the Americas. To aid the reader in this criticism, Mackinder's own first and last words on this subject are printed in the additional papers annexed to this edition. His earliest conception of the Heartland, which he then called "The Geographical Pivot of History," was addressed to the Royal Geographical Society in 1904. His final statement, entitled "The Round World and the Winning of the Peace," was published in *Foreign Affairs*, July, 1943. At that time he expressed his conviction that his "concept of the Heartland . . . is more valid and useful today than it was either twenty or forty years ago." Mackinder died in his home in Dorset on March 6, 1947. If he had lived one more week, he could have known of America's first great step to assume its present strategic responsibilities. For the Truman Doctrine, promising aid to Greece and to all other countries threatened by communist expansion, was announced on March 12.

Mackinder's prophetic power needs no more comment, for the reader will encounter it on almost every page of this book. The main purpose of this introduction is to raise two

4 H. J. Mackinder, "The Geographical Pivot of History," p. 262.
5 *Democratic Ideals and Reality*, p. 164.
6 Milovan Djilas, *Conversations with Stalin* (New York, 1962), pp. 181-182.

related inquiries which have usually been overlooked in the criticism of Mackinder's thought: first, what were the intellectual foundations of his remarkable prophetic power? and second, how relevant are his principles and methods to the broad study of conflict and cooperation between nations? Mackinder did not achieve his authoritative conclusions by inspired guesswork; he always began from clear, distinct, and comprehensive ideas and won his conclusions by hard and systematic thought. The first additional paper, "The Scope and Method of Geography," was delivered to the Royal Geographical Society in 1887, when he was only twenty-four years old. But even at this early age, the generous range and organizing power of his thought are evident.

Mackinder was a man of many parts. After ten years as Principal of Reading College, he became Director of the London School of Economics from 1903 to 1908. A Member of Parliament between 1910 and 1922, he was also Chairman of the Imperial Shipping Committee from 1920 to 1940, being made a Privy Counsellor in 1925.[7] But Mackinder was first and foremost a great teacher, equally interested in the organization and direction of research, the balance of the undergraduate curriculum, and even the education of the very young. Considering himself as a teacher of citizens of a great democracy, Mackinder aimed at nothing less than the development of a new humanism to bridge a dangerous and growing gap between the sciences and the humane arts. Two generations before C. P. Snow warned of divergence between these two cul-

[7] The authority for Mackinder's life is E. W. Gilbert, Reader in Human Geography in the University of Oxford, especially his "Seven Lamps of Geography: an Appreciation of the Teaching of Halford J. Mackinder" (which includes a bibliography of all Mackinder's published works), *Geography,* Vol. 36 (1951), pp. 21-43, and "The Right Honorable Sir Halford J. Mackinder, P. C., 1861-1947," *Geographical Journal,* Vol. 127 (March 1961), pp. 27-29.

tures, Mackinder was one among several scholars and states-men who saw that means were being perfected while ends were neglected. The root of this problem, as he saw it, was an excess of academic specialization.

In the days of our fathers the ancient classics were the com-mon element in the culture of all men, a ground on which the specialists could meet. The world is changing, and it would seem the classics are also becoming a specialty. Whether we regret the turn which things have taken or whether we rejoice at it, it is equally our duty to find a substitute.[8]

Throughout his life Mackinder opposed any substitution of concentration for education, even going so far as the blunt statement: "All specialization contains the seeds of death." More generously, he understood specialization in research as a kind of sacrifice made for the sake of living and teaching.

To the researcher science is an end in itself, but to the teacher it is a means to an end. The teacher can and should think of the bearing of science on the art of living; in other words, should think of its relation to moral and aesthetic values. To the researcher, as such, that is an irrelevant consideration, per-haps even an impediment.[9]

Alike in teaching and in statesmanship, Mackinder insisted that life be seen whole.

From his first scholarly paper in 1887 to the end of his life, Mackinder held to a faith that geography—"the science of the distribution . . . of things in general on the earth's surface"—might be the element of a new humanism. In our century geographers have traced the features of almost all the earth's surface with diligence and remarkable skill; but

[8] H. J. Mackinder, "On the Scope and Methods of Geography," pp. 239-40.
[9] H. J. Mackinder, "The Progress of Geography in the Field and in the Study During the Reign of King George the Fifth," *Geographical Journal* Vol. 86 (July 1935), p. 7.

the teaching of geography has, with rare exceptions, been
confined within bounds far more modest than those staked
out by the dean of British geographers. *Democratic Ideals
and Reality* was not devoted to the advancement of any
discipline, however, but to the elementary problem of our
time: the preservation of civilized society by means short
of the horrors of great war. In the last few years a bridge
has slowly been built between science and the humanities
by scholars devoted to the diagnosis and prevention of war.
The scholars most immediately responsible for such diagnosis would appear to be the specialists in international
relations, and their colleagues in other disciplines could
reasonably expect them to provide some common principles for the study of international conflict. Many valuable
generalizations have been achieved within the discipline of
international relations, but it is possible that no author has
surpassed the simplicity and, therefore, the range and force
of Mackinder's understanding of the ebb and flow of political movement. Perhaps Mackinder may come to be recognized as one of the founders of the newest, and yet the old-
est, humanism: Survival, the survival of men within the
order of civilization.

Considering Mackinder's thought on political motion in
general, he could be said to begin by reminding himself
that all political events are perceived upon the curved
surface of the earth and within the stream of time.

[It was] once remarked that the true geographer thinks in
shapes. Might we not complete the idea with the statement
that the true historian thinks in movements—movements upon
the shapes of the geographer? Both of them see with the mind's
eye.[10]

Now seeing with the mind's eye is imagination. Until the

[10] H. J. Mackinder, *The Development of Geographical Teaching out of
Nature Study* (London, 1908), p. 7.

geographer has a space machine (as he soon will have) and
the historian has a time machine (who knows?), they cannot
see more than the fringe of their subjects; they must per-
force rely upon their imagination. "Geography, rightly understood, is a matter of imagination. Its great function in
education, along with history, is to extend, and make precise and flexible, the imagination."[11] The extension of
imagination is also the province of literature; that is, imagi-
native literature, which can create, as Shakespeare did,
worlds within a globe. It follows that geography, like history, is "an art of expression parallel to and complementary
to the literary arts."[12]

Some students of politics may be dismayed at this analogy. Awed by the precision and power of science based
upon mathematics, are we to retreat into imagination—and
a literary imagination at that? Let us retreat as far as Aristotle's *Poetics*. The philosopher believed that the excellence of drama and poetry is determined not by spectacles
or flourishes, but by the rational strength of the plot; that
is, the degree of necessity, or at least probability in the
sequence of actions. According to Aristotle, the highest arts
of literary expression must be based upon sustained reasoning power. So Mackinder, calling for the extension and
disciplining of imagination, is aware that the excellence of
geography and historiography is determined in the first
place by rational power, including the skillful use of relevant sciences.

The simplest picture of the world, as outlined in "The
Scope and Method of Geography," he achieves with the
aid of Newton's laws of motion. Mackinder begins with
three concentric spheres of rock, water, and air. From the

[11] H. J. Mackinder, *The Teaching of Geography and History: A Study
in Method* (London, 1914), p. 3.

[12] H. J. Mackinder, "Geography—an art and a philosophy," *Geography*
Vol. 42 (1942), p. 129.

introduction of the sun's heat and the rotation of the earth, the system of trade winds can be deduced, as can other great world forces from the introduction of the earth's varying inclination and orbit. But during the slow cooling of the earth, great masses of rock, heavily wrinkled and furrowed, were thrust up to form the arbitrary shapes which we call the continents. It is the study of these great irregularities which distinguishes the geographer (and all those who build upon his work) from the scientist.

Consider now the nature of geographical as compared with scientific research. The physicist or chemist has before him myriads of repetitions of the same phenomena. He abstracts irrelevant aspects and isolates the relevant, and infers a law, such that he can foretell and in suitable cases produce with certainty given results from given causes. But the geographer seeks to decipher the pattern of a unique phenomenon, the surface of this globe. There can for him be no question of law in the physical sense, since there is no repetition of the pattern. Geography no more repeats itself than does History, and though there may be similarities of distribution on the earth's surface, they can but give ground for statistical generalizations, with probabilities, not certainties, for their effect. On the other hand Pattern is complex in the sense that causes of different orders are working together to produce interconnected results. The object of the geographer is to understand the concrete complexity, not to abstract and reduce to simplicity. Both geographer and scientist proceed no doubt by analysis with a view to subsequent synthesis, but the synthesis of the strict scientist is of like with like, whereas that of the geographer is of unlikes.[13]

As a means to grasping this huge pattern, Mackinder was one of the first to advocate the intensive study of the great natural regions of the world; but he never forgot to remind the regional specialist that the only complete region is the whole of the earth's surface.

[13] H. J. Mackinder, *Geographical Journal*, Vol. 86, p. 8.

Upon this unique and uneven surface Mackinder traced the greatest political movements recorded in history. *Democratic Ideals and Reality* is based upon a theory of political motion considered under two main categories: growth and expansion—that is, economic growth within a settled territory and expansion into new territories. This theory can be summed up as two principles, an unprecedented condition, and two conclusions:

The principles:

1. The unequal growth of nations is in large measure the result of the uneven distribution of fertility and strategic opportunity upon the face of the globe.[14]
2. Society reposes on the fact that man is a creature of habit. By interlocking the various habits of many men, society obtains a structure which may be compared with that of a running machine. . . . [Most of] the power of modern man over nature is due to the fact that society is a Going Concern, or, in the language of the engineer, has momentum.[15]

The new condition:

1. Whether we think of the physical, economic, military or political interconnection of things on the surface of the globe, we are now for the first time presented with a closed system. . . . There is no longer elasticity of expansion in the lands beyond the pale. Every shock, every disaster or superfluity, is now felt even to the antipodes.[16]

The conclusions:

1. The great wars of history . . . are the outcome, direct or indirect, of the unequal growth of nations.[17]
2. The grouping of lands and seas, and of fertility and nat-

14 *Democratic Ideals and Reality*, p. 2.
15 ibid., pp. 8-9.
16 ibid., p. 29.
17 ibid., p. 1-2.

ural pathways is such as to lend itself to the growth of empires, and in the end of a single world empire.[18]

Scholarship is supposed to mean the art of leisure, but today's students of world affairs must work and worry under great pressure; they must read a great deal, often in books of uneven quality. The subject is complex; the objective, urgent. So it is not hard to pass over a few brief sentences which may cover a mountain—or a chasm—of thought. But Mackinder's principles deserve, and even demand, patience and reflection; first, because the entire book is based upon them, but, more importantly, because these principles are the measure of a great deal that has been written on world politics. As an aid to criticism, it can be pointed out that Machiavelli's *Discourses on Livy* is based upon the first principle cited; so is Thucydides' great history, which also incorporates the first conclusion. Perhaps the most striking parallels are to be found in Lenin's *Imperialism*, which contains a theory of great wars caused by the uneven growth of industrial nations within a closed political system. From this similar ground, however, Lenin and Mackinder arrive at radically different conclusions.

Mackinder is in no sense a determinist, as can be readily seen from the careful qualifications written into each of his listed principles. He studied the powerful influences exerted by geographical conditions and economic inertia, but he did so in order to counter such influences in the name of national and individual freedom. As for the crudities of Social Darwinism and, by implication, Marxism, he states, "human victory consists in our rising superior to such mere fatalism."[19] The question is how unequal nations can be shaped to survive and grow without danger to themselves or to their neighbors. To this question Mackinder provides

[18] ibid., p. 2.
[19] ibid., p. 2.

two main answers: first, a global balance of power designed to check expansion from the Heartland, and, second, the deliberate control of economic growth in accord with a universal plan.

Writing as a statesman, Mackinder criticized the merely juridical and abstract characteristics of the League of Nations. To complete his analysis of the Heartland peril in 1919, he recommended the adequate subdivision of Eastern Europe into separate nations. In addition to doing justice to national aspirations, he perceived that the main strategic objective of the tier of newly-freed nations—from the Baltic States and Poland through Czechoslovakia and Yugoslavia—was to protect prostrate Russia "for at least one generation" against German penetration.[20] Again and again in 1919, he insisted that the key strategic issue was preventing the dominance of Eastern Europe, the great lowland gateway to the Heartland, by any single great power. "What a pity," he wrote in 1943, that "the alliance, negotiated after Versailles, between the United States, the United Kingdom and France was not implemented! What trouble and sadness that might have saved!"[21] The main issue that prevented such an alliance was English and American refusal to support France in two fundamental and related strategic commitments: first, to guarantee the frontiers of Poland and Czechoslovakia and second, to regard the German re-militarization of the Rhineland as an act of war. But the island democracies refused, at that time, to think strategically or to advance their frontiers so far inland.

Next only to the elementary need for survival, the nations of the world are today committed to economic growth; indeed, they are in awe of economic growth, and it is rare for any contemporary statesman to warn that unlimited and uncontrolled growth is fraught with danger. Believing

[20] ibid., p. 158.
[21] H. J. Mackinder, "The Round World and Winning the Peace," p. 275.

that the unequal growth of nations is a major cause of great wars, Mackinder proposes that international organization commit itself to "that economic ideal which was foreshadowed by the great American statesman, Alexander Hamilton—the ideal of the truly independent nation, balanced in all its development."[22] The alternative method of controlling unequal economic growth in order to prevent war is offered by Lenin: in theory, a universal and enlightened master plan; in practice, permanent war economies in Russia and China.

As a true liberal statesman, Mackinder goes beyond the freedom of nations to his final concern, the freedom of men. Reasoning downward from the freedom of nations, or upward from the freedom of men, he comes to the same conclusion: freedom "must have and keep a balanced life." It is exactly at this point that Mackinder calls on the humane arts, particularly the Socratic ideal of a balanced community, to redress the imbalance permitted in modern times by the irresponsible practices of *laissez-faire* economics. Aristotle, in his *Ethics*, asserts that the study of politics is the sovereign science, because it levies upon all other arts and sciences for the common good, and ends with an invocation of friendship, the element of community. Mackinder calls upon the creative sciences and the controlling arts to unite for the preservation of civilized society, believing that the needs of both free men and free nations can best be served in balanced growth, and his greatest book concludes with a most typically English touch —a postscript in praise of neighborliness.

The influence of Mackinder's thought has been wide and profound. In America and in England, since 1942, most studies of global strategy or political geography have been based, in whole or in part, upon his theories. Mac-

---

[22] *Democratic Ideals and Reality*, p. 176.

kinder's remarkable and unfortunate influence upon German geopolitics has already been mentioned, but it should be noted that Haushofer relied primarily on the 1904 lecture, "The Geographical Pivot of History." Since Mackinder believed that Russia occupied the strongest natural seat of power in the world, his influence upon Soviet thought is an important and intriguing question. During the first years of the First World War, there was some discussion of his 1904 lecture in *Morskoi Sbornik*, organ of the Tsarist mercantile marine, but there is no evidence that any of Mackinder's work has ever been published in the Soviet Union. A distinction must be made, however, between what is taught in the regular Soviet universities and what is taught in the secret Party schools. For example, Pavlovitch, influential in the Pan-Asian movement which arose in the 1920's, was a student of Mackinder's writing. But any direct influence of Mackinder in the Soviet Union is almost certainly minimal compared with the considerable indirect influence exercised through Haushofer, who in the 1920's regularly sent geo-political analyses to Stalin.[23]

Most criticism of Mackinder's thought has centered upon the Heartland concept and the effects of new technology upon strategy. One immediate response to Mackinder's first statement of his main thesis in 1904 was the remarkable and prophetic criticism of R. S. Amery. After complimenting Mackinder for organizing "the whole of history and the whole of ordinary politics under one comprehensive idea," Amery went on to observe:

. . . both the sea and the railway are going in the future—it may be near or it may be somewhat remote—to be supplemented by the air as a means of locomotion, and when we come to that . . . a great deal of this geography must lose its

[23] For this information I am indebted to Dr. B. Nicolaevsky. See his remarkable article, "Russia, Japan, and the Pan-Asiatic Movement to 1925," *The Far Eastern Quarterly*, Vol. 8 (May 1949), pp. 259-295.

importance, and the successful powers will be those who have the greatest industrial base. It will not matter whether they are in the center of a continent or on an island; those people who have the industrial power and the power of invention and of science will be able to defeat all others.[24]

All this only one year after the Wright brothers' first powered flight! Let us hope that the present stalemate in strategic air forces will continue, thus mitigating the full, terrible effects of science and industry turned towards war. Meanwhile, the struggle in the peninsulas of the World Island continues by other means.

Other criticisms of the Heartland (which are listed in the bibliography) turn upon Mackinder's underestimation of the resistant power of peninsular states, especially in alliance with the United States, and upon the details of Soviet strength within the Heartland. Undoubtedly, the reader of this book will perceive many of these qualifications for himself. Finally, in thinking about the Heartland concept, it is wise to bear in mind Mackinder's own warning:

The catch phrase and the oft-repeated metaphor produce a certain kind of pleasure in the reader, the pleasure of recognition by the mind's ear. It is a musical pleasure in its essence, but it is fatal to original thought. Those . . . metaphors were vivid and stimulating once, when first coined to express the visions in the author's mind. Now, owing to repetition, they have the effect of a lullaby. The verbal memory is less suggestive and less subtle than the visual memory.[25]

In other words, a globe and an economic atlas provide the best road to recreating, in today's political context, the thought which empowers this masterpiece.

E. M. Earle introduced the 1942 edition of this book

[24] From the discussion of Mackinder's "Geographical Pivot of History," *Geographical Journal*, Vol. 23 (1904), p. 441.

[25] H. J. Mackinder, *The Teaching of Geography and History*, p. 8.

with the comment that it has "the rare quality of timeless-ness." Mackinder's work will endure in part because of the grandeur of his theme, and in part because of the simplicity of his thought and the clarity of his style. But these qualities are not, in themselves, sufficient to make a book time-less. The inner force of this book, the spirit which keeps it alive, is the author's honesty and magnanimity. Mackinder sought to establish democratic ideals the hard way—the only way they can be established—through honest understanding and just control of the realities of our world.

Anthony J. Pearce
New York University

June, 1962

MAJOR CRITICISMS OF MACKINDER'S STRATEGICAL THEORIES*

Nicolas J. Spykman. *The Geography of the Peace*. New York: Harcourt Brace, 1944.

Hans W. Weigert and Vilhjalmur Stefansson (editors). *Compass of the World: A Symposium on Political Geography*. New York: Macmillan, 1945, pp. 148-214.

Hans W. Weigert, Vilhjalmur Stefansson, and Richard E. Harrison (editors). *New Compass of the World: A Symposium on Political Geography*. New York: Macmillan, 1949, pp. 30-171.

Charles Kruszewski, "The Pivot of History," *Foreign Affairs*, Vol. 32 (April, 1954), pp. 388-401.

W. Gordon East and A. E. Moodie (editors). *The Changing World: Studies in Political Geography*. New York: World Book Co., 1956, pp. 432-449.

Dennis R. Mills, "The U.S.S.R.: A Re-Appraisal of Mackinder's Heartland Concept," *The Scottish Geographical Magazine*. Vol. 72 (Dec., 1956), pp. 144-152.

Hans W. Weigert and others. *Principles of Political Geography*. New York: Appleton-Century-Crofts, 1957, pp. 209-290.

Bernard Semmel, "Sir Halford Mackinder: Theorist of Imperialism," *The Canadian Journal of Economics and Political Science*, Vol. 24 (Nov., 1958), pp. 554-561.

W. A. Douglas Jackson. *Russo-Chinese Borderlands*. New York: D. Van Nostrand, 1962.

* Listed in order of publication.

Chapter One

PERSPECTIVE

OUR memories are still full of the vivid detail of an all-absorbing warfare; there is, as it were, a screen between us and the things which happened earlier even in our own lives. But the time has at last come to take larger views, and we must begin to think of our long war as of a single great event, a cataract in the stream of history. The last four years have been momentous, because they have been the outcome of one century and the prelude to another. Tension between the nations had slowly accumulated, and, in the language of diplomacy, there has now been a *détente*. The temptation of the moment is to believe that unceasing peace will ensue merely because tired men are determined that there shall be no more war. But international tension will accumulate again, though slowly at first; there was a generation of peace after Waterloo. Who among the diplomats round the Congress table at Vienna in 1814 foresaw that Prussia would become a menace to the world? Is it possible for us so to grade the stream bed of future history as that there shall be no more cataracts? That, and no smaller, is the task before us if we would have posterity think less meanly of our wisdom than we think of that of the diplomats of Vienna.

The great wars of history—we have had a world war about every hundred years for the last four centuries—

are the outcome, direct or indirect, of the unequal growth of nations, and that unequal growth is not wholly due to the greater genius and energy of some nations as compared with others; in large measure it is the result of the uneven distribution of fertility and strategical opportunity upon the face of the globe. In other words, there is in nature no such thing as equality of opportunity for the nations. Unless I wholly misread the facts of geography, I would go further, and say that the grouping of lands and seas, and of fertility and natural pathways, is such as to lend itself to the growth of empires, and in the end of a single world-empire. If we are to realize our ideal of a League of Nations which shall prevent war in the future, we must recognize these geographical realities and take steps to counter their influence. Last century, under the spell of the Darwinian theory, men came to think that those forms of organization should survive which adapted themselves best to their natural environment. To-day we realize, as we emerge from our fiery trial, that human victory consists in our rising superior to such mere fatalism.

Civilization is based on the organization of society so that we may render service to one another, and the higher the civilization the more minute tends to be the division of labor and the more complex the organization. A great and advanced society has, in consequence, a powerful momentum; without destroying the society itself you cannot suddenly check or divert its course. Thus it happens that years beforehand detached observers are able to predict a coming clash of societies which are following convergent paths in their development. The historian commonly prefaces his narrative of war with an account of the blindness of men who refused to see the writing on the wall, but the fact is, that, like every other going concern, a national society can be shaped to a desired career while it is young, but when it is old its character is fixed and it is incapable of any great change in its mode of existence. To-day all the nations of the world are about to start afresh; is it within the reach of human forethought so to set their courses as that, notwithstanding geographical temptation, they shall not clash in the days of our grandchildren?

In our anxiety to repudiate the ideas historically associated with the balance of power, is there not perhaps some danger that we should allow merely juridical conceptions to rule our thoughts in regard to the League of Nations? It is our ideal that justice should be done between nations, whether they be great or small, precisely as it is our ideal that there should be justice between men, whatever the difference of their positions in society. To maintain justice as between individual men the power of the state is invoked, and we now recognize, after the failure of international law to avert the Great War, that there must be some power or, as the lawyers say, some sanction for the maintenance of justice as between nation and nation. But the power which is necessary for the rule of law among citizens passes easily into tyranny. Can we establish such a world power as shall suffice to keep the law between great and small states, and yet shall not grow into a world-tyranny? There are two roads to such a tyranny, the one the conquest of all other nations by one nation, the other the perversion of the very international power itself which may be set up to coerce the lawless nation. In our great replanning of human society we must recognize that the skill and opportunity of the robber are prior facts to the law of robbery. In other words, we must envisage our vast problem as business men dealing with realities of growth and opportunity, and not merely as lawyers defining rights and remedies.

My endeavor, in the following pages, will be to measure the relative significance of the great features of our globe as tested by the events of history, including the history of the last four years, and then to consider how we may best adjust our ideals of freedom to these lasting realities of our earthly home. But first we must recognize certain tendencies of human nature as exhibited in all forms of political organization.

Chapter Two

SOCIAL MOMENTUM

"To him that hath shall be given"

IN the year 1789 the lucid French people, in its brain-town of Paris, saw visions, generous visions—Liberty, Equality, Fraternity. But presently French idealism lost its hold on reality, and drifted into the grip of fate, in the person of Napoleon. With his military efficiency Napoleon restored order, but in doing so organized a French power the very law of whose being was a denial of liberty. The story of the great French Revolution and Empire has influenced all subsequent political thought; it has seemed a tragedy in the old Greek sense of a disaster predestined in the very character of revolutionary idealism.

When, therefore, in 1848, the peoples of Europe were again in a vision-seeing mood, their idealism was of a more complex nature. The principle of Nationality was added to that of Liberty, in the hope that liberty might be secured against the overreaching organizer by the independent spirit of nations. Unfortunately, in that year of revolutions, the good ship Idealism again dragged her anchor, and by and by was swept away by fate, in the person of Bismarck. With his Prussian efficiency Bismarck perverted the new ideal of German nationality, just as Napoleon had perverted the simpler

French ideals of liberty and equality. The tragedy of
national idealism, which we have just seen consum-
mated, was not, however, predestined in the disorder
of liberty, but in the materialism, commonly known as
Kultur, of the organizer. The French tragedy was the
simple tragedy of the breakdown of idealism; but the
German tragedy has, in truth, been the tragedy of the
substituted realism.

In 1917 the democratic nations of the whole earth
thought they had seen a great harbor light when the
Russian Czardom fell and the American Republic came
into the war. For the time being, at any rate, the
Russian Revolution has gone the common revolutionary way, but we still put our hope in universal
democracy. To the eighteenth-century ideal of liberty,
and the nineteenth-century ideal of nationality, we have
added our twentieth-century ideal of the League of
Nations. If a third tragedy were to ensue, it would be
on a vast scale, for democratic ideals are to-day the
working creed of the greater part of humanity. The
Germans, with their Real-Politik, their politics of
reality—something other than merely practical politics
—regard that disaster as being sooner or later inevitable.
The war lord and the Prussian military caste may have
been fighting for the mere maintenance of their power,
but large and intelligent sections of German society
have acted under the persuasion of a political philosophy which was none the less sincerely held because
we believed it to be wrong. In this war German antici-
pations have proved wrong in many regards, but that
has been because we have made them so by a few wise
principles of government, and by strenuous effort, not-

withstanding our mistakes in policy. Our hardest test has yet to come. What degree of international reconstruction is necessary if the world is long to remain a safe place for democracies? And in regard to the internal structure of those democracies, what conditions must be satisfied if we are to succeed in harnessing to the heavy plow of social reconstruction the ideals which have inspired heroism in this war? There can be no more momentous questions. Shall we succeed in soberly marrying our new idealism to reality?

.   .   .   .

Idealists are the salt of the earth; without them to move us, society would soon stagnate and civilization fade. Idealism has, however, been associated with two very different phases of temper. The older idealisms, such as Buddhism, Stoicism, and Mediaeval Christianity, were based on self-denial; the Franciscan Friars vowed themselves to chastity, poverty, and service. But modern democratic idealism, the idealism of the American and French Revolutions, is based on self-realization. Its aim is that every human being shall live a full and self-respecting life. According to the preamble of the American Declaration of Independence, all men are created equal and endowed with the rights of liberty and the pursuit of happiness.

These two tendencies of idealism have corresponded historically with two developments of reality. In older times the power of nature over man was still great. Hard reality put limits to his ambitions. In other words, the world as a whole was poor, and resignation was the only general road to happiness. The few could, no doubt, obtain some scope in life, but only at the cost of the serfdom of the many. Even the so-called Democracy of Athens and the Platonic Utopia were based on domestic and industrial slavery. But the modern world is rich. In no small measure man now controls the forces of nature, and whole classes, formerly resigned to their fate, have become imbued with the idea that with a fairer division of wealth there should be a nearer approach to equality of opportunity.

This modern reality of human control over nature, apart from which democratic ideals would be futile, is not wholly due to the advance of scientific knowledge and invention. The greater control which man now wields is conditional, and not absolute like the control of nature over man by famine and pestilence. Human riches and comparative security are based to-day on the division and co-ordination of labor, and on the constant repair of the complicated plant which has replaced the simple tools of primitive society. In other words, the output of modern wealth is conditional on the maintenance of our social organization and capital. Society is a Going Concern, and no small part of our well-being may be compared with the intangible "goodwill" of a business. The owner of a business depends on the habits of his customers no less than on the regular running of the machinery in his factory; both must be kept in repair, and when in repair they have the value of the Going Concern; but should the business stop, they have merely a break-up value—the machinery becomes so much scrap metal, and the goodwill is reduced to the book debts.

Society reposes on the fact that man is a creature of habit. By interlocking the various habits of many men, society obtains a structure which may be compared with that of a running machine. Mrs. Bouncer was able to form a simple society for the occupation of a room, because Box slept by night and Cox by day, but her society was dislocated when one of her lodgers took a holiday, and for the nonce changed his habit. Let any-one try to realize what would happen to himself if all those on whom he depends—the postmen, railwaymen, butchers, bakers, printers, and very many others—were suddenly to vary their settled routines; he will then begin to appreciate in how great a degree the power of modern man over nature is due to the fact that society is a Going Concern, or, in the language of the engineer, has momentum. Stop the running long enough to throw men's habits out of gear with one another, and society would quickly run down to the simple reality of control by nature. Vast numbers would die in consequence.

Productive power, in short, is a far more important element of reality in relation to modern civilization than is accumulated wealth. The total visible wealth of a civilized country, notwithstanding the antiquity of some of its treasures, is generally estimated as equal to the output of not more than seven or eight years. The significance of this statement does not lie in its precise accuracy, but in the rapid growth of its practical meaning for modern men, owing to their dependence on a machinery of production, mechanical and social, which in the past four or five generations has become increasingly delicate and complicated. For every advance in the application of science there has been a corresponding change in social organization. It was by no mere coincidence that Adam Smith was discussing the division of labor when James Watt was inventing the steam engine. Nor, in our own time, is it by blind coincidence that beside the invention of the internal combustion engine—the key to the motor-car, submarine, and aeroplane—must be placed an unparalleled extension of the credit system. Lubrication of metal machinery depends on the habits of living men. The assumption of some scientific enthusiasts that the study of the humane arts has ceased to be important will not bear examination; the management of men, high and low, is more difficult and more important under the conditions of modern reality than it ever was.

We describe the managers of the social machine as organizers, but under that general term are commonly included two distinct categories. In the first place, we have administrators, who are not strictly organizers at all—begetters, that is to say, of new organs in an organism. It is the function of the administrator to keep the running social machine in repair and to see to its lubrication. When men die, or for reasons of ill-health or old age retire, it is his duty to fill the vacant places with men suitably trained beforehand. A foreman of works is essentially an administrator. A judge administers the law, except in so far as in fact, though not in theory, he may make it. In the work of the administrator, pure and simple, there is no idea of progress. Given a certain organization, efficiency is his ideal —perfect smoothness of working. His characteristic disease is called "Red Tape." A complicated society, well administered, tends in fact to a Chinese stagnation by the very strength of its momentum. The goodwill of a long-established and well-managed business may often be sold for a large sum in the market. Perhaps the most striking illustration of social momentum is to be seen in the immobility of the markets themselves. Every seller wishes to go where buyers are in the habit of congregating in order that he may be sure of a purchaser for his wares. On the other hand, every buyer goes, if he can, to the place where sellers are wont to assemble in order that he may buy cheaply as a result of their competition. The authorities have often tried in vain to decentralize the markets of London.

In order to appreciate the other type of organizer, the creator of social mechanism, let us again consider for a moment the common course of revolutions. A Voltaire criticizes the running concern known as French Government; a Rousseau paints the ideal of a happier society; the authors of the great *Encyclopédie* prove that the material bases for such a society exist. Presently the new ideas take possession of some well-meaning enthusiasts —inexperienced, however, in the difficult art of changing the habits of average mankind. They seize an opportunity for altering the structure of French society. Incidentally, but unfortunately, they slow down its running. Stoppage of work, actual breakage of the implements of production and government, removal of practiced administrators, and substitution of misfitting amateurs combine to reduce the rate of production of the necessaries of life, with the result that prices rise, and confidence and credit fall. The revolutionary leaders are, no doubt, willing enough to be poor for a time in order to realize their ideals, but the hungry millions rise up around them. To gain time the millions are led to suspect that the shortage is due to some interference of the deposed powers, and the Terror inevitably follows. At last men become fatalists, and, abandoning ideals, seek some organizer who shall restore efficiency. The necessity is reinforced by the fact that foreign enemies are invading the national territory, and that less production and relaxed discipline have reduced the defensive power of the state. But the organizer needed for the task of reconstruction is no mere administrator; he must be able to design and make, and not merely to repair and lubricate social machinery. So Carnot, who "organizes victory," and Napoleon with his Code Civil, win eternal fame by creative effort.

The possibility of organization in the constructive sense depends on discipline. Running society is constituted by the myriad interlocking of the different habits of many men; if the running social structure is to be altered, even in some relatively small respect, a great number of men and women must simultaneously change various of their habits in complementary ways. It was impossible to introduce daylight saving except by an edict of government, for any partial adherence to the change of hour would have thrown society into confusion. The achievement of daylight saving was, therefore, dependent on social discipline, which is thus seen to consist not in the habits of men but in the power of simultaneous and correlated change of those habits. In an ordered state the sense of discipline becomes innate, and the police are but rarely called upon to enforce it. In other words, social discipline, or the alteration of habit at will or command, itself becomes a habit. Military discipline, in so far as it consists of single acts at the word of command, is of a simpler order, but the professional soldier knows well the difference between habitual discipline and even the most intelligent fighting by quick-trained men.

In times of disorder the interlocking of productive habits breaks down step by step, and society as a whole becomes progressively poor, though robbers of one kind or another may for a while enrich themselves. Even more serious, however, is the failure of the habit of discipline, for that implies the loss of the power of recuperation. Consider to what a pass Russia was brought by a year of cumulative revolutions; her condition was like that terrible state of paralysis when the mind still sees and directs, but the nerves fail to elicit any response from the muscles. A nation does not die when so smitten, but the whole mechanism of its society must be reconstituted, and that quickly, if the men and women who survive its impoverishment are not to forget the habits and lose the aptitudes on which their civilization depends. History shows no remedy but force upon which to found a fresh nucleus of discipline in such circumstances; but the organizer who rests upon force tends inevitably to treat the recovery of mere efficiency as his end. Idealism does not flourish under his rule. It was because history speaks plainly in this regard, that so many of the idealists of the last two generations have been internationalist; the military recovery of discipline is commonly achieved either by conquest from another national base or incidentally to a successful national resistance to foreign invasion.

The great organizer is the great realist. Not that he lacks imagination—very far from that; but his imagination turns to "ways and means," and not elusive ends. His is the mind of Martha and not of Mary. If he be a captain of industry the counters of his thought are labor and capital; if he be a general of armies they are units and supplies. His organizing is aimed at intermediate ends—money if he be an industrial, and victory if he be a soldier. But money and victory are merely the keys to ulterior ends, and those ulterior ends remain elusive for him throughout. He dies still making money, or, if he be a victorious soldier, weeps like Alexander because there are no more worlds to conquer. His one care is that the business or the army which he has organized shall be efficiently administered; he is hard on his administrators. Above all, he values the habit of discipline; his machine must answer promptly to the lever.

The organizer inevitably comes to look upon men as his tools. His is the inverse of the mind of the idealist, for he would move men in brigades and must therefore have regard to material limitations, whereas the idealist appeals to the soul in each of us, and souls are winged and can soar. It does not follow that the organizer is careless of the well-being of the society beneath him; on the contrary, he regards that society as so much man-power to be maintained in efficient condition. This is true whether he be militarist or capitalist, provided that he be farsighted. In the sphere of politics the organizer views men as existing for the state—for the "Leviathan" of the Stuart philosopher Hobbes. But the democratic idealist barely tolerates the state as a necessary evil, for it limits freedom.

In the established democracies of the West, the ideals of freedom have been transmuted into the prejudices of the average citizen, and it is on these "habits of thought" that the security of our freedom depends, rather than on the passing ecstasies of idealism. For a thousand years such prejudices took root under the insular protection of Britain; they are the outcome of continuous experiment, and must be treated at least with respect, unless we are prepared to think of our forefathers as fools. One of these prejudices is that it is unwise to take an expert as minister of state. In the present time of war, when freedom even in a democracy must yield to efficiency, there are those who would have us say that the experts whom we have for the time being installed in some of the high offices should be succeeded henceforth by experts, and that our prejudice is antiquated. None the less even in war time Britain has returned to a Civilian Minister for War! The fact is, of course, that the inefficiencies of the normally working British Constitution are merely the obverse of the truth that democracy is incompatible with the organization necessary for war against autocracies. When the present Chilean Minister first came to England he was entertained by some members of the House of Commons. Referring to the Mother of Parliaments, as seen from the far Pacific, and to the chronic grumbling in regard to Parliamentary government which he found on his arrival in London, he exclaimed, "You forget that one of the chief functions of Parliaments is to prevent things being done!"

The thought of the organizer is essentially strategical, whereas that of the true democrat is ethical. The organizer is thinking how to use men; but the democrat is thinking of the rights of men, which rights are so many rocks in the way of the organizer. Undoubtedly the organizer must be a master, for, given the waywardness of human nature and the inveteracy of habit, he would make little progress otherwise. But he is a bad supreme master, because of his "ways and means" mind.

The Nemesis of democratic idealism, if it break from the bonds of reality, is the supreme rule of the organizer and of blind efficiency. The organizer begins innocently enough; his executive mind revolts from the disorder, and above all from the indiscipline around him. Soldierly efficiency undoubtedly saved Revolutionary France. But such is the impetus of the going concern, that it sweeps forward even its own creator. To improve the efficiency of his man-power he must in the end seek to control all its activities—working and thinking, no less than fighting. He is in supreme command, and inefficiency is pain to him. Therefore Napoleon added to his Grand Army and his Code Civil, also his Concordat with the Papacy, whereby the priest was to become his servant. He might have enjoyed lasting peace after the Treaty of Amiens, but must needs continue to prepare war. Finally he was impelled to his Moscow, just as a great money-maker will overreach himself and end in bankruptcy.

Bismarck was the Napoleon of the Prussians, their man of blood and iron, yet he differed from his French prototype in certain regards which, for our present purpose, are worth attention. His end was unlike the end of Napoleon. There was no banishment to Elba after a Moscow, no imprisonment in St. Helena after a Waterloo. True that, after thirty years at the helm, the old pilot was dropped in 1890 by a new captain with a mind to piracy, but it was because of his caution and not because of vaulting ambition. Both Napoleon and Bismarck had supreme minds of the "ways and means" order, but there was something more in Bismarck. He was not merely the great business man, which is Emerson's description of Napoleon. No statesman ever adjusted war to policy with a nicer judgment than Bismarck. He fought three short and successful campaigns, and made three treaties of peace, from each of which ensued a harvest of advantage to Prussia. Yet what different treaties they were! After the War of 1864 against Denmark, Bismarck took Schleswig and Holstein, with the idea, beyond question, of a Kiel Canal. After the War of 1866 against Austria he refused to take Bohemia, and thereby so offended his king that they were not fully reconciled until after the victories of 1870. There can be no doubt that in this clemency Bismarck foresaw a time when Prussia might need the alliance of Austria. In 1871, after Sedan and the Siege of Paris, Bismarck yielded to the pressure of the military party, and took Lorraine as well as Alsace.

The great Chancellor had, in truth, what the Prussian, as a rule, lacks, an insight into the minds of other nations than his own. His methods were psychological by preference. Once he had achieved German unity under Prussia, he waged no more wars. Yet he accomplished great things—for a time he ruled Europe—and his method was no mere exploitation of military prestige. At the Berlin Congress of 1878 he secured the occupation of the provinces of Bosnia and Herzegovina for Austria, and thereby deepened the rivalry of Austria and Russia in the Balkan Peninsula. At the same Berlin

Congress he privately incited France to occupy Tunis, and when France presently effected that occupation, Italy, as he foresaw, was sharply wounded. The Dual Alliance with Austria followed in 1879, and the Triple Alliance with Austria and Italy in 1881. It was as though he had sent his sheep-dog round his flock to drive his sheep to him. By subtleties of the same order he antagonized France and Britain, and also Britain and Russia. So, too, did he deal in his domestic policy. In 1886 he ceased from struggling with the Vatican, and brought over the Catholic party to his support, thereby neutralizing the socialist tendency in the industrial but Catholic province of the Rhineland, and the particularist tendency in the Catholic kingdom of Bavaria in the south.

The true parallel is to be drawn not between Napoleon and Bismarck, but between Napoleon and the entire Prussian ruling caste. The end of that caste, which we are now witnessing, is like the end of Napoleon; the blindly organizing man goes to his Moscow, and the blindly organizing state to its Armageddon. Kultur is the name given to the philosophy and education which imbued a whole race with the "ways and means" mind. The French are an artistic, and therefore an idealistic people; Napoleon prostituted their idealism with the glory of his genius. Bismarck, on the other hand, was the child of materialistic Kultur, but, greater than the average of his race, he could reckon also with spiritual forces.

Kultur had its origin not in the victories of Frederick the Great, but in the defeat of Jena. The rule of Frederick in the eighteenth century was a personal rule like that of Napoleon, whereas the Prussia of the nineteenth century, behind whatever other pretense, was governed by an oligarchy of intellectual "experts"—staff officers, bureaucrats, professors. Frederick, sole organizer, raised only administrators, with the result that when he died he left Prussia a mere mechanism, to be broken on the field of Jena.

In the very winter of Jena the philosopher Fichte came to lecture in Berlin, while it was still in the occupation of the French.[1] There was no university in the Prussian capital of those days, and the lectures were delivered not to young students, but to the maturest brains of the country in the fever of a great crisis. Fichte taught the philosophy of patriotism at a time when the German universities were devoted to the abstract worship of knowledge and art. In the next few years, between 1806 and 1813, was established that close connection between the army, the bureaucracy, and the schools, or, in other words, between the needs of government and the aims of education, which constituted the essence and perverse strength of the Prussian system. Universal military service was correlated with universal compulsory schooling, inaugurated in Prussia two generations before the English Education Act of 1870; the University of Berlin, with a brilliant professoriate, was established as sister to the Great General Staff. Thus knowledge in Prussia was no longer pursued mainly for its own sake, but as a means to an end, and that end was the success of a state which had experienced bitter disaster. It was a camp-state, moreover, in the midst of a

[1] See *The Evolution of Prussia,* by Marriott and Grant Robertson. Clarendon Press, 1915.

plain, without the natural bulwarks of a Spain, a France, or a Britain. The end determines the means, and since the Prussian end was military strength, based of necessity on stark discipline, the means were inevitably materialistic. Judged from the standpoint of Berlin, it was a wonderful thing to have impressed Kultur, or *strategical mentality,* on the educated class of a whole people, but from the standpoint of civilization at large it was a fatal momentum to have given to a nation—fatal, that is to say, in the long run, either to civilization or that nation.

We have had for a byword in these times the German war map. It may be questioned, however, whether most people in Britain and America have fully realized the part played by the map in German education during the past three generations. Maps are the essential apparatus of Kultur, and every educated German is a geographer in a sense that is true of very few Englishmen or Americans. He has been taught to see in maps not merely the conventional boundaries established by scraps of paper, but permanent physical opportunities— "ways and means" in the literal sense of the words. His Real-Politik lives in his mind upon a mental map. The serious teaching of geography in German high schools and universities dates from the very beginning of Kultur. It was organized in the generation after Jena, mainly by the labors of four men—Alexander von Humboldt, Berghaus, Carl Ritter, and Stieler—who were attached to the new University of Berlin and to the since famous map-house of Perthes of Gotha. To this day, notwithstanding all that has been done by two or three exceptional map-houses in this country, if you want a good map, conveying accurately and yet graphically the fundamental contrasts, you must have resort as often as not to one of German origin. The reason is that in Germany there are many cartographers who are scholarly geographers and not merely surveyors or draftsmen. They can exist, because there is a wide public educated to appreciate and pay for intelligently drawn maps.[1]

In this country we value the moral side of education, and it is perhaps intuitively that we have neglected materialistic geography. Before the war not a few teachers, within my knowledge, objected to geography as a subject of education, on the ground that it tended to promote imperialism, just as they objected to physical drill because it tended to militarism. We may laugh at such excesses of political caution, as men of former centuries scoffed at the anchorites who secreted themselves from the world, but the protest in each case was against an excess in the opposite direction.

Berlin-Bagdad, Berlin-Herat, Berlin-Pekin—not heard as mere words, but visualized on the mental relief map —involve for most Anglo-Saxons a new mode of thought, lately and imperfectly introduced among us by the rough maps of the newspapers. But your Prussian, and his father, and his grandfather have debated such concepts all their lives, pencil in hand. In arranging the detailed terms of peace, our statesmen will, no doubt, have the advice of excellent geographical experts, but the German representatives will have behind them not

[1] In my Address to the Geographical Section of the British Association at Ipswich in 1895 will be found an account of the rise of the German schools of geography.

merely a few experts but a great geographically in-
structed public, long familiar with every important
aspect of the questions which will arise, and quick to
give a farsighted support to their leaders. This may
easily become a decisive advantage, especially should
our people pass into a magnanimous frame of mind. It
would be a curious thing if the successes of Talleyrand
and Metternich, in the secret diplomacy of 1814, were
repeated by the spokesmen of the defeated states of our
own time under the conditions imposed upon diplomacy by popular government! [1]

The map habit of thought is no less pregnant in the
sphere of economics than it is in that of strategy. True
that *laissez-faire* had little use for it, but the "most
favored nation" clause which Germany imposed on defeated France in the Treaty of Frankfurt had quite a
different meaning for the strategical German mind to
that which was attached to it by honest Cobdenites. The
German bureaucrat built upon it a whole structure of
preferences for German trade. Of what use to Britain
under her northern skies was the most favored nation
clause when Germany granted a concession to Italy in
the matter of import duties on olive oil? Would there
not also be railway trucks to be returned to Italy which
might as well return loaded with German exports? The
whole system of most voluminous and intricate commercial treaties between Germany and her neighbors

[1] It is true that there is a "horse-sense" of geography among those
of us who have traveled. It is true, also, that we keep atlases in our
offices and libraries, to be consulted as we would consult a dictionary
for the spelling of a word. But correct spelling does not always imply
literary power! A trained sense of geographical perspective is essential
to the mode of thought here in question.

was based on a minute study of commercial routes and of the lie of productive areas. The German official was thinking in the concrete detail of "living," while his British counterpart was absorbed in the negative principle of "letting live."

. . . .

Kaiser Wilhelm told us that this war was a struggle between two views of the world. "View" is characteristic of the organizer; he sees things from above. Kipling agreed with the Kaiser, but in the language of simple men below, when he declared that there is human feeling and German feeling. The organizer, as organizer, is inevitably inhuman, or rather unhuman. No doubt both Kaiser and poet exaggerated in order to emphasize opposing tendencies; even a democracy must have organizers, just as there must be some remnant of kindliness even among the students of Kultur. The real question is as to which shall have the last word in the state—the idealists or the organizers. Internationalists are in futile revolt against all organization when they would have war of the proletariat on the bourgeoisie.

Democracy refuses to think strategically unless and until compelled to do so for purposes of defense. That, of course, does not prevent democracy from declaring war for an ideal, as was seen during the French Revolution. One of the inconsistencies of our pacifists to-day is that they so often urge intervention in the affairs of other nations. In the Middle Ages vast unorganized crowds set out to march against the infidel and perished fecklessly by the way. It was not from lack of warning that the Western democracies were unprepared for the present war. At the same moment, early in this century, to cite only the case of Great Britain, three honored voices were appealing to our sovereign people and were not heard: Lord Rosebery called for efficiency, Mr. Chamberlain for economic defense, and Lord Roberts for military training. Democracy implies rule by consent of the average citizen, who does not view things from the hilltops, for he must be at his work in the fertile plains. There is no good in railing at the characteristics of popular government, for they are its qualities and no mere defects. President Wilson admits them when he says we must make the world a safe place henceforth for democracies. They were no less admitted in the British House of Commons when responsible ministers took pride in the fact that, save in respect of the defensive force of the navy, we were not prepared for the war.

The democrat thinks in principles, be they—according to his idiosyncrasy—ideals, prejudices, or economic laws. The organizer, on the other hand, plans construction, and, like an architect, must consider the ground for his foundations and the materials with which he will build. It must be concrete and detailed consideration, for bricks may be most suitable for his walls, but stone for his lintels, and timber and slate for his roof. If it be a state which he is erecting—not, be it noted, a nation which is growing—he must carefully consider the territory which it is desirable to occupy and the social structures—not economic laws—which are to his hand as the result of history. So he opposes his strategy to the ethics of the democrat.

Fierce moralists allow no extenuation for sin however persistent the temptation, and great undoubtedly must be the reward in heaven for the slum-dweller who "keeps straight." But practical reformers give much of their thought to the housing problem! Of late our political moralists have been very fierce. They preached the narrow way of "no annexations, no indemnities." In other words, they refused to reckon with the realities of geography and economics. Had we but faith as a grain of mustard seed in average human nature, could we not remove the mountains!

Practical sense, however, warns us that it would be wise to seize the present opportunity, when for once the democratic nations are efficiently armed to make the world a safe place for democracies when going about their ordinary business. In other words, we must see to the housing problem of our coming League of Nations. We must reckon presciently with the realities of space and time, and not be content merely to lay down on paper good principles of conduct. The good may not always appear the same even to those who are now allies, and will pretty surely appear not good, for a time at least, to our present enemies.

"No annexations, no indemnities" was no doubt a rallying cry not meant by its authors to support existing tyrannies. But it is surely legitimate to remark that there is a wide difference between the attitude of the lawyer with his presumptions unless there be proof to the contrary, and that of the business man untied by formulae. The one does things, and the other, at best, allows them to be done.

In the past, democracy has looked with suspicion on the activities even of popular governments, and therein has shown a wise self-knowledge. It used to be thought, and sooner or later will be thought again, that the main function of the state in free countries is to prevent tyrannous things from being done whether by offenders at home or invaders from abroad. Average citizenship is not a likely base for daring innovations. Adventurers, sole or corporate, must therefore be left to blaze the way to progress. In military and bureaucratic states it is otherwise; Napoleon could be a pioneer, as might have been Joseph II if his conservative subjects had not successfully revolted against him. In Prussia all progress has been state engineered, but then progress there has meant merely increase of efficiency.[1]

To save democracy, however, in its recent jeopardy we suspended the very safeguards of democracy, and allowed our governments to organize us not merely for defense but for offense. Had the war been short, this would have been a mere parenthesis in history. But it has been long, and social structures have wasted in part, and in part have been diverted to new uses, so that habits and vested interests have dissolved, and all society is as clay in our hands, if only we have the cunning to mold it while it is still yielding. But the art of the clay-molder, as of the worker in hot metal, lies not merely in knowing what he would make, but also in allowing for the properties of the material in which he is working. He must not only have artistic aims, but also technical knowledge; his human initiative must reckon with reality; he must cultivate his "ways and means" mind, while he tries to retain his ideals of form.

As the artist endeavors to his dying day to learn ever

[1] Twelve years ago I met a Prussian staff officer who told me that he spent his life trying to save half an hour on mobilization.

more about the medium in which he works—and not merely more in a scientific sense, but in a practical "tactile" way, gaining, as we say, greater command over his material—so has it been with the knowledge of humanity at large in regard to the realities of the round world on which we must practice the intricate art of living together. It is not merely that we have amassed vast encyclopaedias of fact, but that, as we live through each new epoch, we see all the past and all the present with new eyes and from new standpoints. It is obvious that these four years of war have wrought a change in human outlook the like of which was not effected in all the previous life of those of us who have gray hairs. Yet, when we look back with our present knowledge, is it not clear that the currents of thought now running so tumultuously were already setting in gently some twenty years ago? In the last years of last century and the first of this, the organizers at Berlin and the minorities in London and Paris had already discerned the new drift of the straws.[1]

I propose trying to depict some of the realities, geographical and economic, in their twentieth-century perspective. The facts will most of them be old and familiar. But, in the language of the Mediaeval schoolmen, there is a great difference between *vera causa* and *causa causans*—mere academic learning and the realization which impels to action.

[1] Mr. Chamberlain resigned from the Cabinet in order to free himself as a leader in September, 1903, and Lord Roberts resigned from commander-in-chief with a similar idea in January, 1904.

Chapter Three

THE SEAMAN'S POINT OF VIEW

*"And God said, Let the waters be gathered
together in one place"*

THE physical facts of geography have remained substantially the same during the fifty or sixty centuries of recorded human history. Forests have been cut down, marshes have been drained, and deserts may have broadened, but the outlines of land and water, and the lie of mountains and rivers have not altered except in detail. The influence of geographical conditions upon human activities has depended, however, not merely on the realities as we now know them to be and to have been, but in even greater degree on what men imagined in regard to them. The ocean has been one throughout history, but for effective human purposes there were two oceans, western and eastern, until the Cape of Good Hope was rounded only four hundred years ago. So did it happen that Admiral Mahan in the closing years of last century could still base a new message in regard to sea-power on a text from the first chapter of Genesis. The ocean was one ocean all the time, but the practical meaning of that great reality was not wholly understood until a few years ago—perhaps it is only now being grasped in its entirety.

Each century has had its own geographical perspective. Men still living, though past the age of military service, were taught from a map of the world on which nearly all the interior of Africa was a blank; yet last year General Smuts could address the Royal Geographical Society on the German ambition to control the world from the now explored vantage-ground of Central Africa. The geographical perspective of the twentieth century differs, however, from that of all the previous centuries in more than mere extension. In outline our geographical knowledge is now complete. We have lately attained to the North Pole, and have found that it is in the midst of a deep sea, and to the South Pole, and have found it upon a high plateau. With those final discoveries the book of the pioneers has been closed. No considerable fertile new land, no important mountain range, and no first-class river can any more be the reward of adventure. Moreover, the map of the world had hardly been sketched before claims to the political ownership of all the dry land had been pegged out. Whether we think of the physical, economic, military, or political interconnection of things on the surface of the globe, we are now for the first time presented with a closed system. The known does not fade any longer through the half-known into the unknown; there is no longer elasticity of political expansion in lands beyond the pale. Every shock, every disaster or superfluity, is now felt even to the antipodes, and may indeed return from the antipodes, as the air waves from the eruption of the volcano Krakatoa in the year 1883 were propelled in rings over the globe until they converged to a point in the opposite hemisphere, and thence di-

verged again to meet once more over Krakatoa, the seat
of their origin. Every deed of humanity will henceforth
be echoed and re-echoed in like manner round the
world. That, in the ultimate analysis, is why every considerable state was bound to be drawn into the recent
war, if it lasted, as it did last, long enough.

To this day, however, our view of the geographical
realities is colored for practical purposes by our pre-
conceptions from the past. In other words, human society is still related to the facts of geography not as
they are, but in no small measure as they have been
approached in the course of history. It is only with an
effort that we can yet realize them in the true, the complete, and therefore detached, perspective of the twentieth century. This war has taught us rapidly, but there
are still vast numbers of our citizens who look out on
to a vivid Western foreground, but only to a very dim
Eastern background. In order therefore to appreciate
where we now stand, it will be worth while to consider
shortly the stages by which we have arrived. Let us
begin with the succeeding phases of the seaman's outlook.

. . . .

Imagine a vast tawny desert, raised a few hundred
feet above the sea level. Imagine a valley with precipi-
tous rocky slopes trenched into this desert pleateau, and
the floor of the valley carpeted with a strip of black
soil, through the midst of which winds northward for
five hundred miles a silvery navigable river. That river
is the Nile flowing from where the granite rocks of
Assouan break its navigability at the first cataract to

where its waters divide at the head of the Delta. From desert edge to desert edge across the valley is a crow-fly distance of some ten or twenty miles. Stand on one of the brinks with the desert behind you; the rocky descent falls from your feet to the strip of plain below, and

away over the floods of the summer-time, or the green of the growing winter-time, or the golden harvests of the spring, you are faced by the opposing wall of rock rising to the other desert. The recesses in those rock fronts were carved long ago into cavernous temples and tombs, and the salients into mighty effigies of kings and gods. Egypt, in this long sunken belt, was anciently civilized because all the essential physical advantages were

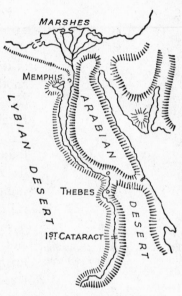

Fig. 1.—A river-world apart.

here combined for men to work upon. On the one hand were a rich soil, abundant water, and a powerful sunshine; hence fertility for the support of a population in affluence. On the other hand was a smooth waterway within half a dozen miles or less of every field in the country. There was also motive power for shipping, since the river current carried vessels northward, and the Etesian winds—known on the ocean as the trade-winds—brought them southward again. Fertility and a line of communications—man-power and facilities for its organization; there are the essential ingredients for a kingdom.

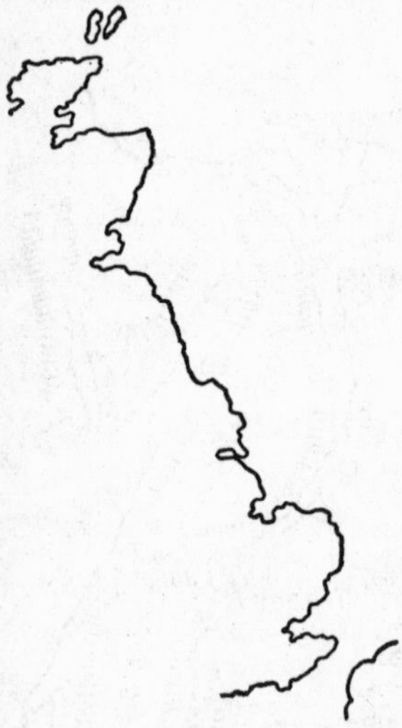

FIG. 2.—A coastal navigation drawn to the same scale as the river navigation on p. 31.

We are asked to picture the early condition of Egypt as that of a valley held by a chain of tribes, who fought with one another in fleets of great war canoes, just as later tribes have fought on the river Congo in our own time. Some one of these tribes, having defeated its neighbors, gained possession of a longer section of the valley, a more extensive material basis for its man-power, and on that basis organized further conquests. At last the whole length of the valley was brought under a single rule, and the kings of all Egypt established their palace at Thebes. Northward and southward, by boat on the Nile, traveled their administrators—their messengers and their magistrates. Eastward and westward lay the strong defense of the deserts, and at the northern limit, against the sea pirates, a belt of marsh round the shore of the Delta.[1]

Now carry your mind to the "Great Sea," the Medi-

[1] See *The Dawn of History* by Professor J. L. Myres.

terranean. You have there essentially the same physical ingredients as in Egypt but on a larger scale, and you have based upon them not a mere kingdom but the Roman Empire. From the Phoenician coast for two thousand miles westward lies the broad water-way to its mouth at Gibraltar, and on either hand are fertile shorelands with winter rains and harvest sunshine. But there is a distinction to be made between the dwellers along the Nile banks and those along the Mediterranean shores. The conditions of human activity are relatively uniform in all parts of Egypt; each of the constituent tribes would have its farmers and its boatmen. But the races round the Mediterranean became specialized; some were content to till their fields and navigate their rivers at home, but others gave most of their energy to seamanship and foreign commerce. Side by side, for instance, dwelt the home-staying, corn-growing Egyptians and the adventurous Phoenicians. A longer and more sustained effort of organization was therefore needed to weld all the kingdoms of the Mediterranean into a single political unit.

Modern research has made it plain that the leading seafaring race of antiquity came at all times from that square of water between Europe and Asia which is known alternatively as the Aegean Sea and the Archipelago, the "Chief Sea" of the Greeks. Sailors from this sea would appear to have taught the Phoenicians their trade in days when as yet Greek was not spoken in the "Isles of the Gentiles." It is of deepest interest for our present purpose to note that the center of civilization in the pre-Greek world of the Aegean, according both to the indications of mythology and the recent excavations, was in the Island of Crete. Was that the first base of sea-power? From that home did the seamen fare who, sailing northward, saw the coast of the rising sun to their right hand, and of the setting sun to their left hand, and named the one Asia and the other Europe? Was it from Crete that the sea-folk settled round the other shores of the Aegean "sea-chamber," forming to this day a coastal veneer of Greek population in front of peoples of other race a few miles inland? There are so many islands in the Archipelago that the name has become, like the Delta of Egypt, one of the common descriptive terms of geography. But Crete is the largest and most fruitful of them. Have we here a first instance of the importance of the larger base for sea-power? The man-power of the sea must be nourished by land fertility somewhere, and other things being equal—such as security of the home and energy of the people—that power will control the sea which is based on the greater resources.

The next phase of Aegean development teaches apparently the same lesson. Horse-riding tribes of Hellenic speech came down from the north into the peninsula which now forms the mainland of Greece, and settled, Hellenizing the early inhabitants. These Hellenes advanced into the terminal limb of the peninsula, the Peloponnese, slenderly attached to the continent by the isthmus of Corinth. Thence, organizing sea-power on their relatively considerable peninsular base, one of the Hellenic tribes, the Dorians, conquered Crete, a smaller though completely insular base.

Some centuries passed, during which the Greeks sailed round the southern headlands of the Peloponnese into the Ionian Sea, and colonized along the shores of that sea also. So the peninsula came to be a citadel in the midst of the Greek sea-world. Along the outer shores of the twin waters, Aegean and Ionian, the Greek colonists were but a fringe exposed to attack from behind. Only in the central peninsula were they relatively, although as the sequel shows not absolutely, safe.

To the eastern, outer shore of the Aegean the Persians came down from the interior against the Greek cities by the sea, and the Athenian fleet carried aid from the peninsular citadel to the threatened kinsfolk over the water, and issue was joined between sea-power and land-power. A Persian sea-raid was defeated at Marathon, and the Persians then resorted to the obvious strategy of baffled land-power; under King Xerxes they marched round, throwing a bridge of boats over the Dardanelles, and entered the peninsula from the north, with the idea of destroying the nest whence the wasps emerged which stung them and flew elusively away. The Persian effort failed, and it was reserved for the half-Greek, half-barbaric Macedonians, established in the root of the Greek Peninsula itself, to end the first cycle of sea-power by conquering to south of them the Greek sea-base, and then marching into Asia, and through Syria into Egypt, and on the way destroying Tyre of the Phoenicians. Thus they made a "closed sea" of the Eastern Mediterranean by depriving both the Greeks and the Phoenicians of their bases. That done, the Macedonian king, Alexander, could advance light-heartedly into Upper Asia. We may talk of the mobility of ships and of the long arm of the fleet, but, after all, sea-power is fundamentally a matter of appropriate

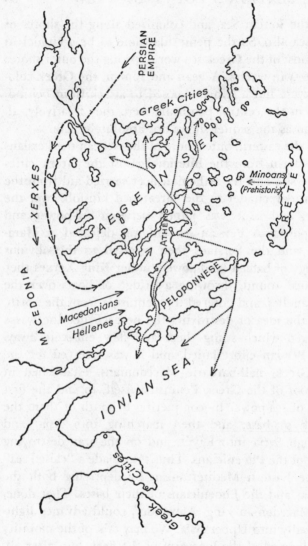

FIG. 3.—The Greek seas, Aegean and Ionian, showing the Cretan insular sea base, and the Greek peninsular sea base; also the march of Xerxes to outflank the sea power of Athens.

bases, productive and secure. Greek sea-power passed through the same phases as Egyptian river-power. The end of both was the same; without the protection of a navy, commerce moved securely over a water-way because all the shores were held by one and the same land-power.

. . . .

Now we go to the Western Mediterranean. Rome there began as a fortified town on a hill, at the foot of which was a bridge and a river-wharf. This hill-bridge-port-town was the citadel and market of a small nation of farmers, who tilled Latium, the "broad land" or plain, between the Apennines and the sea. "Father" Tiber was for shipping purposes merely a creek, navigable for the small sea-craft of those days, which entered thus from the coast a few miles into the midst of the plain, but that was enough to give Rome the advantage over her rivals, the towns crowning the Alban and Etruscan hills of the neighborhood. Rome had the bridge and the inmost port just as had London.

Based on the productivity of Latium, the Romans issued from the Tiber to traffic round the shores of the Western Mediterranean. Soon they came into competition with the Carthaginians, who were based on the fertility of the Mejerdeh Valley in the opposite promontory of Africa. The First Punic or Phoenician War ensued, and the Romans victoriously held the sea. They then proceeded to widen their base by annexing all the peninsular part of Italy as far as the Rubicon River.

In the Second Punic War, the Carthaginian general, Hannibal, endeavored to outflank the Roman sea-power by marching round it, as Xerxes and Alexander had done in regard to the sea-powers opposed to them. He carried his army over the western narrows from Africa into Spain, and then advanced through Southern Gaul into Italy. He was defeated, and Rome annexed

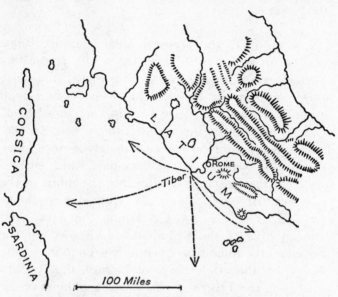

Fig. 4.—Latium, a fertile sea base.

the Mediterranean coasts of Gaul and Spain. By taking Carthage itself in the Third Punic War, she made a "closed sea" of the Western Mediterranean, for all the shores were held by one and the same land-power.

There remained the task of uniting the controls of the western and eastern basins of the Mediterranean, connected by the Sicilian Strait and the Strait of Messina. The Roman legions passed over into Macedonia and thence into Asia, but the distinction between Latin

West and Greek East remained, as was evident when civil war came to be waged between the Roman governors of the West and the East, Caesar and Antony. At the sea-fight of Actium, one of the decisive battles of the world's history, the Western fleet of Caesar destroyed the Eastern fleet of Antony. Thenceforth for five centuries the entire Mediterranean was a "closed sea"; and we think in consequence of the Roman Empire as chiefly a land-power. No fleet was needed, save a few police vessels, to maintain as complete a command of the arterial sea-way of the Mediterranean as ever the kings of Egypt exercised over their Nile-way. Once more land-power terminated a cycle of competition upon the water by depriving sea-power of its bases. True that there had been the culminating sea-battle of Actium, and that Caesar's fleet had won the reward of all finally successful fleets, the command over all the sea. But that command was not afterwards maintained upon the sea, but upon the land by holding the coasts.

.   .   .   .

When Rome had completed the organization of her power round the Mediterranean, there followed a long transitional epoch, during which the oceanic development of Western civilization was gradually preparing. The transition began with the Roman road system, constructed for the greater mobility of the marching legions.

After the close of the Punic Wars four Latin-speaking provinces encircled the Western Mediterranean—Italy, Southern Gaul, Eastern and Southern Spain, and Carthaginian Africa. The outer boundary of the African province was protected by the Sahara desert, and Italy had in rear the Adriatic moat, but in Gaul and

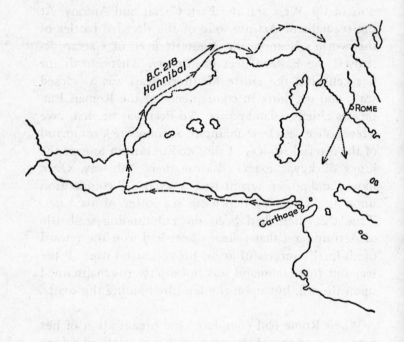

FIG. 5.—Two famous marches for the purpose of outflanking

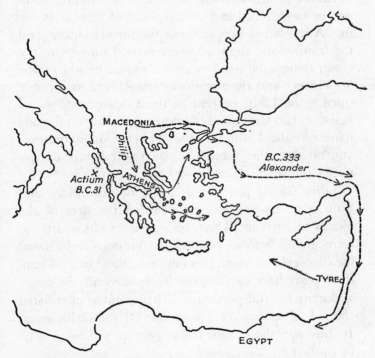

MACEDONIA

Philip

Actium
B.C. 31

ATHENS

B.C. 333
Alexander

TYRE

EGYPT

sea power; also a victory which "closed" the Mediterranean.

Spain Rome found herself the uncomfortable neighbor of independent Celtic tribes. Thus the familiar dilemma of empire presented itself; to advance and end the menace, or to entrench and shut it out, but leave it in being. A still virile people chose the former course, and the frontier and the roads were carried through to the ocean along a thousand miles of frontage between Cape St. Vincent and the mouths of the Rhine. As a consequence the Latin portion of the Empire came to be based on two features of physical geography: on the one hand was the Latin Sea—the Western Mediterranean; and on the other hand was the Latin Peninsula, between the Mediterranean and the ocean.[1]

Julius Caesar penetrated to the Bay of Biscay, and built a fleet wherewith he defeated the fleet of the Veneti of Brittany. Then, because the Celts of Britain were giving help to their Gallic kinsmen, he crossed the Channel and smote them in their island base. A hundred years later the Romans conquered all the lower and more fruitful portion of Britain, and so eliminated the risk of the rise of a sea-power off the Gallic coast. In this way the Channel also became a "closed sea," controlled by land-power.

After four centuries the land-power of Rome waned, and the seas on either side of the Latin Peninsula then soon ceased to be "closed." The Norsemen raided over the North Sea from their fiords, and through the Channel, and through the Straits of Gibraltar, even into the recesses of the Mediterranean, enveloping with their

[1] I do not know whether these names, Latin Sea and Latin Peninsula, have been used beforehand. It seems to me that they serve to crystallize important generalizations, and I propose using them henceforth.

sea-power the whole great peninsula. They seized forward bases in the islands of Britain and Sicily, and even nibbled at the mainland edges in Normandy and Southern Italy.

At the same time the Saracen camel-men came down from Arabia and took Carthage, Egypt, and Syria from the Empire—the provinces, that is to say, south of the Mediterranean. Then they launched their fleets on the water, and seized part of Sicily and part of Spain for overseas bases. Thus the Mediterranean ceased to be the arterial way of an empire, and became the frontier moat dividing Christendom from Islam. But the greater sea-power of the Saracen enabled them to hold Spain, though north of the water, just as at an earlier time the greater sea-power of Rome had enabled her to hold Carthage, though south of the water.

For a thousand years Latin Christendom was thus imprisoned in the Latin Peninsula and its appendant island of Britain. Fifteen hundred miles northeastward, measured in a straight line, trends the oceanic coast from the Sacred Promontory of the ancients to the Straits of Copenhagen, and fifteen hundred miles eastward, measured in the same way, lies the sinuous Mediterranean coast from the Sacred Promontory to the Straits at Constantinople. A lesser peninsula advances towards the main peninsula at each strait, Scandinavia on the one hand, and Asia Minor on the other; and behind the land bars so formed are two land-girt basins, the Baltic and Black Seas. If Britain be considered as balancing Italy, the symmetry of the distal end of the main peninsula is such that you might lay a Latin cross upon it with the head in Germany, the arms in Britain and Italy, the feet in Spain, and the center in France, thus typifying that ecclesiastical empire of the five nations which, though shifted northward, was the medi-

FIG. 6.—The Latin sea, showing the Roman territory after the Punic Wars.

eval heir of the Roman Caesars. Towards the East, however, where the Baltic and Black Seas first begin to define the peninsular character of Europe, the outline is less shapely, for the Balkan Peninsula protrudes southward, only tapering finally into the historic little peninsula of Greece.

Is it not tempting to speculate on what might have happened had Rome not refused to conquer eastward of the Rhine? Who can say that a single mighty sea-

FIG. 7.—The Latin peninsula, occupied by the modern Romance nations.

power, wholly Latinized as far as the Black and Baltic Seas, would not have commanded the world from its peninsular base? But classical Rome was primarily a Mediterranean and not a peninsular power, and the Rhine-Danube frontier must be regarded as demarking a penetration from the Mediterranean coast rather than as the incomplete achievement of a peninsular policy.

It was the "opening" again of the seas on either hand which first compacted Europe in the peninsular sense. Reaction had to be organized, or the pressures from north and south would have obliterated Christendom. So Charlemagne erected an empire astride of the Rhine, half Latin and half German by speech, but wholly Latin ecclesiastically. With this empire as base the Crusades were afterwards undertaken. Seen in large perspective at this distance of time, and from the seaman's point of view, the Crusades, if successful, would have had for their main effect the "closing" once more of the Mediterranean Sea. The long series of these wars, extending over two centuries, took two courses. On the one hand, fleets were sent out from Venice and Genoa to Jaffa and Acre on the Syrian coast; on the other hand, armies marched through Hungary, along the famous "corridor" of the Morava and Maritza Valleys, and through Constantinople and Asia Minor into Syria. The comparison is obvious between these campaigns of the Crusaders by land, from a German base round to the back of the Mediterranean Sea, and the similar campaign of Alexander from his Macedonian base. A good many parallels might, indeed, be drawn between the half-Greek Macedonians and the half-Latin Germans. No Greek of the full blood but looked upon a Macedonian as a sort of bastard! But his position in the broad root of the Greek Peninsula enabled the Macedonian to conquer the Greek sea-base, as the position of the German in the broad root of the greater Latin Peninsula has always made him dangerous to the Latin sea-bases beyond the Rhine and the Alps.

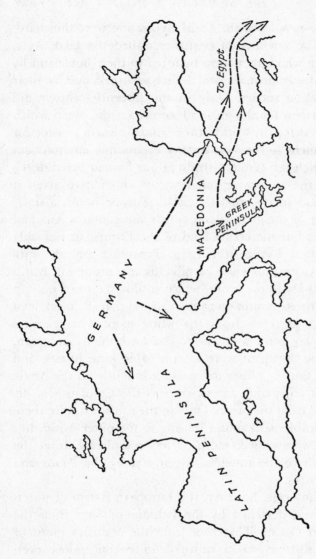

Fig. 8.—Showing Germany in the neck of the Latin peninsula, and Macedonia in the neck of the Greek peninsula.

The peoples of the Latin civilization were thus hardened by a winter of centuries, called the Dark Ages, during which they were besieged in their homeland by the Mohammedans, and failed to break out by their Crusading sorties. Only in the fifteenth century did time ripen for the great adventure on the ocean which was to make the world European. It is worth pausing for a moment to consider further the unique environment in which the Western strain of our human breed developed the enterprise and tenacity which have given it the lead in the modern world. Europe is but a small corner of the great island which also contains Asia and Africa, but the cradle land of the Europeans was only a half of Europe—the Latin Peninsula and the subsidiary peninsulas and islands clustered around it. Broad deserts lay to the south, which could be crossed only in some three months on camel back, so that the black men were fended off from the white men. The trackless ocean lay to the west, and to the north the frozen ocean. To the northeast were interminable pine forests, and rivers flowing either to ice-choked mouths in the Arctic Sea or to inland waters, such as the Caspian Sea, detached from the ocean. Only to the southeast were there practicable oasis routes leading to the outer world, but these were closed, more or less completely, from the seventh to the nineteenth century, by the Arabs and the Turks.

In any case, however, the European system of waterways was detached by the Isthmus of Suez from the Indian Ocean. Therefore from the seaman's point of view Europe was a quite definite conception, even though the landsman might think of it as merging with

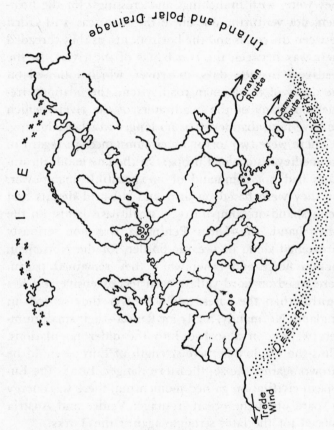

FIG. 9.—The river and coast ways of the seaman's Europe. The land surface of all Europe measures less than 2 per cent of the surface of the globe. This was the prison of medieval Christendom, but the sea base of modern Christendom.

Asia. It was a world apart, but within that world was ample fertility, and in its water-paths a natural provision for the intimacy of a family of nations. Water-paths they were, with branchings and crossings, for the boatmen, not venturing out on to the high seas, still sailed between the coasts and the horizon, just as they threaded their way between the two banks of the rivers. In the relatively roadless days, moreover, which followed on the decay of the Roman road system, the boatmen frequented many of the headwaters of the rivers, which we have now abandoned as no longer worth navigating.

There were two fortunate circumstances in regard to the medieval siege of Europe. On the one hand, the Infidels had not command of inexhaustible man-power, for they were based on arid and sub-arid deserts and steppes, and on comparatively small oasis lands; on the other hand, the Latin Peninsula was not seriously threatened along its oceanic border, for the Norsemen, though fierce and cruel while they remained pagan, were based on fiord valleys even less extensive and less fruitful than the oases, and wherever they settled—in England, Normandy, Sicily, or Russia—their small numbers were soon absorbed into the older populations. Thus the whole defensive strength of Europe could be thrown against the southeastern danger. But as the European civilization gained momentum, there was energy to spare upon the ocean frontage; Venice and Austria sufficed for the later struggle against the Turks.

After the essays, without practical result, of the Norsemen to force their way through the northern ice of Greenland, the Portuguese undertook to find a seaway to the Indies round the coast of Africa. They were inspired to the venture by the lead of Prince Henry, "the Navigator," half Englishman and half Portuguese. At first sight it seems strange that pilots like Columbus, who had spent their lives on coasting voyages, often going from Venice to Britain, should so long have delayed an exploration southward as they issued from the Straits of Gibraltar. Still more strange does it appear that when at last they had set themselves to discover the outline of Africa, it took them two generations of almost annual voyaging before Da Gama led the way into the Indian Ocean. The cause of their difficulties was physical. For a thousand miles, from the latitude of the Canary Islands to that of Cape Verde, the African coast is a torrid desert, because the dry trade-wind there blows off the land without ceasing. It might be a relatively easy matter to sail southward on that steady breeze, but how was the voyage back to be accomplished by ships which could not sail near the wind like a modern clipper, and yet dared neither sail out on to the broad ocean across the wind, nor yet tediously tack their way home off a coast with no supplies of fresh food and water, in a time when the plague of scurvy had not yet been mastered?

Once the Portuguese had found the ocean-way into the Indian seas, they soon disposed of the opposition of the Arab dhows. Europe had taken its foes in rear; it had sailed round to the rear of the land, just as Xerxes, Alexander, Hannibal, and the Crusaders had marched round to the rear of the sea.

From that time until the opening of the Suez Canal in 1869, the seamen of Europe continued in ever-increasing number to round the Cape, and to sail northward on the eastern ocean as far as China and Japan. Only one ship, the *Vega* of the Swedish Baron Nordenskiold, has to this day made the passage round the north of Asia—with infinite risk, and in two years—and she happens not to have circumnavigated the Triple Continent, for she returned home through the Suez Canal. Nor was the overland journey to the Indies undertaken, except as an adventure, until last century. The trade to the Indies was conducted by coasting—no doubt in a bold way, from point to point, round the great southward promontory whose shores were European and African on the one side, and African and Asiatic on the other. From the point of view of the traffic to the Indies, the world was a vast cape, standing out southward from between Britain and Japan. This world-promontory was enveloped by sea-power, as had been the Greek and Latin promontories beforehand: all its coasts were open to ship-borne trade or to attack from the sea. The seamen naturally chose for the local bases of their trading or warfare small islands off the continental coast, such as Mombasa, Bombay, Singapore, and Hongkong, or small peninsulas, such as the Cape of Good Hope and Aden, since those positions offered shelter for their ships and security for their depots. When grown bolder and stronger they put their commercial cities, such as Calcutta and Shanghai, near the entry of great river-ways into productive and populous marketlands. The seamen of Europe, owing to their greater mobility, have thus had superiority for some four centuries over the landsmen of Africa and Asia.

The passing of the imminent danger to Christendom, because of the relative weakening of Islam, was, no

doubt, one of the reasons for the break-up of Medieval
Europe at the close of the Middle Ages; already in 1493
the Pope had to draw his famous line through the ocean,
from Pole to Pole, in order to prevent Spanish and
Portuguese seamen from quarreling. As a result of this
break-up, there arose five competing oceanic powers—
Portuguese, Spanish, French, Dutch, and English—in
the place of the one power
which would, no doubt,
have been the ideal of
the Crusaders.

Thus the outcome of a
thousand years of tran-
sition, from the ancient
to the modern conditions
of sea-power, is such as to
prompt a comparison be-
tween the Greek and
Latin Peninsulas, each

FIG. 10.—The World-Promontory.

with its offset island. Peninsular Greece and insular
Crete anticipated in their relations the Latin Peninsula
and the island of Britain. Under the Dorians the greater
resources of the peninsular mainland were utilized for
the conquest of Crete, but at a later time the rivalry of
Sparta and Athens prevented a full exploitation of the
peninsula as a sea-base. So in the case of the greater
peninsula and greater island, Britain was conquered
and held by Rome from the peninsular mainland; but
when the Middle Ages were closing, several rival sea-
bases occupied the Latin Peninsula, each of them open
to attack from the land behind, as Athens and Sparta
had been open to the Macedonian invasion. Of these

Latin sea-bases, one, Venice, fronted towards Islam, while the others contended with internecine feuds for the command of the ocean, so that in the end the lesser British insular base, faced by no united peninsular base, became the home of a power which enveloped and contained the greater peninsula.

Within Great Britain itself it is true that there was not effective unity until the eighteenth century, but the facts of physical geography have determined that there should always be a predominant English people in the south of the island, whether as foe or partner of the Scottish and Welsh peoples. From Norman days, until the growth of the modern industries upon the coal-fields, the English nation was almost uniquely simple in its structure. It is that which makes English history the epic story that it is, until the histories of Scotland and Ireland come to confuse their currents with it. One fertile plain between the mountains of the west and north and the narrow seas to the east and south, a people of farmers, a single king, a single parliament, a tidal river, a single great city for central market and port—those are the elements on which the England was built whose warning beacons blazed on the hilltops from Plymouth to Berwick-on-Tweed, in that night of Elizabeth's reign when the Spanish Armada had entered the Channel. On a smaller scale, Latium, the Tiber, the city, the senate, and the people of Rome once presented a similar unity and a similar executive strength. The real base historically of British sea-power was our English plain—fertile and detached; coal and iron from round the borders of the plain have been added in later times. The white ensign of the Royal Navy is with some historic justice the flag of St. George, with a "difference" for the minor partners.

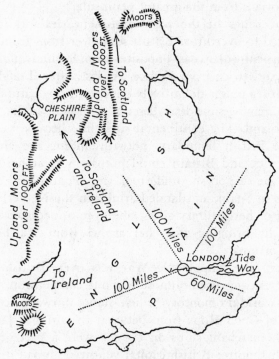

Fig. 11.—The English plain, a fertile sea base.

Every characteristic of sea-power may be studied in British history during the last three centuries, but the home-base, productive and secure, is the one thing essential to which all things else have been added. We are told that we should thank God daily for our Channel, but as I looked out over the glorious harvest of this English plain in this critical year 1918, it seemed to me that our thanksgiving *as a seafaring people* should be no less for our fruitful soil. Insular Crete had to yield to the Dorians from the greater peninsula.

Four times in the past three centuries was it attempted to overthrow British sea-power from frontages on the peninsular coast opposite—from Spain, from Holland, and twice from France. At last, after Trafalgar, British sea-power definitively enveloped the Latin Peninsula, having subsidiary bases at Gibraltar, Malta, and Heligoland. The continental coast line became the effective British boundary, notwithstanding the enemy privateers, and Britain could prepare war at her ease upon the sea. So she undertook the "Peninsular" campaigns in Spain, and landed armies in the Netherlands in aid of her military allies. She even anticipated Gallipoli by bringing away her armies from Walcheren and Corunna.

When the Napoleonic War was over, British sea-power encompassed, almost without competition, that great world-promontory which stands forward to the Cape of Good Hope from between Britain and Japan. British merchant ships on the sea were a part of the British Empire; British capital ventured abroad in foreign countries was a part of British resources, controlled from the city of London and available for the maintenance of power on and over the seas. It was a proud and lucrative position, and seemed so secure that the mid-Victorian folk thought it almost in the natural order of things that insular Britain should rule the seas. We were, perhaps, not quite a popular people in the rest of the world; our position behind a Channel seemed an unfair advantage. But warships cannot navigate the mountains, and since the French wars of the Plantagenets we have not sought to make permanent European conquests, so that, on the whole, we may hope that the verdict of foreign historians on our Britain of the nineteenth century may resemble that of the famous schoolboy who described his headmaster as "a beast, but a just beast."

Perhaps the most remarkable outcome of British sea-power was the position in the Indian Ocean during the generation before the war. The British "Raj" in India depended on support from the sea, yet on all the waters between the Cape of Good Hope, India, and Australia, there was habitually no British battleship or even first-class cruiser. In effect, the Indian Ocean was a "closed sea." Britain owned or "protected" most of the coast lines, and the remaining frontages were either on islands, as the Dutch East Indies, or on territories such as Portuguese Mozambique and German East Africa, which, although continental, were inaccessible under existing conditions by land-way from Europe. Save in the Persian Gulf, there could be no rival base for sea-power which combined security with the needful resources, and Britain made it a declared principle of her policy that no sea-base should be established on either the Persian or Turkish shores of the Persian Gulf. Superficially there is a striking similarity between the closed Mediterranean of the Romans, with the Legions along the Rhine frontier, and the closed Indian Ocean, with the British army on the northwest frontier of India. The difference lay in the fact that, whereas the closing of the Mediterranean depended on the Legions, the closing of the Indian seas was maintained by the long arm of sea-power itself from the home-base.

. . . .

In the foregoing rapid survey of the vicissitudes of sea-power, we have not stayed to consider that well-worn theme of the single mastery of the seas. Everyone now realizes that owing to the continuity of the ocean and the mobility of ships, a decisive battle at sea has immediate and far-reaching results. Caesar beat Antony at Actium, and Caesar's orders were enforceable forthwith on every shore of the Mediterranean. Britain won her culminating victory at Trafalgar, and could deny all the ocean to the fleets of her enemies, could transport her armies to whatsoever coast she would and remove them again, could carry supplies home from foreign sources, could exert pressure in negotiation on whatsoever offending state had a sea-front. Our concern here has been rather in regard to the bases of sea-power and the relation to these of land-power. In the long run, that is the fundamental question. There were fleets of war canoes on the Nile, and the Nile was closed to their contention by a single land-power controlling their fertile bases through all the length of Egypt. A Cretan insular base was conquered from a larger Greek peninsular base. Macedonian land-power closed the Eastern Mediterranean to the warships both of Greeks and Phoenicians by depriving them impartially of their bases. Hannibal struck overland at the peninsular base of Roman sea-power, and that base was saved by victory on land. Caesar won the mastery of the Mediterranean by victory on the water, and Rome then retained control of it by the defense of land frontiers. In the Middle Ages Latin Christendom defended itself on the sea from its peninsular base, but in modern times, because competing states grew up within that peninsula, and there were several bases of sea-power upon it, all open to attack from the land, the mastery of the seas passed to a power which was less broadly based, but on an island —fortunately a fertile and coal-bearing island. On sea-power, thus based, British adventurers have founded an overseas empire of colonies, plantations, depots, and protectorates, and have established, by means of sea-borne armies, local land-powers in India and Egypt. So impressive have been the results of British sea-power that there has perhaps been a tendency to neglect the warnings of history and to regard sea-power in general as inevitably having, because of the unity of the ocean, the last word in the rivalry with land-power.

.   .   .   .   .   .

Never has sea-power played a greater part than in the recent war and in the events which led up to it. Those events began some twenty years ago with three great victories won by the British fleet without the firing of a gun. The first was at Manila, in the Pacific Ocean, when a German squadron threatened to intervene to protect a Spanish squadron, which was being defeated by an American squadron, and a British squadron stood by the Americans. Without unduly stressing that single incident, it may be taken as typical of the relations of the Powers during the war between Spain and America, which war gave to America detached possessions both in the Atlantic and Pacific, and led to her undertaking the construction of the Panama Canal, in order to gain the advantages of insularity for the mobilization of her warships. So was a first step taken towards the reconciliation of British and American hearts. Moreover the Monroe Doctrine was upheld in regard to South America.

The second of these victories of the British fleet was when it held the ocean during the South African War, of such vital consequence to the maintenance of the British rule in India; and the third was when it kept the ring round the Russo-Japanese War, and incidentally kept the door open into China. In all three cases history would have been very different but for the intervention of the British fleet. None the less—and perhaps as a consequence—the growth of the German fleet under the successive Navy Laws, induced the withdrawal of the British battle squadrons from the Far East and from the Mediterranean, and co-operation in those seas with the Japanese and French sea-powers.

The Great War itself began in the old style, and it was not until 1917 that the new aspects of reality became evident. In the very first days of the struggle the British fleet had already taken command of the ocean, enveloping, with the assistance of the French fleet, the whole peninsular theater of the war on land. The German troops in the German colonies were isolated, German merchant shipping was driven off the seas, the British expeditionary force was transported across the Channel without the loss of a man or a horse, and British and French supplies from over the ocean were safely brought in. In a word, the territories of Britain and France were made one for the purpose of the war, and their joint boundary was advanced to within gun-shot range of the German coast—no small offset for the temporary, though deeply regretted, loss of certain French departments. After the battle of the Marne the true war map of Europe would have shown a Franco-British frontier following the Norwegian, Danish, German, Dutch, and Belgian coasts—at a distance of three miles in the case of the neutral coasts—and then running as a sinuous line through Belgium and France to the Jura border of Switzerland. West of that boundary, whether by land or sea, the two Powers could make ready their defense against the enemy. Nine months later Italy dared to join the Allies, mainly because her ports were kept open by the Allied sea-power.

On the Eastern front also the old style of war held. Land-power was there divided into two contending forces, and the outer of the two, notwithstanding its incongruous Czardom, was allied with the sea-power of the democratic West. In short, the disposition of forces repeated in a general way that of a century earlier, when British sea-power supported the Portuguese and Spaniards in "the Peninsula," and was allied with the autocracies of the Eastern land-powers. Napoleon fought on two fronts, which in the terms of to-day we should describe as Western and Eastern.

In 1917, however, came a great change, due to the entry of the United States into the war, the fall of the Russian Czardom, and the subsequent collapse of the Russian fighting strength. The world-strategy of the contest was entirely altered. We have been fighting since, and can afford to say it without hurting any of our allies, to make the world a safe place for democracies.

So much as regards idealism. But it is equally important that we should bear in mind the new face of reality. We have been fighting lately, in the close of the war, a straight duel between land-power and sea-power, and sea-power has been laying siege to land-power. We have conquered, but had Germany conquered she would have established her sea-power on a wider base than any in history, and in fact on the widest possible base. The joint continent of Europe, Asia, and Africa, is now effectively, and not merely theoretically, an island. Now and again, lest we forget, let us call it the World-Island in what follows.

One reason why the seamen did not long ago rise to the generalization implied in the expression "World-Island," is that they could not make the round voyage of it. An ice-cap, two thousand miles across, floats on the polar sea, with one edge aground on the shoals off the north of Asia. For the common purposes of navigation, therefore, the continent is not an island. The seamen of the last four centuries have treated it as a vast promontory stretching southward from a vague north, as a mountain peak may rise out of the clouds from hidden foundations. Even in the last century, since the opening of the Suez Canal, the eastward voyage has still been round a promontory, though with the point at Singapore instead of Cape Town.

This fact and its vastness have made men think of the Continent as though it differed from other islands in more than size. We speak of its parts as Europe, Asia, and Africa in precisely the same way that we speak of the parts of the ocean as Atlantic, Pacific, and Indian. In theory even the ancient Greeks regarded it as insular, yet they spoke of it as the "World." The school children of to-day are taught of it as the "Old World," in contrast with a certain pair of peninsulas which together constitute the "New World." Seamen speak of it merely as "the Continent," the continuous land.

Let us consider for a moment the proportions and relations of this newly realized Great Island.[1] It is set as it were on the shoulder of the earth with reference to the North Pole. Measuring from Pole to Pole along the central meridian of Asia, we have first a thousand miles of ice-clad sea as far as the northern shore of Siberia, then five thousand miles of land to the southern point of India, and then seven thousand miles of sea to the Antarctic cap of ice-clad land. But measured along the meridian of the Bay of Bengal or of the Arabian Sea, Asia is only some three thousand five hundred miles across. From Paris to Vladivostok is six thousand miles, and from Paris to the Cape of Good Hope is a similar distance; but these measurements are on a globe twenty-six thousand miles round. Were it not for the ice impediment to its circumnavigation, practical seamen would long ago have spoken of the Great Island by some such name, for it is only a little more than one-fifth as large as their ocean.

The World-Island ends in points northeastward and southeastward. On a clear day you can see from the northeastern headland across Bering Strait to the beginning of the long pair of peninsulas, each measuring about one twenty-sixth of the globe, which we call the

[1] It would be misleading to attempt to represent the statements which follow in map form. They can only be appreciated on a globe. Therefore they are illustrated by diagrams; see Figs. 12 and 13.

Americas. Superficially there is no doubt a certain re-
semblance of symmetry in the Old and New Worlds;
each consists of two peninsulas, Africa and Euro-Asia
in the one case, and North and South America in the
other. But there is no real likeness between them. The
northern and northeastern shores of Africa for nearly
four thousand miles are so intimately related with the
opposite shores of Europe and Asia that the Sahara constitutes a far more effective break in social continuity
than does the Mediterranean. In the days of air navigation which are coming, sea-power will use the water-
way of the Mediterranean and Red Seas only by the
sufferance of land-power, a new amphibious cavalry,
when the contest with sea-power is in question.

But North and South America, slenderly connected
at Panama, are for practical purposes insular rather than
peninsular in regard to one another. South America
lies not merely to south, but also in the main to east
of North America; the two lands are in echelon, as soldiers would say, and thus the broad ocean encircles
South America, except for a minute proportion of its
outline. A like fact is true of North America with reference to Asia, for it stretches out into the ocean from
Bering Strait so that, as may be seen upon a globe,
the shortest way from Pekin to New York is across
Bering Strait, a circumstance which may some day have
importance for the traveler by railway or air. The third
of the new continents, Australia, lies a thousand miles
from the southeastern point of Asia, and measures only
one sixty-fifth of the surface of the globe.

Thus the three so-called new continents are in point
of area merely satellites of the old continent. There is

one ocean covering nine-twelfths of the globe; there is one continent—the World-Island—covering two-twelfths of the globe; and there are many smaller islands, whereof North America and South America are, for effective purposes, two, which together cover the remaining one-twelfth. The term "New World" implies, now that we can see the realities and not merely historic appearances, a wrong perspective.

The truth, seen with a broad vision, is that in the great world-promontory, extending southward to the Cape of Good Hope, and in the North American sea-base we have, on a vast scale, yet a third contrast of peninsula and island to be set beside the Greek peninsula and the island of Crete, and the Latin Peninsula and the British Island. But there is this vital difference, that the world-promontory, when united by modern overland communications, is in fact the World-Island, possessed potentially of the advantages both of insularity and of incomparably great resources.

Leading Americans have for some time appreciated the fact that their country is no longer a world apart, and President Wilson had brought his whole people round to that view when they consented to throw themselves into the war. But North America is no longer even a continent; in this twentieth century it is shrinking to be an island. Americans used to think of their three millions of square miles as the equivalent of all Europe; some day, they said, there would be a United States of Europe as sister to the United States of America. Now, though they may not all have realized it, they must no longer think of Europe apart from Asia and Africa. The Old World has become insular, or in other words a unit, incomparably the largest geographical unit on our globe.

There is a remarkable parallelism between the short history of America and the longer history of England; both countries have now passed through the same succession of colonial, continental, and insular stages. The Angle and Saxon settlements along the east and south coast of Britain have often been regarded as anticipating the thirteen English colonies along the east coast of North America; what has not always been remembered is that there was a continental stage in English history to be compared with that of Lincoln in America. The wars of Alfred the Great and William the Conqueror were in no small degree between contending parts of England, with the Norsemen intervening, and England was not effectively insular until the time of Elizabeth, because not until then was she free from the hostility of Scotland, and herself united, and therefore a unit, in her relations with the neighboring continent. America is to-day a unit, for the American people have fought out their internal differences, and it is insular, because events are compelling Americans to realize that their so-called continent lies on the same globe as *the* Continent.

Picture upon the map of the world this war as it has been fought in the year 1918. It has been a war between Islanders and Continentals, there can be no doubt of that. It has been fought on the Continent, chiefly across the landward front of peninsular France; and ranged on the one side have been Britain, Canada, the United States, Brazil, Australia, New Zealand, and Japan—all insular. France and Italy are peninsular, but

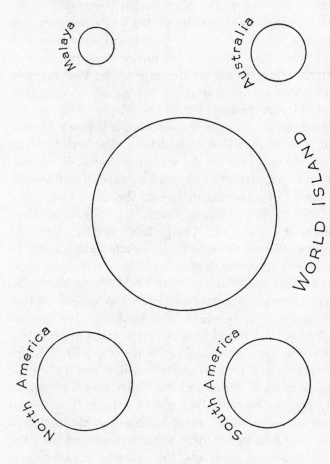

FIG. 12.—These circles represent the relative areas of the World Island and its satellites.

even with that advantage they would not have been in
the war to the end had it not been for the support of
the Islanders. India and China—so far as China has
been in the war on the Manchurian front—may be regarded as advanced guards of British, American, and
Japanese sea-power. Dutch Java is the only island of
large population which is not in the Western Alliance,
and even Java is not on the side of the Continentals.
There can be no mistaking the significance of this
unanimity of the islanders. The collapse of Russia has
cleared our view of the realities, as the Russian Revolution purified the ideals for which we have been fighting.

The facts appear in the same perspective if we consider the population of the globe. More than fourteen-
sixteenths of all humanity live on the Great Continent,
and nearly one-sixteenth more on the closely offset
islands of Britain and Japan. Even to-day, after four
centuries of emigration, only about one-sixteenth live in
the lesser continents. Nor is time likely to change these
proportions materially. If the middle west of North
America comes presently to support, let us say, another
hundred million people, it is probable that the interior
of Asia will at the same time carry two hundred millions more than now, and if the tropical part of South
America should feed a hundred million more, then the
tropical parts of Africa and the Indies may not improb-
ably support two hundred millions more. The Congo
forest alone, subdued to agriculture, would maintain
some four hundred million souls if populated with the
same density as Java, and the Javanese population is
still growing. Have we any right, moreover, to assume
that, given its climate and history, the interior of Asia

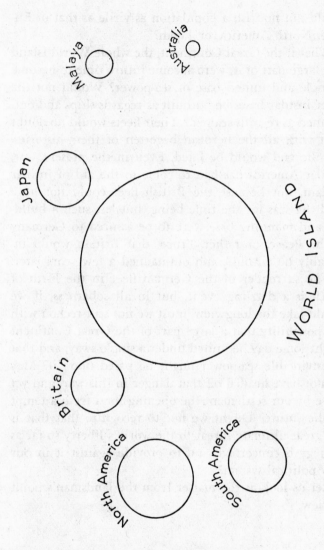

FIG. 13.—These circles represent the relative populations of the World Island and its satellites.

would not nourish a population as virile as that of Europe, North America, or Japan?

What if the Great Continent, the whole World-Island or a large part of it, were at some future time to become a single and united base of sea-power? Would not the other insular bases be outbuilt as regards ships and outmanned as regards seamen? Their fleets would no doubt fight with all the heroism begotten of their histories, but the end would be fated. Even in the present war, insular America has had to come to the aid of insular Britain, not because the British fleet could not have held the seas for the time being, but lest such a building and manning base were to be assured to Germany at the Peace, or rather Truce, that Britain would inevitably be outbuilt and outmanned a few years later.

The surrender of the German fleet in the Firth of Forth is a dazzling event, but in all soberness, if we would take the long view, must we not still reckon with the possibility that a large part of the Great Continent might some day be united under a single sway, and that an invincible sea-power might be based upon it? May we not have headed off that danger in this war, and yet leave by our settlement the opening for a fresh attempt in the future? Ought we not to recognize that that is the great ultimate threat to the world's liberty so far as strategy is concerned, and to provide against it in our new political system?

Let us look at the matter from the landsman's point of view.

Chapter Four

THE LANDSMAN'S POINT OF VIEW

FOUR centuries ago the whole outlook of mankind was changed in a single generation by the voyages of the great pioneers, Columbus, Da Gama, and Magellan. The idea of the unity of the ocean, beforehand merely inferred from the likeness of the tides in the Atlantic and Indian waters, suddenly became a part of the mental equipment of practical men. A similar revolution is in progress in the present generation in the rapid realization of the unity of the Continent owing to modern methods of communication by land and air. The islanders have been slow to understand what is happening. Britain went into the war for the defense of her neighbors, Belgium and France, seeing vaguely perhaps that she was herself threatened through their danger, but almost unanimous in her decision only because of a moral tie, her bond in regard to Belgium. America was shocked by the *Lusitania* tragedy, and was ultimately brought in because of the general infringement of the rights of neutrals by the German submarines. Neither of the Anglo-Saxon nations at first clearly saw the strategical meaning of the war. Theirs was an external view of the Continent, like that of the seaman who named the Guinea, Malabar, Coromandel, and Murman "Coasts." Neither in London nor in New York were international politics commonly discussed in the way in which they are discussed in the cafés of Continental Europe. In order, therefore, to appreciate the Continental view we must remove our standpoint from without to within the great ring of the "Coasts."

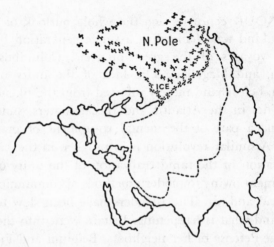

FIG. 14.—Showing the great part of Asia and Europe whose rivers flow either to the icy north, or into salt lakes without exit to the ocean; also how Africa faces Europe and Asia for 4000 miles. (Equal areas projection.)

Let us begin by "brigading" our data, for only so shall we be able to reason conveniently about the realities which the Continent presents for strategical thought. When you are thinking of large things you must think on broad lines; the colonel of a battalion thinks in companies, but the general of a division in brigades. For the purpose of forming our brigades, however, it will be necessary at the outset to go into some degree of geographical detail.

. . . .

The northern edge of Asia is the inaccessible coast, beset with ice except for a narrow water lane which opens here and there along the shore in the brief summer owing to the melting of the local ice formed in the winter between the grounded floes and the land. It so happens that three of the largest rivers in the world, the Lena, Yenisei, and Obi, stream northward through Siberia to this coast, and are therefore detached for practical purposes from the general system of the ocean and river navigations.[1] South of Siberia are other regions at least as large, drained into salt lakes having no outlet to the ocean; such are the basins of the Volga and Ural Rivers flowing to the Caspian Sea, and of the Oxus and Jaxartes to the Sea of Aral. Geographers usually describe these inward basins as "Continental." Taken together, the regions of Arctic and Continental drainage measure nearly a half of Asia and a quarter of Europe, and form a great continuous patch in the north and center of the continent. That whole patch, extending right across from the icy, flat shore of Siberia to the torrid, steep coasts of Baluchistan and Persia, has been inaccessible to navigation from the ocean. The opening of it by railways—for it was practically roadless beforehand—and by aeroplane routes in the near future, constitutes a revolution in the relations of men to the

[1] This is true up to the present time, though, with the aid of modern ice-breakers, the efforts which are being made, especially by Tyneside enterprise, to open a direct route to the mouths of the Obi and Yenisei may perhaps result in the establishment of a seaborne summer traffic to Western Siberia.

larger geographical realities of the world. Let us call this great region the Heartland of the Continent.

The north, center, and west of the Heartland are a plain, rising only a few hundred feet at most above sea level. In that greatest lowland on the globe are included Western Siberia, Turkestan, and the Volga basin of Europe, for the Ural Mountains, though a long range, are not of important height, and terminate some three hundred miles north of the Caspian, leaving a broad gateway from Siberia into Europe. Let us speak of this vast plain as the Great Lowland.

Southward the Great Lowland ends along the foot of a tableland, whose average elevation is about half a mile, with mountain ridges rising to a mile and a half. This tableland bears upon its broad back the three countries of Persia, Afghanistan, and Baluchistan; for convenience we may describe the whole of it as the Iranian Upland. The Heartland, in the sense of the region of Arctic and Continental drainage, includes most of the Great Lowland and most of the Iranian Upland; it extends therefore to the long, high, curving brink of the Persian Mountains, beyond which is the depression occupied by the Euphrates Valley and the Persian Gulf.

Now let us travel in imagination to the west of Africa. There, between the latitudes of the Canary and Cape Verde Islands, is a desert coast: it was the character of that coast, it will be remembered, which so long baffled the efforts of the medieval sailors to make the southward voyage round Africa. With a breadth of a thousand miles the Sahara spreads thence across the north of Africa from the Atlantic Ocean to the Valley of the Nile. The Sahara is not everywhere an utter desert;

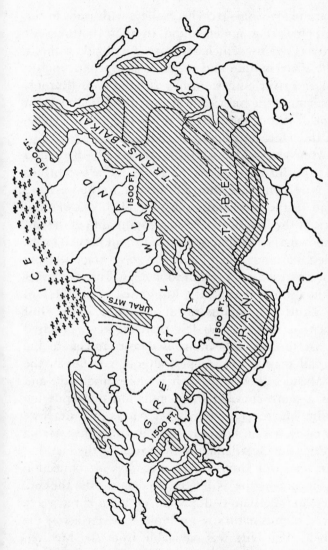

Fig. 15.—The Great Lowland, which is seen to extend westward into Europe, beyond the limits of the Heartland. The boundary of the Heartland in the east is here shown as including the lofty plateau courses of the Pacific and Indian rivers.

there are many oases—trenched valleys with wells to the water percolating underground in their bottoms, or hilly tracts against which at times the clouds gather— but these are minute and scattered exceptions upon a barren and riverless area nearly as large as all Europe. The Sahara is the most unbroken natural boundary in the world; throughout history it has been a barrier between the white and the black men.

Between the Sahara and the Heartland there is a broad gap which is occupied by Arabia. The two brinks of the Nile Valley are known as Libyan to the west and Arabian to the east; and away beyond the Lower Euphrates, at the foot of the Persian Mountains, is the district known as Arabistan or the country of the Arabs. In complete harmony, therefore, with local usage, Arabia may be regarded as spreading for eight hundred miles from the Nile to beyond the Euphrates. From the foot of the Taurus Mountains, north of Aleppo, to the Gulf of Aden, it measures no less than eighteen hundred miles. As to one-half, Arabia is desert, and as to the other half mainly dry steppes; although it lies in the same latitudes as the Sahara, it is more productive and carries a more considerable population of wandering Bedouin. Moreover, it has larger oases, and therefore larger cities. What, however, most distinguishes Arabia both from the Heartland and the Sahara is the fact that it is traversed by three great water-ways in connection with the ocean—the Nile, the Red Sea, and the Euphrates and Persian Gulf. None of these three ways, however, affords naturally a complete passage across the arid belt. The Nile was navigable from the Mediterranean only to the first cataract, midway across the

desert, though locks have now been constructed at Assouan which give access as far as the second cataract;
and the navigation of the Euphrates ascends only to a
point a hundred miles from the Mediterranean. To-day
it is true that the Suez Canal unites the Mediterranean
to the Red Sea, but it was not only the isthmus which
formerly impeded through traffic by this route; persistent north winds of the trade-wind current blow down
the northern end of the Red Sea, which is beset with
rocks, and sailing ships do not willingly attempt the
northward voyage to the Canal, which would therefore
have been relatively useless but for steam navigation.
The former Red Sea route to the Mediterranean was
from Kosseir on the west coast over the desert to the
Nile at Keneh, and then down the Nile; that was the
way followed by the British army when sent from India
to Egypt more than a hundred years ago, at the time of
the Napoleonic invasion of Egypt and Palestine.

It follows from the foregoing description that the
Heartland, Arabia, and the Sahara together constitute
a broad, curving belt inaccessible to seafaring people,
except by the three Arabian water-ways. This belt extends completely across the great continent from the
Arctic to the Atlantic shores. In Arabia it touches the
Indian Ocean, and, as a consequence, divides the remainder of the Continent into three separate regions
whose rivers flow to the ice-free ocean. These regions
are the Pacific and Indian slopes of Asia; the peninsulas
and islands of Europe and the Mediterranean; and the
great promontory of Africa south of the Sahara. The
last-named differs from the other two regions in a very
important respect. Its larger rivers, the Niger, Zambesi,

Fig. 16.—The World Island, divided into six

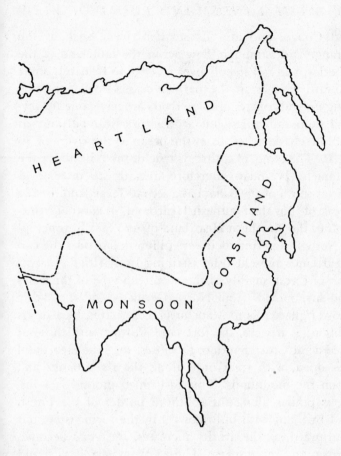

natural regions. (Equal areas projection.)

and Congo, and also its smaller rivers, such as the Orange and Limpopo, flow across the tableland of the interior, and fall steeply over its edge to relatively short seaward reaches in the narrow coastal lowlands. The long upland courses of these rivers are navigable for several thousand miles, but are for practical purposes as completely detached from the ocean as the rivers of Siberia. The same, of course, is true of the Nile above the cataracts. We may, therefore, regard the interior of Africa south of the Sahara as a second Heartland. Let us speak of it as the Southern Heartland, in contra-distinction to the Northern Heartland of Asia and Europe.

Notwithstanding their very different latitudes the two Heartlands present other striking similarities. A great belt of forest, mainly of the evergreen type of the pines and firs, spreads from North Germany and the Baltic shore right across to Manchuria, connecting by a forest ribbon, as it were, the forests of Europe with those of the Pacific Coast. South of this forest zone the Heartland lies open, with trees only along the river banks and upon the mountains. This vast, open ground is a luscious prairie along the southern border of the forest, and brilliant with bulb flowers in the spring-time, but southward, as the aridity increases, the grass becomes coarser and more sparse. The whole grassland, rich and poor, is conveniently spoken of as the steppes, although that name properly belongs only to the less fertile southern tracts which surround the desert patches of Turkestan and Mongolia. The steppes were probably the original habitat of the horse, and in their southern parts, of the two-humped camel (Fig. 18).

The Southern Heartland also has its wide open grasslands, which in the Sudan gradually increase in fertility from the edge of the Sahara towards the tropical forest of the Guinea Coast and the Congo. The forests do not spread completely across to the Indian Ocean, but leave a belt of grassy upland which connects the grasslands of the Sudan with those of South Africa, and this immense, open ground, thus continuous from the Sudan to the Cape Veldt, is the home of the antelopes, zebras, and other large, hoofed game, which correspond to the wild horses and wild asses of the Northern Heartland. Though the zebra has not been successfully domesticated, and the South African natives had no usual beast of burden, yet the horse and the one-humped camel of Arabia were early introduced into the Sudan. In both Heartlands, therefore, although to a greater extent in the Northern than in the Southern, mobility by the aid of animals has been available to replace the riverwise and coastwise mobility of the ships of the Atlantic and Pacific coastlands.

The Northern Heartland adjoins Arabia, as we have seen, for many hundred miles where the Iranian Upland drops to the Euphrates Valley; the Southern Heartland, at its northeastern corner in Abyssinia and Somaliland, grasps, though with an interval of sea, the southern fertile angle of Arabia, known as Yemen. So the steppes of Arabia, enframing its deserts, serve as a passage-land between the Northern and Southern Heartlands; and there is also the way by the banks of the Nile through Nubia. Thus it will be realized that the Northern Heartland, Arabia, and the Southern Heartland afford a broad, grassy way for horsemen and camel-men from Siberia through Persia, Arabia, and Egypt into the Sudan, and that but for the tsetse-fly and other plagues men would probably have penetrated on horseback and camel-back southward almost to the Cape of Good Hope.

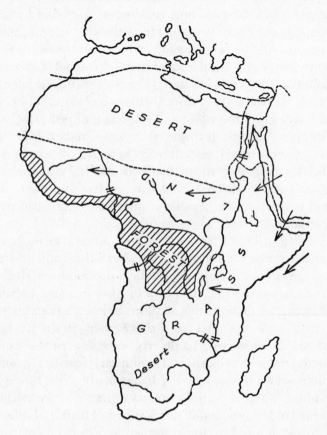

Fig. 17.—The southern Heartland. = River falls. ← Lines of Arab invasion.

Outside Arabia, the Sahara, and the two Heartlands, there remain in the World-Island only two comparatively small regions, but those two regions are the most important on the globe. Around the Mediterranean, and in the European peninsulas and islands, there dwell four hundred million people, and in the southern and eastern coastlands of Asia, or, to use the historic expression, in the Indies, there dwell eight hundred million people. In these two regions, therefore, are three-quarters of the people of the world. From our present point of view the most pertinent way of stating this great fact is to say that four-fifths of the population of the Great Continent, the World-Island, live in two regions which together measure only one-fifth of its area.

These two regions resemble one another in certain other very important respects. In the first place, their rivers are for the most part navigable continuously from the ocean. In the Indies we have this series of large rivers descending to the open sea; Indus, Ganges, Brahmaputra, Irrawady, Salwen, Menam, Mekong, Songho, Sikiang, Yangtse, Hoangho, Peiho, Liauho, Amur. Most of them are navigable from their mouths for some hundreds of miles; a British battleship once steamed up the Yangtse to Hankow, five hundred miles from the sea. There is not much space for such large rivers in peninsular Europe, but the Danube, Rhine, and Elbe carry a great traffic in direct connection with the ocean. Mannheim, three hundred miles up the Rhine, was one of the principal ports of Europe before the war; barges a hundred yards long and of a thousand tons burden lay beside its wharves. For the rest, the peninsulation of Europe, which limits the develop-

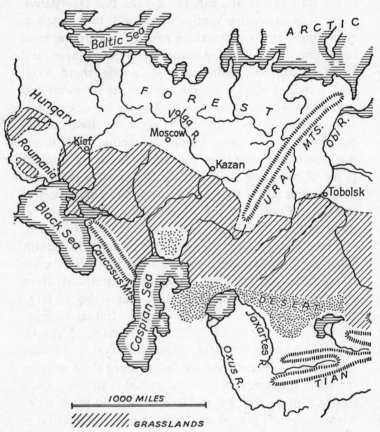

FIG. 18.—The steppes.

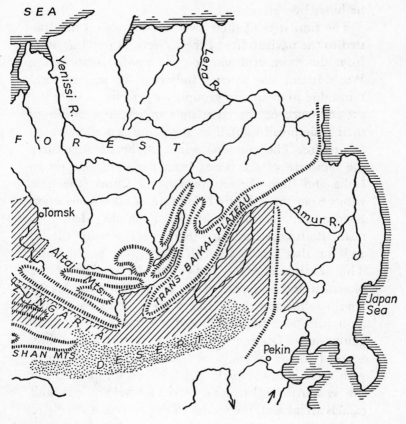

/////// Grasslands.

ment of rivers, itself offers even greater facilities for mobility by water.

The similarity of these two "Coastlands" is not limited to the navigability of their rivers. If we clear away from the more arid zone on the rainfall map of the World-Island the patches indicative of merely local rains, due to mountain groups, we perceive at once the pre-eminence of the coastlands in fertility, owing to their widespread rainfall on the plains as well as in the mountains. The monsoon winds of the summer carry the moisture of the ocean from the southwest on to India and from the southeast on to China; the west winds from the Atlantic bring rain at all seasons upon Europe, and in the winter-time upon the Mediterranean. Both coastlands are therefore rich with tillage, and for that reason nourish their great populations. Thus Europe and the Indies are the regions of the plowmen and shipmen; whereas the Northern Heartland, Arabia, and the Southern Heartland have for the most part been unplowed, and are inaccessible to sea-going ships. On the other hand, they are naturally adapted to the mobility of horsemen and camel-men, with their herds of cattle and flocks of sheep. Even on the savannahs of tropical Africa, where horses and camels are absent, the wealth of the natives is chiefly of cattle and sheep. These are, of course, broad generalizations, with many local exceptions; they are none the less truly and sufficiently descriptive of immense geographical realities.[1]

.   .   .   .

[1] Realities, that is to say, that have conditioned history, and have thus led to the present distribution of population and civilization. These same realities have to-day begun to take on new aspects, owing to the higher organization of food production on the richer grasslands.

Let us now call history to our aid, for no practical idea, no idea which moves men to action, can be grasped statically; we must come to it with a momentum of thought either from our own experience or from the his-

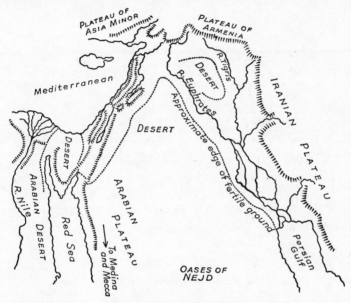

FIG. 19.—Northern Arabia.

tory of the race. The oases of the East count in poetry as the gardens of the world, only because they are approached over the desert!

Recorded history begins in the great oases round the north of Arabia. The first international politics of which we have definite knowledge were concerned with the intercourse between two states which had grown up on the alluvial flats of the Lower Euphrates and Lower Nile; the maintenance of dykes to keep out the water, and of canals to distribute water, inevitably gives an impulse to social order and discipline. There was a certain difference in the two civilizations which may well have been the basis of interchange between them. In Egypt the rocky sides of the relatively narrow valley

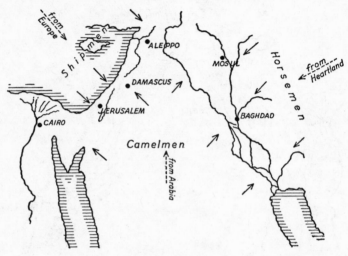

FIG. 20.—The mobile conquerors of the plowed lands.

offered stone for building, and the papyrus reed afforded a material for writing; whereas, building was of brick in the broad plain of Babylonia, and clay tablets bore the cuneiform inscriptions. The road between the two countries ran westward from the Euphrates across the Syrian angle of the Arabian Desert, past the wells of Palmyra, to Damascus, which was built in the oasis formed by the streams Abana and Pharpar descending from Anti-Lebanon and Hermon. From Damascus there were alternative ways into Egypt; the lower by the coast, and the upper along the edge of the desert plateau east of the Jordan Valley. Aloof, on the rocky ridge of Judea, between these upper and lower ways, was the hill fortress of Jerusalem.

In a monkish map, contemporary with the Crusades, which still hangs in Hereford Cathedral, Jerusalem is marked as at the geometrical center, the navel, of the world, and on the floor of the Church of the Holy Sepulchre at Jerusalem they will show you to this day the precise spot which is the center. If our study of the geographical realities, as we now know them in their completeness, is leading us to right conclusions, the medieval ecclesiastics were not far wrong. If the World-Island be inevitably the principal seat of humanity on this globe, and if Arabia, as the passage-land from Europe to the Indies and from the Northern to the Southern Heartland, be central in the World-Island, then the hill citadel of Jerusalem has a strategical position with reference to world-realities not differing essentially from its ideal position in the perspective of the Middle Ages, or its strategical position between ancient Babylon and Egypt. As the war has shown, the Suez Canal carries the rich traffic between the Indies and Europe to within striking distance of an army based on Palestine, and already the trunk railway is being built through the coastal plain by Jaffa, which will connect the Southern with the Northern Heartland. Who owns Damascus, moreover, will have flank access to the alternative route between the oceans down the Euphrates Valley. It cannot be wholly a coincidence that in the selfsame region should be the starting point of history and the crossing point of the most vital of modern highways.

In the dawn of history we find the children of Shem, the Semites, conquering the cultivated margins of the Arabian deserts; there is no small similarity between the ring of their settlements round the sea of sand, and the settlements of the Greeks round the Aegean Sea. The invasion of the Promised Land from beyond the Jordan by the Beni-Israel, the Children of Israel, was probably but one of many like descents of the Bedouin. The Chaldees, from whose city of Ur on the desert border Abraham migrated along the beaten track into Palestine, were Semites who supplanted the non-Semitic Accadians in the land

FIG. 21.—A medieval wheel-map.

which became Babylonia; and the dynasty of the Shepherd Kings in Egypt was also apparently of Semitic origin. So it came about that all the peoples of Arabia—Arabs, Babylonians, Assyrians, Syrians, Phoenicians, and Hebrews—spoke dialects of the same Semitic family of speech. To-day Arabic is the universal tongue from the Taurus to the Gulf of Aden, and from the Persian Mountains to the oases in the Sahara west of the Nile.

The Arabian tableland drops steeply to the sea shores around in all directions save one; northeastward it shelves gradually down to the depression occupied by the Euphrates and the Persian Gulf. That depression is eighteen hundred miles long, from the gorge by which the Euphrates issues from its source valley in the Armenian Plateau to the Strait of Ormuz at the mouth of the Persian Gulf; throughout its length it is overlooked by the range of the Persian Mountains, the high Iranian brink of the Heartland. One of the great events of classical history was when the Persian Highlanders came down on to the Euphrates plain under their King Cyrus, and, after conquering Babylon, passed on by the Syrian road through Damascus to the conquest of Egypt.

The gorge by which the Euphrates escapes from the Armenian Upland is more than eight hundred miles in a direct line from the river mouth and only a little more than one hundred miles from the northeastern corner of the Mediterranean Sea near Aleppo. Immediately west of this gorge the high upland of Armenia, some one and a half miles in average elevation, drops to the much lower peninsular tableland of Asia Minor. A second great event in classical history was when the Macedonians, under King Alexander, having crossed the Dardanelles and traversed the open center of Asia Minor, descended by the Taurus passes into Cilicia, and struck through Syria into Egypt, and then from Egypt back through Syria to the Euphrates, and down the Euphrates to Babylon. It is true that Alexander thus led his Macedonians overland into Arabia, but their attack was really based on sea-power, as is evident from the rapid rise which ensued of the great Greek-speaking ports of Alexandria and Antioch, the coastal capitals, that is to say, of seamen going inland.

If these facts be considered with a geographical eye, a belt of fertility will be seen extending northwestward up the Euphrates, then curving to southward along the

rain-gathering mountains of Syria, and ending westward in Egypt. It is a populous belt, for it is inhabited
by the settled plowmen. Except for two intervals of
sterility, the trunk road of antiquity ran through its
corn fields from Babylon to Memphis. The key to some
of the greater events of ancient history is to be found
in the subjection of the peoples of this agricultural strip
now to this and now to that neighboring race of superior mobility. From the south, with all the depth of
Arabia behind them, the camel-men advanced northeastward against Mesopotamia, northwestward against
Syria, and westward against Egypt; from the northeast,
with all the vast depth of the Heartland behind them,
the horsemen came down from the Iranian Upland into
Mesopotamia; and from the northwest, whether across
the peninsula of Asia Minor or directly to the Levantine
shore, came the shipmen against Syria and Egypt, having behind them all the water-ways of Europe.[1]

In Asia the Romans did but take over the western
portion of the Macedonian conquests. As the Rhine and
Danube, defended by the Legions, marked the extent
of Roman penetration northward from the Mediterranean, so the Upper Euphrates, where it flows from
north to south before bending southeastward, marked
the limit, defended by other Legions, of their eastward
penetration from the Mediterranean. The Roman Empire was, in fact, in the large sense, a local empire; it
belonged wholly to the Atlantic Coastland. The further
provinces which had been under the Macedonian sway
fell in Roman times to the Parthians, successors of the

[1] See Fig. 20 on p. 88.

Persians, who in their turn descended from Iran upon Mesopotamia.

Once more came the opportunity of the camel-men. Inspired by the preaching of Mohammed, the Arabs of the central oasis of Nejd, and of its western extension in the Hedjaz of Mecca and Medina, sent forth the Saracen armies, who drove the Parthians from Mesopotamia, and the Romans from Syria and Egypt, and established a chain of inland capitals—Cairo, Damascus, and Bagdad—in the ancient trackway of fertility. From this fertile base the Saracen power was carried into all the regions around in such manner as to make a bid for a true world-empire. Northeastward the Mohammedans ascended from Bagdad into Iran by the same passway which had guided the Parthians and Persians downward, and they spread even into Northern India. Southward they crossed from the Yemen headland of Arabia to the African coast south of the Sahara, and penetrated on their camels and horses through the whole breadth of the Sudan. Thus, like a vast eagle, their empire of land-power spread its wings from the Arabian Centerland, on the one hand over the Northern Heartland, far into the depths of Asia, and on the other hand over the Southern Heartland equally far into the depths of Africa.

But the Saracens were not content with a dominion based only on the means of mobility proper to their steppes and deserts; like their predecessors, the Phoenicians and Shebans, they took to the sea. Westward they traveled along the north coast of Africa, both on sea and land, until they came to two countries, Barbary and Spain, whose broad tablelands, neither utterly sterile like the Sahara, nor yet forested like most of the European peninsula, repeated in some degree the conditions of their own homeland. On the other hand, eastward from Yemen, at the mouth of the Red Sea, and from Oman, at the mouth of the Persian Gulf, they sailed on the summer monsoon to the Malabar coast of India, and even to the far Malay Islands, and returned home on the winter monsoon. Thus the Arab dhows sketched out a sea-empire, extending from the Straits of Gibraltar to the Straits of Malacca, from the Atlantic gate to the Pacific gate.

This vast Saracen design of a northward and southward dominion of camel-men crossed by a westward and eastward dominion of shipmen was vitiated by one fatal defect; it lacked in its Arabian base the necessary man-power to make it good. But no student of the realities, about which must turn the strategical thought of any government aspiring to world-power, can afford to lose sight of the warning thus given by history.

. . . .

The Saracen Empire was overthrown, not from Europe or the Indies, but from the Heartland in the north —a significant fact. Arabia is sea-girt or desert-girt in every other direction but towards the Heartland. The western sea-power of the Arabs was no doubt countered from Venice and Genoa, and their eastern sea-power was subdued by the Portuguese after they had rounded the Cape of Good Hope, but the downfall of the Saracens in Arabia itself was due to Turkish land-power. We must give some further consideration to the characteristics of the great Northern Heartland, and in the first place to those of the long grassy zone which, south of the forest zone, extends across its whole breadth, overlapping westward and eastward some distance into the adjoining parts of the two Coastlands.

The steppes begin in the center of Europe, where the Hungarian Plain is completely surrounded by a ring of forested mountains, the Eastern Alps and the Carpathians.[1] To-day fields of wheat and maize have in large part replaced the native grass, but a hundred years ago, before the railways had brought markets within reach, the sea-like levels of Hungary east of the Danube were a prairie land, and the wealth of the Hungarians was almost exclusively in horses and cattle. Beyond the forrested barrier of the Carpathians begin the steppes of the main belt, spreading eastward, with the shore of the Black Sea to the south and the edge of the Russian forest to the north. The forest edge crosses the Russian Plain sinuously, but in a generally oblique direction, from the northern end of the Carpathians in the fiftieth parallel of latitude to the foot of the Ural range in the fifty-sixth parallel. Moscow stands a short way within the forest, where are the broad clearings which constituted all of inhabited Russia until the recent colonization of the steppe southward. As far as the Volga and the Don the wheat fields have now in large measure replaced the steppe grass, but until a hundred years ago the Cossack outposts of Russia were still based on the Dnieper and Don Rivers, the trees along whose banks alone broke the vast levels of waving grass or of snow.

The forests which clothe the end of the Ural Mountains form a promontory southward into the open steppes, but the grass is continuous through the gateway

[1] See Fig. 18 on p. 84-85.

of plain which leads from Europe into Asia between the Ural range and the northern end of the Caspian Sea. Beyond this gateway the steppes expand again to even greater breadth than in Europe. To the north of them are still the forests, but to the south are now the deserts and sub-arid steppes of Turkestan. The Trans-Siberian railway traverses the grassy zone from Chelyabinsk, the station at the eastern foot of the Ural Mountains where the lines from Petrograd and Moscow unite, to Irkutsk on the Angara River just below its exit from Lake Baikal. Wheat fields are beginning in large measure to replace the grass along the line of the railway, but the thread of settled population is still a narrow one, and the Tartar and Khirghiz horsemen are still nomad over wide areas.

The edge of the forest bends southward along the boundary between Western and Eastern Siberia, for Eastern Siberia is filled with forested mountains and hills, which fall in elevation gradually from the Transbaikalian Plateau into the northeastern promontory of Asia towards Bering Strait. The grassy zone bends south with the forest and continues eastward over the lower level of the Mongolian Upland. The slope upward from the Great Lowland into Mongolia is through the "Dry Strait" of Zungaria, between the Tianshan Mountains on the south and Altai Mountains on the north. Beyond Zungaria the steppes, now at upland level, continue round the southern edge of the forested Altai and Transbaikalian Mountains, with the Gobi Desert to the south of them, until they reach the upper tributaries of the Amur River. There is a forest belt along the eastern, outward face of the Kingan range, by which the Mongolian upland drops to the lowland of Manchuria, but there is a last detached grassland in Manchuria, to be compared with the similarly detached grassland of Hungary five thousand miles away at the west end of the steppe belt. Grassy Manchuria does not, however, extend through to the Pacific shore, for there a coast range of mountains, thickly forested, enframes the open country and deflects the eastward-flowing Amur to a northward mouth.

Let us clear this long ribbon of steppes of its modern railways and corn fields, and people it again in imagination with horse-riding Tartars, who are none other than Turks; it is said that the Turkish language of Constantinople can to this day be understood by the Arctic tribe at the mouth of the Lena River. For some recurrent reason—it may have been owing to spells of droughty years—these Tartar mobile hordes have from time to time in the course of history gathered their whole strength together and fallen like a devastating avalanche upon the settled agricultural peoples either of China or Europe. In the west we hear of them first as the Huns, who in the middle of the fifth century after Christ rode into Hungary under a great but terrible leader, Attila. From Hungary they raided in three directions—northwestward, westward, and southwestward. Northwestward they caused so much commotion among the Germans, that those tribes nearest the sea, the Angles and Saxons, were in part driven over the water to a new home in the island of Britain. Westward they penetrated far into Gaul, but were defeated in the great battle of Chalons, where the Frank, the Goth, and the Roman Provincial, standing shoulder to shoulder against the common enemy from the east, began that fusion from which has sprung the modern French people. Southwestward Attila advanced as far as Milan, destroying on the way the important Roman cities of Aquileia and Padua, whose inhabitants fled to the lagoons by the sea and there founded Venice. At Milan Attila was met by Bishop Leo of Rome, and, for whatever reason, went no farther, with the result that the Roman See won a great prestige. Thus can it be said with much truth that from the reaction of the coastmen against this hammer blow from the Heartland, there arose the English and French nationalities, the sea-power of Venice, and the supreme mediaeval institution of the Papacy. Who shall say what great and, let us hope, beneficent things may not grow out of the reaction which has been compelled by the hammer blow of our modern Huns?

The Hunnish raids ceased after a few years, for it is probable that the man-power behind them was not very considerable; the force of a blow may be due as much to its speed as to its weight. But some Hunnish remnants probably lingered in the grassy vacancy of the Hungarian Plain, to be absorbed by new tribes of horsemen advancing westward, the Avars, against whom Charlemagne made war, and presently the Magyars. In the year 1000 these Magyar Turks, who had done much ravaging in Germany during the previous century, were converted to Christianity from Rome, and became thenceforth some sort of a bulwark to Latin Christendom, so that no more Tartars were admitted into Hungary. But the economic life of the Magyars continued in the main to be that of the steppes until less than a hundred years ago.

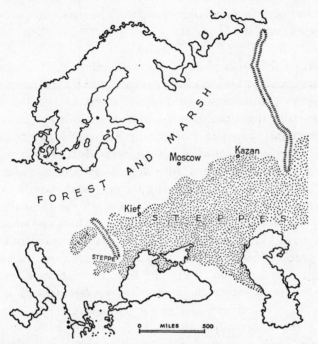

FIG. 22.—Forest and steppes in East Europe. (After a diagram in my paper on "The Geographical Pivot of History" in the *Geographical Journal* for 1904.)

When we reflect that through several centuries of the Dark Ages the Norse pagans in their ships were at piracy on the northern seas, and the Saracen and Moorish infidels in their ships at piracy on the Mediterranean, and that the horse-riding Turks from Asia raided thus into the very heart of the Christian peninsula when it was clasped by hostile sea-power, we have some idea of the pounding, as between pestle and mortar, which went to the making of modern Europe. The pestle was land-power from the Heartland.

.   .   .   .

If these historical events be followed on the map, the strategical fact of decisive meaning which emerges is that the continuous plains of the Great Lowland over-lap from the Continental and Arctic drainage of the Heartland into the east of the European peninsula. There was no impediment to prevent the horsemen from riding westward into regions drained by such wholly European rivers as the Dnieper and Danube. In sharp contrast to this open passage from the Heartland into Europe is the system of mighty barriers which separate the Heartland along its eastern and south-eastern border from the Indies. The populous lands of China proper and India lie round the eastern and southern slopes of the most massive uplands on the globe; the southern face of the Himalaya range, curv-ing for 1,500 miles along the north of India, rises from levels at most only 1,000 feet above the sea to peaks of 28,000 and 29,000 feet. But the Himalaya is only the edge of the Tibetan Plateau, which is as large as France, Germany, and Austria-Hungary put together, and of an average elevation of 15,000 feet, or the peak height of Mont Blanc in the Alps. As compared with such facts as these, the distinction between the lower uplands and the lowlands, between the Iranian Upland, let us say, and the Great Lowland, becomes altogether subordinate. Tibet, with its attendant Himalaya,

Pamirs, Karakoram, Hindu Kush, and Tianshan—call them together the Tibetan Heights—has no parallel on earth for combined height and area, or, in a single word, for massiveness. When the Sahara shall be crossed and recrossed daily by the traffic of civilization, it is probable that Tibet, the "roof of the world," will still deflect round its flanks and widely separate the overland routes into China and India, thus giving a special significance to the northwest frontiers of those two countries.

North of Tibet, a considerable part of which has a continental drainage, and is, therefore, included within the Heartland, spreads the Mongolian Upland, also largely of the Heartland. This Mongolian Upland is of a much lower elevation than Tibet, and is in fact comparable in point of level with the Iranian Upland. Two natural ways come over the arid surface of Mongolia to drop down into the fertile lowland of China; the one through the Province of Kansu, round the northeastern corner of Tibet, to the great city of Sinan, of a million inhabitants; the other directly southeastward from Lake Baikal to Pekin, which city also has about a million inhabitants. Sinan and Pekin, thus just within the Chinese Lowland, are capitals founded by conquerors from the Heartland.

Across the Iranian Upland into India there are also two natural ways, the one over the lofty but narrow spine of the Hindu Kush, down the Cabul Valley, and over the terminal Kaibar Pass to the crossing of the Indus River at Attock; the other through Herat and Kandahar, round the ends of the Afghan ridges, and by the Bolan Gorge down to the Indus. Immediately east of the Indus River is the Indian Desert, extending from

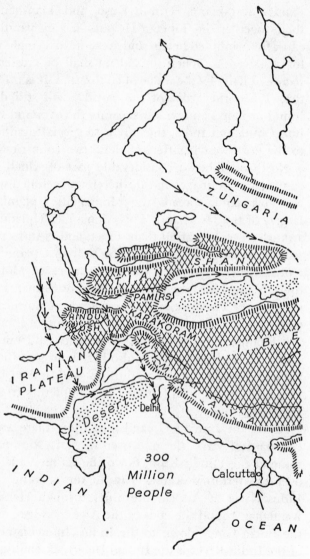

FIG. 23.—The Tibetan heights and the approaches

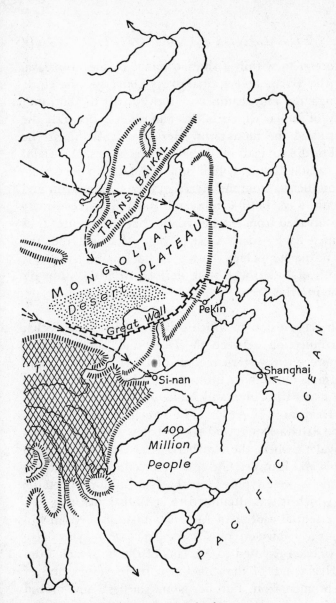

to China and India from the Heartland.

the ocean to within a short distance of the Himalaya, and the Bolan and Kaibar ways converge, therefore, through the antechamber of the Punjab to the inner entry of India, which is the passage left between the desert and the mountains. Here stands Delhi, at the head of the navigation of the Jumna-Ganges, and Delhi is a capital founded, like Sinan and Pekin in China, by conquerors from the Heartland. By these narrow and difficult ways both China and India have repeatedly been invaded from the Heartland, but the empires thus founded have usually soon become detached from the rule of the steppemen. So was it, for instance, with the Moguls of India, who were derived from the Mongols of the interior.

. . . .

The conclusion to which this discussion leads is that the connection between the Heartland, and especially its more open western regions of Iran, Turkestan, and Siberia, is much more intimate with Europe and Arabia than it is with China and India, or yet with the Southern Heartland of Africa. The strong natural frontiers of the Sahara Desert and the Tibetan Heights have no equivalent where the Northern Heartland merges with Arabia and Europe. The close connection of these three regions is well typified by that geographical formula into which it was attempted to crystallize just now certain essential aspects of Mesopotamian and Syrian history; the plowmen of Mesopotamia and Syria have always been exposed to descents of the horsemen from the Heartland, of the camel-men from Arabia, and of the shipmen from Europe. None the less—and indeed just because of its more transitional character—the boundary between the Heartland on the one hand, and Arabia and Europe on the other, is worth following with some care.

FIG. 24.—The Heartland, with the addition of the basins of the Black and Baltic Seas, and the uppermost (plateau) valleys of the Chinese and Indian rivers.

The long range of the Persian Mountains bends westward round the upper end of Mesopotamia and becomes the Taurus Range, which is the high southern brink of the peninsular upland of Asia Minor. The surface of Asia Minor is a patch of steppes, verging on desert in the center, where salt lakes receive some of the streams from the Taurus; but the larger rivers flow northward to the Black Sea. Beyond the break made by the Aegean Sea, we have the great basin of the Danube, also draining into the Black Sea; the head-streams of the Danube tributaries rise almost within sight of the Adriatic, but high on those Illyrian Uplands whose steep outer brink forms the mountain wall above the beautiful Dalmatian coast. That wall we name the Dinaric Alps.

Thus the Taurus and the Dinaric Alps present steep fronts to the Mediterranean and Adriatic, but send long rivers down to the Black Sea. But for the Aegean Sea, breaking through the uplands towards the Black Sea, and but for the Dardanelles, whose current races southward with the water of all the Black Sea rivers, these high, outward fronts of the Taurus and Dinaric Alps would be a single curving range, the edge of a continuous bar of land dividing the inner Black Sea from the outer Mediterranean and Adriatic. Were it not for the Dardanelles that edge would form the border of the Heartland, and the Black Sea and all its rivers would be added to the "Continental" systems of drainage. When the Dardanelles are closed by land-power to the sea-power of the Mediterranean, as they have been in the Great War, that condition of things is in effect realized so far as human movements are concerned.

The Roman emperors put their eastern capital at Constantinople (Istanbul: *ed.*), midway between the Danube and Euphrates frontiers, but Constantinople was to them more than the bridge-town from Europe into Asia. Rome, the Mediterranean Power, did not annex the northern shore of the Black Sea, and that sea, therefore, was itself a part of the frontier of the empire. The steppes were left to the Scythians, as the Turks were then called, and at most a few trading stations were dotted by the seamen along the coast of the Crimea. Thus Constantinople was the point from which Mediterranean sea-power held the middle sea-frontier, as the land-power of the Legions held the western and eastern frontiers along the rivers. Under Rome, sea-power thus advanced into the Heartland, if that term be understood, in a large, a strategical sense, as including Asia Minor and the Balkan Peninsula.

Later history is no less transparent to the underlying facts of geography, but in the inverse direction. Some of the Turks from Central Asia turned aside from the way down into Arabia, and rode over the Median and Armenian Uplands into the open steppe of Asia Minor, and there made their home, just as the Magyar Turks only a century or two earlier rode round the north of the Black Sea into the Hungarian Steppe. Under great leaders of cavalry of the Ottoman dynasty, these Turks crossed the Dardanelles, and, following the "Corridor" of the Maritza and Morava Valleys through the Balkan Mountains, achieved the conquest of Magyar Hungary itself. From the moment that the city of Constantinople fell into Turkish hands in 1453, the Black Sea was closed to the Venetian and Genoese seamen. Under Rome, the realm of the seamen had been advanced to the northern shore of the Black Sea; under the Ottoman Turks the Heartland, the realm of the horsemen, was advanced to the Dinaric Alps and the Taurus. This essential fact has been masked by the extension of

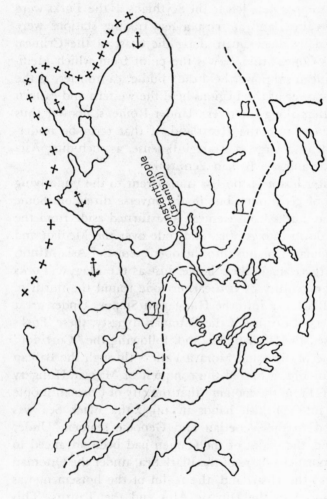

FIG. 25.—Showing the boundary of the Heartland when Mediterranean sea power enters the Black Sea + + + +, and when land power advances from the steppes to the Taurus and Dinaric Alps.

Turkish dominion into Arabia outside the Heartland; but it is evident again to-day when Britain has conquered Arabia for the Arabs. Within the Heartland, the Black Sea has of late been the path of strategical design eastward for our German enemy.

We defined the Heartland originally in accordance with river drainage; but does not history, as thus recounted, show that for the purposes of strategical thought it should be given a somewhat wider extension? Regarded from the point of view of human mobility, and of the different modes of mobility, it is evident that since land-power can to-day close the Black Sea, the whole basin of that sea must be regarded as of the Heartland. Only the Bavarian Danube, of very little value for navigation, may be treated as lying outside.

One more circumstance remains to be added, and we shall have before us the whole conception of the Heartland as it emerges from the facts of geography and history. The Baltic is a sea which can now be "closed" by land-power. The fact that the German fleet at Kiel was responsible for the mines and submarines which kept the Allied squadrons from entering the Baltic does not, of course, in any way vitiate the statement that the closing was by land-power; the Allied armies in France were there by virtue of sea-power, and the German sea defenses of the Baltic were there as a result of land-power. It is of prime importance in regard to any terms of peace which are to guarantee us against future war that we should recognize that under the conditions of to-day, as was admitted by responsible ministers in the House of Commons, the fleets of the islanders could no more penetrate into the Baltic than they could into the Black Sea.

The Heartland, for the purposes of strategical thinking, includes the Baltic Sea, the navigable Middle and Lower Danube, the Black Sea, Asia Minor, Armenia, Persia, Tibet, and Mongolia. Within it, therefore, were Brandenburg-Prussia and Austria-Hungary, as well as Russia—a vast triple base of man-power, which was lacking to the horse-riders of history. The Heartland is the region to which, under modern conditions, sea-power can be refused access, though the western part of it lies without the region of Arctic and Continental drainage. There is one striking physical circumstance which knits it graphically together; the whole of it, even to the brink of the Persian Mountains overlooking torrid Mesopotamia, lies under snow in the winter-time. The line indicative of an *average* freezing temperature for the whole month of January passes from the North Cape of Norway southward, just within the "Guard" of islands along the Norwegian shore, past Denmark, across mid-Germany to the Alps, and from the Alps eastward along the Balkan range. The Bay of Odessa and the Sea of Azof are frozen over annually, and also the greater part of the Baltic Sea. At mid-winter, as seen from the moon, a vast white shield would reveal the Heartland in its largest meaning.

When the Russian Cossacks first policed the steppes at the close of the Middle Ages, a great revolution was effected, for the Tartars, like the Arabs, had lacked the necessary man-power upon which to found a lasting empire, but behind the Cossacks were the Russian plowmen, who have to-day grown to be a people of a hundred millions on the fertile plains between the Black and Baltic Seas. During the nineteenth century, the Russian Czardom loomed large within the great Heartland, and seemed to threaten all the marginal lands of Asia and Europe. Towards the end of the century, however, the Germans of Prussia and Austria determined to subdue the Slavs and to exploit them for the occupation of the Heartland, through which run the land-ways into China, India, Arabia, and the African Heartland. The German military colonies of Kiauchau and East Africa were established as termini of the projected overland routes.

To-day armies have at their disposal not only the Transcontinental Railway but also the motor-car. They have, too, the aeroplane, which is of a boomerang nature, a weapon of land-power as against sea-power. Modern artillery, moreover, is very formidable against ships. In short, a great military power in possession of the Heartland and of Arabia could take easy possession of the crossways of the world at Suez. Sea-power would have found it very difficult to hold the Canal if a fleet of submarines had been based from the beginning of the war on the Black Sea. We have defeated the danger on this occasion, but the facts of geography remain, and offer ever-increasing strategical opportunities to land-power as against sea-power.

It is evident that the Heartland is as real a physical fact within the World-Island as is the World-Island itself within the ocean, although its boundaries are not quite so clearly defined. Not until about a hundred years ago, however, was there available a base of man-power sufficient to begin to threaten the liberty of the

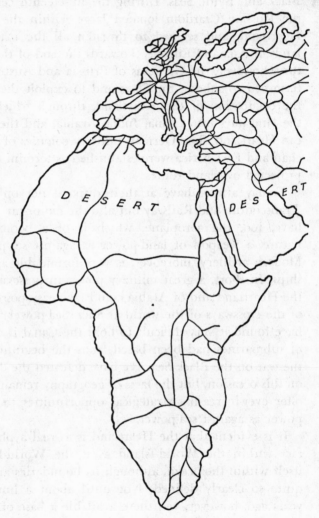

FIG. 26.—The World Island united, as it soon will be, by railways, and by

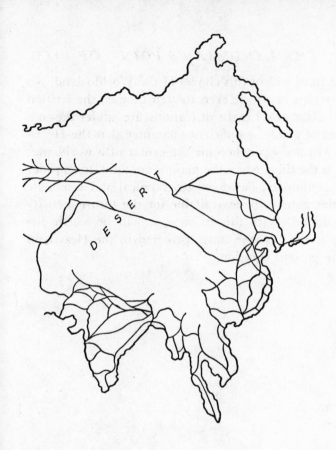

aeroplane routes, the latter for the most part parallel with the main railways.

world from within this citadel of the World-Island. No mere scraps of paper, even though they be the written constitution of a League of Nations, are, under the conditions of to-day, a sufficient guarantee that the Heartland will not again become the center of a world war. Now is the time, when the nations are fluid, to consider what guarantees, based on geographical and economic realities, can be made available for the future security of mankind. With this in view, it will be worth our while to see how the storm gathered in the Heartland on the present occasion.

Chapter Five

THE RIVALRY OF EMPIRES

A MOST interesting parallel might be drawn between the advance of the sailors over the ocean from Western Europe and the contemporary advance of the Russian Cossacks across the steppes of the Heartland. Yermak, the Cossack, rode over the Ural Mountains into Siberia in 1533, within a dozen years, that is to say, after Magellan's voyage round the world. The parallel might be repeated in regard to our own days. It was an unprecedented thing in the year 1900 that Britain should maintain a quarter of a million men in her war with the Boers at a distance of six thousand miles over the ocean; but it was as remarkable a feat for Russia to place an army of more than a quarter of a million men against the Japanese in Manchuria in 1904 at a distance of four thousand miles by rail. We have been in the habit of thinking that mobility by sea far outran mobility upon the land, and so for a time it did, but it is well to remember that fifty years ago ninety per cent of the world's shipping was still moved by sails, and that already the first railway had been opened across North America.

One of the reasons why we commonly fail to appreciate the significance of the policing of the steppes by the Cossacks is that we think vaguely of Russia as extending, with a gradually diminishing density of settlement, from the German and Austrian frontiers for thousands of miles eastward, over all the area colored on the map with one tint and labeled as one country, as far as Bering Strait. In truth Russia—the real Russia which supplied more than eighty per cent of the recruits for the Russian armies during the first three years of the war—is a very much smaller fact than the simplicity of the map would seem to indicate. The Russia which is the homeland of the Russian people, lies wholly in Europe, and occupies only about half of what we commonly call Russia in Europe. The land boundaries of Russia in this sense are in many places almost as definite as are the coasts of France or Spain. Trace a line on the map from Petrograd (Leningrad: *ed.*) eastward along the Upper Volga to the great bend of the river at Kazan, and thence southward along the Middle Volga to the second great bend at Czaritzin, and finally southwestward along the lower river Don to Rostof and the Sea of Azof. Within this line, to south and west of it, are more than a hundred million Russian people. They, the main stock of Russia, inhabit the plain between the Volga and the Carpathians and between the Baltic and Black Seas, with an average density of perhaps one hundred and fifty to the square mile, and this continuous sheet of population ends more or less abruptly along the line which has been indicated.

Northward of Petrograd and Kazan is North Russia, a vast somber forest land with occasional marshes, more than half as large as all the region just defined as the Russian homeland. North Russia has a population of less than two millions, or not three to the square mile. East of the Volga and Don, as far as the Ural Mountains and the Caspian Sea, lies East Russia, about as large as

North Russia, and with a population also of about two millions. But in the Kama Valley, between North and East Russia, is a belt of settled country, extending eastward from Kazan and Samara to the Ural range, and over that range, past the mines of Ekaterinburg, into Siberia, and right across Western Siberia to Irkutsk, just short of Lake Baikal. This belt of population beyond the Volga numbers perhaps twenty millions. The whole of it, from Kazan and Samara to Irkutsk, in so far as it is occupied by plowmen and not by wandering horsemen, is of recent settlement.

The Middle Volga, flowing southward from Kazan to Czaritzin, is a remarkable moat not only to Russia but to Europe. The west shore, known as the Hill Bank, in opposition to the Meadow Bank on the other side, is a hill face, some hundred feet high, which overlooks the river for seven hundred miles; it is the brink of the inhabited plain, here a little raised above the sea level. Stand on the top of this brink, looking eastward across the broad river below you, and you will realize that you have populous Europe at your back, and, in front, where the low meadows fade away into the half sterility of the drier steppes eastward, you have the beginning of the vacancies of Central Asia.

A striking practical commentary on these great physical and social contrasts has been supplied in the last few months by the Civil War in Russia. In all North Russia there are but two or three towns larger than a village, and, since the Bolsheviks are based on the town populations, Bolshevism has had little hold north of the Volga. Moreover the sparse rural settlements, chiefly of foresters, have, in their simple colonial conditions, no grounds for agrarian political feeling, and there is thus no peasant sympathy for the Bolsheviks. As a result, the

FIG. 27.—Showing the limits of the denser Russian population ‑‑‑‑‑.

railway from Archangel to Vologda on the Upper Dwina long remained open for communication with the ocean and the West. The Trans-Siberian line runs from Petrograd through Vologda, and there is a direct line from Moscow to Vologda which may be considered as leaving Russia proper and entering North Russia at the bridge over the Volga at Jaroslav. For these reasons it was that the Allied embassies established themselves at Vologda when they retired from Petrograd and Moscow: apart from the convenience of alternative communications with Archangel and Vladivostok, they were outside Bolshevik Russia.

Even more significant was the action of the Czecho-Slovaks on the Moscow branch of the Trans-Siberian line. Advancing from the Ural Mountains, with the support of the Ural Cossacks, they took Samara at the point where the railway reaches the Meadow Bank, and they seized the great bridge over the river at Syzran. They even penetrated a short way along the line to Penza within the real Russia, but through a rather sparsely populated neighborhood. Also, they struck up the river to Kazan. In truth they were thus hovering round the edge of the real Russia and threatening it from outside. The British expedition from Archangel by boat up the Dwina River to Kotlas, and thence by railway to Vyatka on the Trans-Siberian line, appears a less foolhardy enterprise when seen in the light of these realities.

This definition of the real Russia gives a new meaning not only to the Russia but also to the Europe of the nineteenth century. Let us consider that Europe, with the help of the map. All the more northern regions of Scandinavia, Finland, and Russia, and also East Russia southward to the Caucasus, are excluded as being mere vacancies, and with them the Turkish dominion in the Balkan Peninsula. It will be remembered that Kinglake in *Eöthen*, writing in 1844, considered that he was entering the East when he was ferried across the river

Save to Belgrade. The boundary between the Austrian and Turkish Empires as settled by the Treaty of Belgrade in 1739, was not varied until 1878. Thus the real Europe, the Europe of the European peoples, the Europe which, with its overseas colonies, is Christendom, was a perfectly definite social conception; its landward boundary ran straight from Petrograd to Kazan, and then along a curved line from Kazan by the Volga and Don Rivers to the Black Sea, and by the Turkish frontier to near the head of the Adriatic. At the one end of this Europe is Cape St. Vincent standing out to sea; at the other end is the land cape formed by the Volga elbow at Kazan. Berlin is almost exactly midway between St. Vincent and Kazan. Had Prussia won this war it was her intention that Continental Europe from St. Vincent to Kazan, with the addition of the Asiatic Heartland, should have become the naval base from which she would have fought Britain and America in the next war.

Let us now divide our Europe into East and West by a line so drawn from the Adriatic to the North Sea that Venice and the Netherlands may lie to the west, and also that part of Germany which has been German from the beginning of European history, but so that Berlin and Vienna are to the east, for Prussia and Austria are countries which the German has conquered and more or less forcibly Teutonized. On the map thus divided let us "think through" the history of the last four generations; it will assume a new coherency.

                .   .   .   .

The English Revolution limited the powers of monarchy, and the French Revolution asserted the rights of the people. Owing to disorder in France, and her invasion from abroad, the organizer Napoleon was thrown up. Napoleon conquered Belgium and Switzerland, surrounded himself with subsidiary kings in Spain, Italy,

FIG. 28.—The real Europe, east and west, with the addition of Barbary, the Balkans, and Asia Minor (see pp. 125-126).

and Holland, and made an alliance with the subordinate Federation of the Rhine, or, in other words, with the old Germany. Thus Napoleon had united the whole of West Europe, saving only insular Britain. Then he advanced against East Europe, and defeated Austria and Prussia, but did not annex them, though he compelled them to act as his allies when he afterwards went forward against Russia. We often hear of the vast spaces for Russian retreat which lay behind Moscow; but, in fact, Napoleon at Moscow had very nearly marched right across the inhabited Russia of his time.[1] Napoleon was brought down partly by the exhaustion of his French man-power, but mainly because his realm of West Europe was enveloped by British sea-power, for Britain was able to bring to herself supplies from outside Europe and to cut West Europe off from similar supplies. Naturally she allied herself with the Powers of East Europe, but there was only one way by which she could effectively communicate with them, and that was through the Baltic. This explains her naval action twice at Copenhagen. Owing to her command of the sea, Britain was, however, able to land her armies in Holland, Spain, and Italy, and to sap the Napoleonic strength in rear. It is interesting to note that the culminating victory of Trafalgar and the turning-point of Moscow lay very nearly at the two extremes of our real Europe. The Napoleonic War was a duel between West and East Europe, whose areas and populations were about evenly balanced, but the superiority due to the higher civilization of West Europe was neutralized by British sea-power.

After Waterloo, East Europe was united by the Holy League of the three Powers—Russia, Austria, and Prussia. Each of the three advanced westward a stage, as though drawn by a magnet in that direction. Russia obtained most of Poland, and thus extended a political peninsula into the heart of the physical peninsula of Europe. Austria took the Dalmatian coast, and also Venice and Milan in the mainland of Northern Italy.

[1] And therefore across the territory which could afford supplies to the contending armies.

Prussia obtained a *detached* territory in the old Germany of the West, which territory was divided into the two provinces of the Rhineland and Westphalia. This annexation of Germans to Prussia proved to be a much more significant thing than the addition of Poles to Russia and of Italians to Austria. The Rhineland is an anciently civilized country, and so far Western that it accepted the Code Napoleon for its law, which it still retains. From the moment that the Prussians thus forced their way into West Europe a struggle became inevitable between the liberal Rhineland and the conservative Brandenburg of Berlin. But that struggle was postponed for a time owing to the exhaustion of Europe.

British naval power continued the while to envelop West Europe from Heligoland, Portsmouth, Plymouth, Gibraltar, and Malta. By changes precipitated in the years 1830 to 1832 the temporary reaction in the West was brought to an end, and the middle classes came into power in Britain, France, and Belgium. In the years from 1848 to 1850 the democratic movement spread eastward of the Rhine, and Central Europe was ablaze with the ideas of freedom and nationality, but from our point of view two events, and two only, were decisive. In 1849 the Russian armies advanced into Hungary and put the Magyars back into their subjection to Vienna, thereby enabling the Austrians to reassert their supremacy over the Italians and Bohemians. In 1850 took place that fatal conference at Olmütz when Russia and Austria refused to allow the king of Prussia to accept the All-German Crown which had been offered to him from Frankfurt in the West. Thus the continuing unity of East Europe was asserted, and the liberal movement from the Rhineland was definitely balked.

In 1860 Bismarck, who had been at Frankfurt, and who had also been ambassador in Paris and Petrograd, was called to power at Berlin, and resolved to base German unity not on the idealism of Frankfurt and the West, but on the organization of Berlin and the East. In 1864 and 1866 Berlin overran West Germany, annexing Hanover and thereby opening the way into the Rhineland for Junker militarism. At the same time Berlin weakened her competitor Austria by helping the Magyar to establish the dual government of Austria-Hungary, and by depriving Austria of Venice. France had previously recovered Milan for the West. The War of 1866 between Prussia and Austria was, however, in essence merely a civil war; this became evident in 1872 when Prussia, having shown that her power was irresistible in the war against France, formed the League of the Three Emperors, and thus reconstituted for a time the East Europe of the Holy Alliance. The center of power in East Europe was now, however, Prussia, and no longer Russia, and East Europe had established a considerable Rhenish "Glacis" against West Europe.

For some fifteen years after the Franco-Prussian War Bismarck ruled both East and West Europe. He ruled the West by dividing the three Romance Powers of France, Italy, and Spain. This he accomplished in regard to their relations to Barbary, the "Island of the West" of the Arabs. France had taken the central portion of Barbary, known as Algeria, and by encouraging her to extend her dominion eastward into Tunis and westward into Morocco, Bismarck brought her interests into conflict with those of Italy and Spain. In East Europe there was a somewhat similar rivalry between Russia and Austria in respect of the Balkan Peninsula, but here the effort of Bismarck was to hold his two allies together. Therefore, after making the Dual Alliance with Austria in 1878, Bismarck negotiated his secret Reinsurance Treaty with Russia. He desired a solid East Europe under Prussia control, but a divided West Europe.

·   ·   ·   ·   ·   ·   ·

The events which we have thus briefly called to mind are no mere past and dead history. They show the fundamental opposition between East and West Europe, an opposition which becomes of world significance when we remember that the line through Germany which history indicates as the frontier between East and West is the very line which we have on other grounds taken as demarking the Heartland in the strategical sense from the Coastland.

In West Europe there are two principal elements, the Romance and the Teutonic. As far as the two chief nations, Britain and France, are concerned, there is and can be in modern times no question of conquest of the one by the other. The Channel lies between them. Away back in the Middle Ages it is true that for three centuries French knights ruled England, and that for another century the English tried to rule France. But those relations ended for good when Queen Mary lost Calais. The great wars between the two countries in the eighteenth century were waged primarily to prevent the French monarchy from dominating the continent of Europe. For the rest, they were wars of colonial and commercial rivalry. So far, also, as the Teutonic element along the Rhine is concerned, there was certainly in the past no deep-seated hostility to the French. The Alsatians, though German by speech, became—it is one of the great facts of history operative to this day— French in heart. Even what is now the Rhine province of Prussia accepted, as we have seen, the Code Napoleon.

In East Europe there are also two principal elements, the Teutonic and the Slavonic, but no equilibrium has been established between them as between the Romance and Teutonic elements of West Europe. The key to the whole situation in East Europe—and it is a fact which cannot be too clearly laid to heart at the present moment—is the German claim to dominance over the Slav. Vienna and Berlin, just beyond the boundary of West Europe, stand already within territory that was Slav in the earlier Middle Ages; they represent the first step of the German out of his native country as a conqueror eastward. In the time of Charlemagne the rivers Saale and Elbe divided the Slavs from the Germans, and to this day, only a short distance south of Berlin, is the Circle of Kottbus, where the peasantry still speak Wendish, or the Slav tongue of all the region a few centuries ago. Outside this little Wendish remnant, the Slav peasantry have accepted the language of the German barons who rule them in their large estates. In south Germany, where the peasantry is truly German, the land is held by small proprietors.

No doubt there is a difference of impression made on foreigners by the Austrians and by the Prussians of noble birth; that difference comes, no doubt, from the fact that the Austrians advanced eastward from south German homes, whereas the Prussians came from the harsher north. But in Prussia and Austria alike, the great landowners were autocrats before the war, though we commonly think of the Junker as Prussian only. The peasantry of both countries was in a state of serfdom until a comparatively short time ago.

The territory thrust out by Prussia in northeasterly and southeasterly directions have deep historical meaning for those who read history on the map, and it is history on the map which constitutes one of the great realities with which we must deal in our reconstruction. The map showing the distribution of languages tells in this instance even more than the political map, for it shows three tongues of German speech and not merely two. The first lies northeastward along the Baltic Shore; it represents a German conquest and forced Teutonization of the later Middle Ages. By the coastwise waterway the Hanseatic merchants of Lübeck and the Teutonic knights, no longer occupied in Crusading, conquered all the shorelands to where now stands Petrograd. By subsequent history half of this strip of "Deutschthum" was incorporated with the Berlin monarchy, and the other half became the Baltic provinces of the Russian Czardom. But the Baltic provinces retained, to our days, their German merchant community of Riga, their German University of Dorpat, and their German barons as landlords. Under the Treaty of Brest-Litovsk the German element was again to have ruled in these lands of Courland and Livonia.

The second pathway of the Germans was up the Oder River to its source in the Moravian Gate, the deep valley leading from Poland towards Vienna between the mountains of Bohemia on the one hand, and the Carpathian Mountains on the other hand. The German settlements along the Upper Oder became Silesia, of

FIG. 29.—The surviving islands of Wendish (Slavonic) speech at Kottbus, encircled by the flowing tide of German speech.

which the greater part was taken from Austria by Prussia under Frederick the Great. The salience of these northeastward and southeastward limbs of German-speaking country is still further accentuated by the Polish-speaking Prussian province of Posen in the re-entering angle between them.

The third eastward path of the Germans was down the Danube, and by southward passes also into the

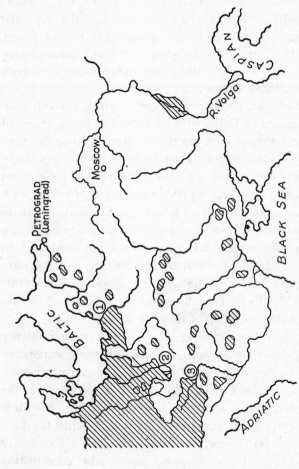

Fig. 30.—Showing the three eastward tongues of German speech, and the scattered German settlements as far as the Volga. (1) Prussia. (2) Silesia. (3) Austria.

Eastern Alps. This has become the Austrian Archduchy about Vienna, and the Carinthian Duchy—German-speaking—in the Austrian Alps. Between the Silesian and Austrian Germans projects westward the province of Bohemia, mainly of Slav speech. Let us not forget that Posen and Bohemia have retained their native tongues, and that the three salients of German speech represent three streams of conquest.

Beyond even the utmost points of these three principal invasions of Deutschthum, there are many scattered German colonies of farmers and miners, some of them of very recent origin. They occur at many points in Hungary, although for political purposes the Germans have there now very much identified themselves with the Magyar tyranny. The Saxons in Transylvania share with the Magyars of that region a privileged position amid a subject population of Rumanian peasants.[1] In Russia a chain of German settlements lies eastward through the north of the Ukraine almost to Kieff. Only on the Middle Volga, about the city of Saratof, do we come to the last patch of these German colonists.

We must not, however, think of German influence among the Slavs as being limited to these extensions of the German tongue, though they are a very powerful factor—since German Kultur has gone wherever the German language has given it entry. The Slav kingdom of Bohemia was completely incorporated into the German imperial system; the king of Bohemia was one of the electors of the emperor under the constitution

[1] The statements here made are left in the form that held before the war, for the memory of them is more potent than the as yet vague regrouping of the future.

which came to an end only in 1806, after the battle of Austerlitz. The Poles, the Czechs, the South Slavs of Croatia, and the Magyars are Roman Catholic—that is to say, of the Latin or western branch of the Church, and this has certainly meant an extension of German influence as against the Greek Church of the Russians. After the siege of Vienna in 1683, the Austrian Germans advanced step by step in the eighteenth century, driving the Turks before them from Hungary, until by the Treaty of Belgrade in 1739, they fixed the line which, for more than a hundred years, afterwards delimited Turkish power towards Christendom. Undoubtedly the Austrians thus rendered a great service to Europe, but the incidental effect, so far as the Croatians, Magyars, Slovaks, and Rumanians of Transylvania were concerned, was merely to substitute the mastery of the German for that of the Turk. When Peter the Great of Russia moved his capital at the beginning of the eighteenth century from Moscow to Petrograd, he went from a Slavonic to a German environment, a fact recorded in the German name St. Petersburg. As a consequence, throughout the eighteenth and nineteenth centuries, German influence was great in Russian government. The Russian bureaucracy, on which the Czardom depended, was, in large measure, recruited from among the cadets of the German baronial families of the Baltic provinces.

Thus East Europe has not consisted, like West Europe, of a group of peoples independent of one another, and—until Alsace was taken by Prussia—without serious frontier questions between them; East Europe has been a great triple organization of German domi-

nation over a mainly Slavonic population, though the
extent of the German power, no doubt, varied in different parts. In this fact we have the key to the meaning
of the *volte-face* of 1895, when was concluded the incongruous Franco-Russian alliance between democracy and
despotism. When Russia allied herself with France
against the Germans, much more was implied than
merely a reshuffling of the cards on the play-table of
Europe. Something fundamental had happened in East
Europe from the point of view of Berlin. Prior to that
great and significant event there had been long bicker-
ings between the Russian and Austrian governments
as the result of their rivalry in the Balkans, but these
were in the nature of family quarrels, no less than was
the short war between Prussia and Austria in 1866.
When Russia advanced to the Danube against Turkey
in 1853 and Austria massed forces to threaten her from
the Carpathians, the friendship of the Holy Alliance,
which had subsisted since 1815, was, no doubt, suspended until Bismarck brought the three despotisms
together again in his Three-Kaiser Alliance of 1872.
But it so happened that, during the interval, Russia
was not in a position to advance afresh against the
Turks, owing to the losses which she had experienced
in the Crimean War, and therefore no irremediable
breach ensued between her and Austria. But the Three-
Kaiser Alliance could not last long after Austria had
given notice of her Balkan ambitions by occupying the
Slav provinces of Bosnia and Herzegovina in 1878.
Some uncomfortable years followed, during which German strength was mounting up, before Russia was con-
vinced that the alternative before her was either an

alliance with the French Republicans or the acceptance of a position of subordination to Germany, like that to which Austria had been reduced.

. . . .

So much in regard to the history of West and East Europe during the Victorian Age. There was, however, a contemporary history of the Not-Europe which we must now bring into our reckoning. The naval warfare which culminated in the battle of Trafalgar had the effect of dividing the stream of the world's history into two separate currents for nearly a century. Britain enveloped Europe with her sea-power, but save in so far as it was necessary at times for her to intervene around the Eastern Mediterranean because of her stake in the Indies, she took no serious part in the politics of the European peninsula. British sea-power, however, also enveloped the great world-promontory which ends in the Cape of Good Hope, and, operating from the sea-front of the Indies, came into rivalry with the Russian-Cossack power, then gradually completing its hold on the Heartland. In the far north the Russians descended the great Amur River to the Pacific coast before the Crimean War. It is usual to attribute the opening of Japan to the action of the American Commodore Perry in 1853, but the presence of the Russians in the island of Sakhalin, and even as far south as Hakodate in Yesso, had done something to prepare the way. In regard to Britain, the most immediate Russian menace was, of course, beyond the northwest frontier of India.

In the nineteenth century Britain did what she liked upon the ocean, for the United States were not yet powerful, and Europe was fully occupied with its wars.

Shipping and markets were the objective of the nation of shopkeepers under the régime of the Manchester school of political thought. The principal new markets offering were among the vast populations of the Indies, for Africa was unexplored, and for the most part went naked, and the Americas were not yet populous. Therefore, while Britain might have annexed almost every coast outside Europe except the Atlantic coast of the United States, she limited herself to calling-ports for her shipping on the ocean road to the Indies, and to such colonial developments in unoccupied regions as were forced on her by her own adventurers, whom she tried in vain to check. But she was compelled to make a steady advance in India, of that kind which old Rome had known so well, when one new province after another was annexed for the purpose of depriving invaders of their bases against the territory already possessed.

The map reveals at once the essential strategic aspects of the rivalry between Russia and Britain during the nineteenth century. Russia, in command of nearly the whole of the Heartland, was knocking at the landward gates of the Indies. Britain, on the other hand, was knocking at the sea gates of China, and advancing inland from the sea gates of India to meet the menace from the northwest. Russian rule in the Heartland was based on her man-power in East Europe, and was carried to the gates of the Indies by the mobility of the Cossack cavalry. British power along the sea frontage of the Indies was based on the man-power of the distant islands in West Europe, and was made available in the East by the mobility of British ships. Obviously there were two critical points in the alternative voyages round from West to East; those points we know to-day as the "Cape" and the "Canal." The Cape lay far removed from all overland threat throughout the nineteenth century; practically South Africa was an island. The Canal was not opened until 1869, but its construction was an event which cast its shadow before. It was the Frenchman, Napoleon, who gave to Egypt, and therefore also to Palestine, its modern importance, just as it was the Frenchman Dupleix, who, in the eighteenth century, showed that it was possible to build an empire in India from the coast inward, on the ruins of the Mogul Empire which had been built from Delhi outward. Both ideas, that of Napoleon and that of Dupleix, were essentially ideas of sea-power, and sprang not unnaturally from France in the peninsula of West Europe. By his expedition to Egypt Napoleon drew the British fleet to the battle of the Nile in the Mediterranean, and also drew the British army from India, for the first time, overseas to the Nile Valley. When, therefore, Russian power in the Heartland increased, the eyes both of Britain and France were necessarily directed towards Suez, those of Britain for obvious practical reasons, and those of France partly for the sentimental reason of the great Napoleonic tradition, but also because the freedom of the Mediterranean was essential to her comfort in the Western peninsula.

But Russian land-power did not reach, in the eyes of people of that time, as far as to threaten Arabia. The natural European exit from the Heartland was by the sea-way through the Straits of Constantinople. We have seen how Rome drew her frontier through the Black Sea, and made Constantinople a local base of her Mediterranean sea-power against the Scythians of the steppes. Russia, under Czar Nicholas, sought to invert this policy, and, by commanding the Black Sea and its south-ward exit, aimed at extending her land-power to the Dardanelles. The effect was inevitably to unite West Europe against her. So it happened that when Russian intrigue had involved Britain in the First Afghan War in 1839, Britain could not view with equanimity the encampment of a Russian army on the Bosporus in order to defend the Sultan from the attack, through Syria, of Mehemet Ali, the insurgent Khedive of Egypt. Therefore Britain and France dealt with Mehemet themselves, by attacking him in Syria in 1840.

In 1854 Britain and France were again involved in action against Russia. France had assumed the protectorate of the Christians in the Near East, and her prestige in that respect was being damaged by Russian intrigue in regard to the Holy Places at Jerusalem. So France and Britain found themselves involved in support of the Turks when the Russian armies came against them on the Danube. Lord Salisbury, shortly before his death, declared that in supporting Turkey we had backed the wrong horse. Is that so certain in regard to the middle of last century? Time is of the essence of international policy; there is an opportunism which is the tact of politics. In regard to things which are not fundamental, is it not recognized that in ordinary social intercourse it is possible to say the right thing at the wrong time? In 1854 it was Russian power, and not yet German power, which was the center of organization in East Europe, and Russia was pressing through the Heartland against the Indies, and by the Straits of Constantinople was seeking to issue from the Heartland into the west, and Prussia was supporting Russia.

In 1876 Turkey was again in trouble and was again backed by Britain, though necessarily without the support of France. The result was to head off Russian power from Constantinople, but at the cost of giving to the Germans their first step towards the Balkan corridor by handing over to Austrian keeping the Slav provinces, hitherto Turkish, of Bosnia and Herzegovina. On that occasion the British fleet, by Turkish sufferance, steamed through the Dardanelles to within sight of the minarets of Constantinople. The great change in the orientation of Russian policy had not yet occurred, and neither Russia nor Britain yet foresaw the economic methods of amassing man-power to which Berlin was about to resort.

When we look back on the course of events during the hundred years after the French Revolution, and consider East Europe as the basis of what was on the whole a single force in the world's affairs, do we not realize that, separate as people of the Victorian Age often thought the politics of Europe from those of the Not-Europe outside, there was, in fact, no such separation? East Europe was in command of the Heartland, and was opposed by the sea-power of Britain round more than three-quarters of the margin of the Heartland, from China through India to Constantinople. France and Britain were commonly allied in action in regard to Constantinople. When, in 1840, there was danger of war in Europe because of the quarrel between the Khedive and the Sultan, instinctively all eyes were turned to the Rhine, where Prussia had established her outpost provinces. Then it was that the German song, the "Wacht am Rhein," was written! But the war threatened against France was not in respect of Alsace and Lorraine, but in support of Russia; in other words, the quarrel was between East and West Europe.

In 1870 Britain did not support France against Prussia. With the after-wisdom of events should we not, perhaps, be justified in asking whether we did not in this instance fail to back the right horse? But the eyes of the islanders were still blinded by the victory of Trafalgar. They knew what it was to enjoy sea-power, the freedom of the ocean, but they forgot that sea-power is, in large measure, dependent on the productivity of the bases on which it rests, and that East Europe and the Heartland would make a mighty sea-base. In the Bismarckian period, moreover, when the center of gravity of East Europe was being shifted from Petrograd to Berlin, it was perhaps not unnatural that contemporaries should fail to realize the subordinate character of the quarrels between the three autocracies, and the fundamental character of the war between Prussia and France.

The recent Great War arose in Europe from the revolt of the Slavs against the Germans. The events which led up to it began with the Austrian occupation of the Slav provinces of Bosnia and Herzegovina in 1878, and the alliance of Russia with France in 1895. The Entente of 1904 between Britain and France was not an event of the same significance; our two countries had co-operated more often than not in the nineteenth century, but France had been the quicker to perceive that Berlin had supplanted Petrograd as the center of danger in East Europe, and our two policies had, in consequence,

been shaped from different angles for a few years. West
Europe, both insular and peninsular, must necessarily
be opposed to whatever Power attempts to organize the
resources of East Europe and the Heartland. Viewed in
the light of that conception, both British and French
policy for a hundred years past takes on a large con-
sistency. We were opposed to the half-German Russian
Czardom because Russia was the dominating, threatening force both in East Europe and the Heartland for
half a century. We were opposed to the wholly German
Kaiserdom, because Germany took the lead in East
Europe from the Czardom, and would then have
crushed the revolting Slavs, and dominated East Europe
and the Heartland. German Kultur, and all that it
means in the way of organization, would have made
that German domination a chastisement of scorpions
as compared with the whips of Russia.

． ． ． ． ． ． ．

Thus far we have been thinking of the rivalry of empires from the point of view of strategical opportunities,
and we have come to the conclusion that the World-
Island and the Heartland are the final geographical
realities in regard to sea-power and land-power, and that
East Europe is essentially a part of the Heartland. But
there remains to be considered the economic reality of
man-power. We have seen that the question of base, not
only secure but also productive, is vital to sea-power;
the productive base is needed for the support of men
not only for the manning of the ships, but for all the
land services in connection with shipping, a fact to-day
more clearly realized in Britain than ever before. In
regard to land-power we have seen that the camel-men

and horsemen of past history failed to maintain lasting empires from lack of adequate man-power, and that Russia was the first tenant of the Heartland with a really menacing man-power.

But man-power does not imply a counting only of heads, though, other things being equal, numbers are decisive. Nor does it depend merely on the number of efficient human beings, though health and skill are of first importance. Man-power—the power of men—is also in these modern days very greatly dependent on organization, or, in other words, on the Going Concern, the social organism. German Kultur, the "ways and means" philosophy, has been dangerous to the outer world because it recognizes both realities, geographical and economic, and thinks *only* in terms of them.

The "political" economy of Britain and the "national" economy of Germany have come from the same fountain, the book of Adam Smith. Both accept as their bases the division of labor and competition to fix the prices at which the products of labor shall be exchanged. Both, therefore, can claim to be in harmony with the dominant tendency of thought in the nineteenth century as expressed by Darwin. They differ only in the unit of competition. In political economy the unit is the individual or firm; in national economy it tends to become the state among states. This was the fact appreciated by List, the founder of German national economy, under whose impulse the Prussian Zollverein or Customs Union was broadened until it included most of Germany. The British political economists welcomed the Zollverein, regarding it as an installment of their own Free Trade. In truth, by removing competition in greater or less degree to the outside, national economy aimed at substituting for the competition of mere men that of great national organizations. In a word, the national economists thought dynamically, but the political economists in the main statically.

This contrast of thinking between Kultur and Democracy was not at first of great practical significance. In the fifties and sixties of last century the Germans were at their wars. The British manufacturer was top dog, and, as Bismarck once said, free trade is the policy of the strong. It was not until 1878, the date of the first scientific tariff, that the economic sword of Germany was unsheathed. That date marks approximately a very great change in the arts of transport to which due weight is not always attached. It was then that British-built railways in America and British steel-built ships on the Atlantic began to carry bulk-cargoes.

What this new fact of the carriage of bulk—wheat, coal, iron ore, petroleum—means will be realized if we reflect that in western Canada to-day a community of a million people raise the cereal food of twenty millions, and that the other nineteen millions are at a distance—in eastern Canada, the eastern United States, and Europe. Prior to 1878 relatively light cargoes of such commodities as cotton, timber, and coal had been transported over the ocean by sailing ship, but the whole bulk of the cargoes of the world was insignificant as measured by the standards of to-day. Germany grasped the idea that under the new conditions it was possible to grow man-power where you would, on imported food and raw material, and therefore in Germany itself, for strategical use.

Up to this time the Germans, like the British, had freely emigrated, but the German no less than the British populations in the new countries made an increased demand for British manufactures. So the British people grew in number at home as well as in the colonies and the United States. Cobden and Bright had foreseen this; they meant to have cheap food and cheap raw materials wherewith to make cheap exports. But the rest of the world looked upon our free trade as a method of empire rather than of freedom; the reverse of the medal was presented to them; they were to be hewers and drawers for Great Britain. The British Islanders unfortunately made the mistake of attributing their prosperity mainly to their free imports, whereas it was chiefly due to their great Going Concern, and the fact that it had been set going before it had competitors. It was because they were "the strong" in 1846, that they could adopt free trade with *immediate* advantage and without serious *immediate* disadvantage.

From 1878 Germany began to build up her manpower by stimulating employment at home. One of her methods was the scientific tariff, a sieve through which imports were "screened," so that they should contain a minimum of labor and especially of skilled labor. But every other means was resorted to for the purpose of raising a Going Concern which should yield a great production at home. The railways were bought by the state, and preferential rates granted. The banks were brought under the control of the state by a system of interlocked shareholding, and credit was organized for industry. Cartels and combines reduced the cost of production and distribution. The result was that about the year 1900 German emigration, which had been steadily falling, ceased altogether, except in so far as balanced by immigration.

The economic offensive was increased by methods of penetration abroad. Shipping lines were subsidized, and banks were used as trade outposts in foreign cities. International combines were organized under German control, very largely with the help of the Jews of Frankfurt. Finally, in 1905, Germany imposed such a system of commercial treaties on seven adjoining nations as meant their economic subjection. One of these nations was Russia, then weak from war and revolution. These treaties are said to have taken ten years to think out —a characteristic efflorescence of Kultur!

The rapid German growth was a triumph of organization, or, in other words, of the strategical, the "ways and means" mentality. The fundamental scientific ideas were, most of them, imported, and the vaunted German technical education was merely a form of organization. The whole system was based on a clear understanding of the reality of the Going Concern—organized manpower.

But the Going Concern is a relentless fact, for the first political attribute of the animal Man is hunger. In the ten years before the war Germany was growing at the rate of a million souls a year—the difference between deaths and births. That meant that the productive Going Concern must not only be maintained, but that its "going" must be constantly accelerated. In the course of forty years the hunger of Germany for markets had become one of the most terrible realities of the world. The fact that the commercial treaty with Russia would come up for renewal in 1916 was probably not unconnected with the forcing of the war; Germany required, at all costs, a subject Slavdom to grow food for her and to buy her wares.

The men who, at Berlin, pulled the lever in 1914, and set free the dammed-up flood of German man-power have a responsibility which has been analyzed and fixed, so far as our information yet goes, with keen research by the unfortunate generation which has had to fight the fearful duel. But before history their guilt will be shared by those who, in years past, set the concern going. In this matter British statesmen and the British people will not be held wholly blameless.

It is the theory of free trade that the different parts of the world should develop on the basis of their natural facilities, and that different communities should specialize and render service to one another by exchanging their products freely. It was firmly believed that free trade thus made for peace and the brotherhood of men. That may have been a tenable theme in the time of Adam Smith and for a generation or two afterwards. But under modern conditions the Going Concern, or, in other words, accumulating financial and industrial strength, is capable of outweighing most natural facilities. The Going Concern of the Lancashire cotton industry is an instance of this on a great scale. A very small difference of price in cheap lines of export will hold or lose a market, and the great Going Concern can best afford to cut prices. Hence Lancashire has maintained her cotton industry for a century against all competitors, though the sources of the raw material and the principal markets for the finished goods are in distant parts of the world. Coal and a moist climate are her only natural facilities, and they can be paralleled elsewhere. The Lancashire cotton industry continues by virtue of momentum.

The result, however, of all specialization is to make growth lopsided. When the stress began after 1878, British agriculture waned, though British industry continued to grow. But presently lopsidedness developed even within British industry; the cotton and ship-building branches still grew, but the chemical and electrical branches did not increase proportionately. It was not only that German penetration designedly robbed us of our key industries, for the ordinary operation of specialization in a world which was becoming industrially active outside Britain was bound to produce some such contrasts. Britain developed vastly those industries into which she gradually concentrated her efforts. Therefore she, no less than Germany, became "market-hungry," for nothing smaller than the whole world was market enough for her in her own special lines.

Britain had no tariff available as a basis for bargaining; in that respect she stood naked before the world. Therefore, when threatened in some vital market, she could but return threats of sea-power. Cobden probably foresaw this in his later days when he declared the need for a strong British navy, but the rank and file of the Manchester School were so persuaded that free trade made for peace that they gave little thought to the special industrial requirements of sea-power; in their view any trade was equally good provided it were profitable. Yet Britain was *fighting* for her South American markets when her fleet maintained the Monroe Doctrine against Germany in the Manila incident, and for her Indian market when her fleet kept Germany at bay during the South African War, and for the open door to her China market when her fleet supported Japan in the Russian War. Did Lancashire realize that it was by force that the free import of cottons was imposed on India? Undoubtedly India has profited vastly on a balance by the British Raj, and no great weight of guilt need rest on the Lancashire conscience in this matter; but the fact remains that repeatedly, both within and without the Empire, free-trading, peace-loving Lancashire has been supported by the *force* of the Empire. Germany took note of the fact and built her fleet, and that fleet in being, and still in being to the end of the war, neutralized a mighty British effort which would have been available otherwise in support of our army in France.

The momentum of the Going Concern is very difficult to change in a democracy. The one hope of the future is that, as a result of the lesson of this war, even democracy may learn to take longer views. In an economically lopsided community the majority is on the overdeveloped side, and it is the majority which chooses the rulers in a democracy. The vested interests as a consequence tend to vest ever deeper: both the interest of labor in earning and buying in particular ways, and of capital in making profit in those same ways; on the average there is nothing to choose between labor and capital in these regards; they both take short views.

But there is the same difficulty of changing the Going Concern in an autocracy, although that difficulty is felt in a different way. The majority in a democracy *will not* change its economic routine, but autocracy often *does not dare* to do so. Germany under the Kaiserdom aimed at a world-empire, and to achieve it resorted to appropriate economic expedients for building up her man-power; presently she dared not change her only too successful policy even when it was forcing her to war, for the alternative was revolution. Like Frankenstein she had constructed an unmanageable monster.

In my belief, both free trade of the *laissez-faire* type and protection of the predatory type are policies of empire, and both make for war. The British and the Germans took seats in express trains on the same line, but in opposite directions. Probably from about 1908 a collision was inevitable; there comes a moment when the brakes have no longer time to act. The difference in British and German responsibility may perhaps be stated thus: the British driver started first, and ran carelessly, neglecting the signals, whereas the German driver deliberately strengthened and armored his train to stand the shock, put it on the wrong line, and at the last moment opened his throttle valves.

The Going Concern is, in these days, the great economic reality; it was used criminally by the Germans, and blindly by the British. The Bolsheviks must have forgotten that it existed.

Chapter Six

THE FREEDOM OF NATIONS

THE Allies have won the war. But how have we won? The process is full of warning. We were saved, in the first place, by the readiness of the British fleet, and by the decision which sent it to sea; so British communications with France were secured. That readiness and decision were the outcome of the British habit of looking to the one thing essential in the midst of many things we leave slipshod; it is the way of the capable amateur. We were saved, in the second place, by the wonderful victory of French genius on the Marne, prepared for by many years of deep thought in the great French *Ecole Militaire;* in other respects the French army was not as ready as it might have been, except in courage. We were saved in the third place by the sacrifice—it was no less—of the old British professional army at Ypres, a name that will stand in history beside Thermopylae. We were saved, in short, by exceptional genius and exceptional heroism from the results of an average refusal to foresee and prepare: eloquent testimony both to the strength and the weakness of democracy.

Then for two years the fighting was stabilized, and became a war of trenches on land and of submarines at sea, a war of attrition in which time told in favor of Britain but against Russia. In 1917 Russia cracked and then broke. Germany had conquered in the East,

but postponed the utter subjection of the Slavs in order first to strike down her Western foes. West Europe
had to call in the help of America, for West Europe
alone would not have been able to reverse the decision
in the East. Again time was needed, because America,
the third of the greater democracies to go to war, was
even less prepared than the other two. And time was
bought by the heroism of British seamen, the sacrifice of
British merchant shipping, and the endurance of the
French and British soldiers against an offensive in
France which all but overwhelmed them. In short, we
once more pitted character and a right insight into
essentials against German organization, and we just
managed to win. At the eleventh hour Britain accepted
the principle of the single strategical command, giving
scope once more to the *École Militaire*.

But this whole record of Western and oceanic fighting, so splendid and yet so humiliating, has very little
direct bearing on the international resettlement. There
was no immediate quarrel between East Europe and
West Europe; the time was past when France would
have attacked Germany to recover Alsace and Lorraine.
The war, let us never forget, began as a German effort
to subdue the Slavs who were in revolt against Berlin.
We all know that the murder of the Austrian (German)
Archduke in Slav Bosnia was the pretext, and that the
Austrian (German) ultimatum to Slav Serbia was the
method of forcing the war. But it cannot be too often
repeated that these events were the result of a fundamental antagonism between the Germans, who wished
to be masters in East Europe, and the Slavs, who refused to submit to them. Had Germany elected to stand

on the defensive on her short frontier towards France, and had she thrown her main strength against Russia, it is not improbable that the world would be nominally at peace to-day, but overshadowed by a German East Europe in command of all the Heartland. The British and American insular peoples would not have realized the strategical danger until too late.

Unless you would lay up trouble for the future, you cannot now accept any outcome of the war which does not finally dispose of the issue between German and Slav in East Europe. You must have a balance as between German and Slav, and true independence of each. You cannot afford to leave such a condition of affairs in East Europe and the Heartland, as would offer scope for ambition in the future, for you have escaped too narrowly from the recent danger.

A victorious Roman general, when he entered the city, amid all the head-turning splendor of a "Triumph," had behind him on the chariot a slave who whispered into his ear that he was mortal. When our statesmen are in conversation with the defeated enemy, some airy cherub should whisper to them from time to time this saying:

Who rules East Europe commands the Heartland:
Who rules the Heartland commands the World-Island:
Who rules the World-Island commands the World.

.   .   .   .

Viscount Grey once attributed the whole tragic course of recent events to the breach of the public law of Europe when Austria tore up the Treaty of Berlin by annexing Bosnia and Herzegovina in 1908. Undoubtedly that was a milestone in history, but the original occupation of these two Slav provinces of Turkey by Austria in 1878, under that very Berlin Treaty, was perhaps nearer to the source. It meant to the Slav mind notice that the Prussian German stood behind the Austrian German in his advance over the country for which the Slav had fought with the Turk; for the War of 1876, it must be remembered, which led up to the Congress of Berlin, began with a rising of the Slavs of Bosnia and Herzegovina against Turkey, and became European because of the sympathy of the neighboring Slavs of Serbia and Montenegro, which impelled them also to fight against the Turk. After 1878 there followed a few years of Russian hesitancy while Germany was beginning to build up her man-power. Then, in 1895, came the alliance between the Czardom and the French Republic. France needed an ally because of the still open Alsatian wound in her side; Russia needed an ally because of the German bully by her side. Russia and France were not immediate neighbors, so that the incompatibility of democracy and autocracy was not under the circumstances an impediment sufficient to forbid the marriage. But it was none the less some measure of the need in which Russia stood.

In 1905, when Russia was weak after the Japanese War and her first revolution, Germany imposed upon her a punishing tariff. In 1907 Russia went so far, in consequence, as to accept an understanding even with Britain, her rival of two generations and the ally of her late enemy, Japan. Again we have evidence of the stress that was on her, especially if we remember the German influences in her court and bureaucracy.

When, therefore, in 1908, Austria took that further action in regard to Bosnia and Herzegovina to which Viscount Grey attached such importance, she dealt a blow where there were already bruises. The little neighbor Serbia protested, and the big sister Russia supported her, for it meant the definite closing of the door to the historic aspirations of Serbian nationality, proudly held ever since the great defeat of Kossovo in the fourteenth century. But the Kaiser of Berlin put on his "shining armor" at Vienna, and shook his "mailed fist" in the face of the Czar at Petrograd. A few more uncomfortable years, and then, in 1912, came the First Balkan War, when the united Balkan Slavs overthrew the German-trained Turkish army. In 1913 the Bulgarian Slavs, instead of submitting the dispute in regard to the division of the territory taken from Turkey to the arbitration of the Czar, as had been provided by the Treaty of the Balkan Alliance, were persuaded by German intrigue to attack the Serbian Slavs. The Second Balkan War ensued, in which the Bulgarians were defeated owing to the intervention of the Rumanians, and the Treaty of Bukharest registered a severe check to German ambition, and gave new hope to the subject Slavs of Austria.

The very remarkable report sent from Berlin to Paris, three months after the Treaty of Bukharest, by M. Jules Cambon, the French ambassador, makes it clear that Germany had then decided to obtain by her own sword, whenever an opportunity could be made, the position which she had failed to win vicariously. Accumulating evidence goes to show that within a week of the murder of the Archduke Franz Ferdinand, Germany had decided to seize that pretext in order to force the issue. Austria sought to impose such terms of punishment on Serbia for her assumed complicity in the murder as no free nation could accept, and when Serbia had gone to the utmost limit of concession, and even Austria hesitated, Germany hastened to fasten her quarrel on Russia, the ultimate reserve of all Slavdom. Had Russia submitted, as in 1908, she would have gone into the question of the renewal of the Tariff Treaty with Germany in 1916 with no option but a surrender into economic slavery. All this is a familiar story, but it is necessary to keep it clearly in mind, if we are to appreciate the fact that the key to the resettlement is in the East, though the decisive fighting has been in the West.

How came it that Germany made the double mistake of invading France and of invading her through Belgium? Germany knew the weakness of Russia; there was no illusion of the "steam roller" for her. Her choice of the more difficult offensive must have been on the assumption that the British democracy probably, and the American democracy certainly, were, from her point of view, asleep. She meant the German superman to rule the world, and she thought she saw a short cut to her end, in the place of the longer path through the Heartland, the command of which would fall to her inevitably, could she but deprive the islanders of their "bridge-head" in France. But there was another and even stronger reason for what she did; she was in the grip of economic fate. She was out against the Slavs for markets, for raw materials, and for wider fields to till; a million people were being added annually to her stay-at-home, kept-at-home family. But to develop that mighty Going Concern of her man-power, so strong for conquest if she could keep it going, but so insatiably hungry, she had built up Hamburg, and all that Hamburg stood for in the way of overseas adventure and home industries. Hamburg had her own momentum, and it was not eastward. Thus German strategy was biased by political necessity.

The result was that Berlin committed a fundamental mistake; she fought on two fronts without fully making up her mind on which front she meant to win. You may strike at the two flanks of your enemy, the right and the left, but, unless your force is sufficient to annihilate, you must decide beforehand which stroke is to be the feint and which the real attack. Berlin had not decided between her political objectives—Hamburg and overseas dominion, or Bagdad and the Heartland—and therefore her strategical aim also was uncertain.

.   .   .   .

The German blunder, under compelling destiny, having given us victory, it is essential that we should focus our thought on the stable resettlement of the affairs of East Europe and the Heartland. If we accept anything less than a complete solution of the Eastern Question in its largest sense we shall merely have gained a respite, and our descendants will find themselves under the necessity of marshaling their power afresh for the siege of the Heartland. The essence of the resettlement must be territorial, for in East Europe, and in still greater measure in the remainder of the Heartland, we have to deal with regions whose economic development has only commenced. Unless you look forward, the growth of the peoples will by and by unbalance your settlement.

No doubt it may be urged that German mentality will be altered by German defeat. He would be a sanguine man, however, who would trust the future peace of the world to a change in the mentality of any nation. Look back to old Froissard or to Shakespeare, and you will find your Englishman, Scotsman, Welshman, and Frenchman with all their essential characteristics already fixed. The Prussian is a definite type of humanity with his good and his bad points, and we shall be wise if we act on the assumption that his kind will breed true to its type. However great the defeat which in the end we may have inflicted on our chief enemy, we should only be cheapening our own achievement if we did not recognize in the North German one of the three or four most virile races of mankind.

Even with revolution in Germany let us not be too sure in regard to its ultimate effect. The German revolutions of 1848 were almost comic in their futility. Since Bismarck there has only been one German chancellor with political insight, and he—Von Bülow—has declared in his book on *Imperial Germany* that "the German has always accomplished his greatest works under strong, steady, and firm guidance." The end of the present disorder may only be a new ruthless organization, and ruthless organizers do not stop when they have attained the objects which they at first set before them.

It will be replied, of course, that though Prussian mentality remain unchanged, and though a really stable Prussian democracy be slow in its development, yet that Germany will, in any case, be so impoverished that she cannot do harm for the better part of a century to come. Is there not, however, in that idea a misreading of the real nature of riches and poverty under modern conditions? Is it not productive power which now counts rather than dead wealth? Shall we not all of us—and now in some degree even the Americans also—have spent our dead capital, and shall we not all of us, the Germans included, be starting again in the productive race practically from scratch? The world was astonished at the rapidity with which France recovered from her disaster of 1870, but the power of industrial production was as nothing then to what it is now. Sober calculation in regard to Britain leads to the conclusion that her increased productive power, owing to reorganization and new methods compelled by the war, should far exceed the interest and sinking fund even of her vast war debts. No doubt you have the Paris Resolutions, and can deny to a refractory Germany the raw materials wherewith to compete with you. If you resort to that method, however, you postpone your League of Nations, and you remain a League of Allies. Are you certain, moreover, that you would win in an economic war? You might undoubtedly handicap Germany, but a handicap may only lead to greater effort. Did not Napoleon limit the Prussian army after Jena to 42,000 men with the colors, and was not the Prussian effort to circumvent his prohibition the origin of the whole modern system of short-service national armies? Economic war, with Germany exploiting the Slavs, and presently the Heartland, would in the long run merely serve to emphasize the distinction between the Continent and the Islands, and between land-power and sea-power, and no one who contemplates the unity of the Great Continent under modern railway conditions can view unconcernedly either the preparation for the world war which would be inevitable, or the ultimate result of that war.

We, the Western nations, have incurred such tremendous sacrifices in this conflict that we cannot afford to trust to anything that *may* happen at Berlin; we must be secure in any case. In other words, we must settle this question between the Germans and Slavs, and we must see to it that East Europe, like West Europe, is divided into self-contained nations. If we do that, we shall not only reduce the German people to its proper position in the world, a great enough position for any single people, but we shall also have created the conditions precedent to a League of Nations.

You plead that if we inflict a decisive peace we shall leave such bitter feelings that no workable League of Nations can ensue. You have in mind, of course, the results of the annexation of Alsace in 1871. But the lessons of history are not to be learned from a single instance. The great American Civil War was fought to a finish, and to-day the southerners are as loyal to the Union as are the northerners; the two questions of Negro slavery and of the right of particular states to secede from the Federation were finally decided, and ceased to be the causes of quarrel. The Boer War was fought to a finish, and to-day General Smuts is an honored member of the British Cabinet. The War of 1866, between Prussia and Austria, was fought to a finish, and within a dozen years Austria had formed the Dual Alliance with Prussia. If you do not now secure the full results of your victory and close this issue between the German and the Slav, you will leave ill-feeling which will not be based on the fading memory of a defeat, but on the daily irritation of millions of proud people.

　　•　　　　•　　　　•　　　　•　　　　•　　　　•

The condition of stability in the territorial rearrangement of East Europe is that the division should be into three and not into two state-systems. It is a vital necessity that there should be a tier of independent states between Germany and Russia.[1] The Russians are, and for one, if not two, generations must remain, hopelessly incapable of resisting German penetration on any basis but that of a military autocracy, unless they be shielded from direct attack. The Russian peasantry cannot read; they have obtained the only reward they looked for when they sided with the revolutionaries of the towns, and now as small proprietors they hardly know how to manage their own countrysides. The middle class have so suffered that they were ready to accept order even from the hated Germans. As for the workmen of the towns, only a small minority of the Russian population—but because of their relative education and of their command of the centers of communication the rulers to-day of the country—Kultur knows well how to "influence" them. In the opinion of those who know Russia best, autocratic rule of some sort is almost in-

[1] The details of the discussion of the territorial resettlement which will follow will, of course, become in large measure obsolete with the announcement of the decisions of the Peace Congress. My object is not, however, so much to debate certain solutions of the problems immediately confronting us, as to give a concrete aspect to the general idea which I am endeavoring to build up. My purpose will still be served if it is borne in mind that what I have written on these particulars represents the outlook at Christmas, 1918.

evitable if she is to depend on her own strength to cope with the Germans.

The Slav and kindred nations which inhabit the borderland between the Germans and the Russians are, however, of a very different caliber. Consider the Czechs: have they not stood proof against Bolshevism and asserted their capacity of nationhood under amazing conditions in Russia? Have they not shown the most extraordinary political capacity in creating anew and maintaining Slav Bohemia, though beset on three sides by Germany and on the fourth side by Hungary? Have they not also made Bohemia a hive of modern industry and a seat of modern learning? They, at any rate, will not lack the will to order and to independence.

Between the Baltic and the Mediterranean you have these seven non-German peoples, each on the scale of a European state of the second rank—the Poles, the Bohemians (Czechs and Slovaks), the Hungarians (Magyars), the South Slavs (Serbians, Croatians, and Slovenes), the Rumanians, the Bulgarians, and the Greeks. Of these, two are among our present enemies—the Magyars and the Bulgarians. But the Magyars and Bulgarians are engirt by the other five peoples, and neither of them will be powerful for harm without Prussian support.

Let us count over these seven peoples. First we have the Poles, some twenty million of them, with the river Vistula for their arterial water-way, and the historic cities of Cracow and Warsaw. The Poles are a more generally civilized people than the Russians, even in that part of Poland which has been tied to Russia; in the Prussian province of Posen they have enjoyed the advantages of Kultur, without some of the debasement which Kultur brought to the master German. Undoubtedly there are strong currents of party among the Poles, but now that the Polish aristocracy of Galicia is no longer bribed to the support of the Hapsburg throne by leave to oppress the Ruthenians of East Galicia, at least one motive of party, one vested interest, should have disappeared.

By some means the new Poland must be given access to the Baltic Sea, not only because that is essential to her economic independence, but also because it is desirable to have Polish ships on the Baltic, which strategically is a closed sea of the Heartland, and, further, there must be a complete territorial buffer between Germany and Russia. Unfortunately the province of East Prussia, mainly German by speech and Junker by sentiment, would be detached from Germany by any strip of Poland going down to the sea. Why should we not contemplate an exchange of peoples as between Prussia east of the Vistula, and Polish Posen? [1] During this war we have undertaken much vaster things, both in the way of mere transport and also of organization. In the past, in order to deal with such difficulties, diplomatists have resorted to all manner of "servitudes" as the land lawyers would say. But rights-of-way over other people's property usually become inconvenient and lead to disputes. Would it not pay humanity to bear the

[1] Since I wrote this paragraph, M. Venizelos, in an interview with a *Times* correspondent, dated Paris, January 14, 1919, has used these words: "This would still leave some hundreds of thousands of Greeks under Turkish rule in the center of Asia Minor. For this there is only one cure, and that is to encourage a *wholesale and mutual transfer of population.*"

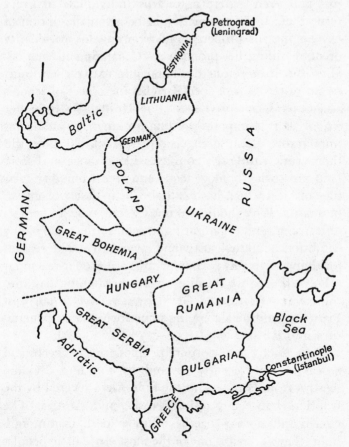

FIG. 31.—The middle tier of states between Germany and Russia. Many boundary questions have still to be determined.

cost of a radical remedy in this case, a remedy made just and even generous towards individuals in every respect? Each proprietor should be given the option of exchanging his property and retaining his nationality or of retaining his property and changing his nationality. But if he selects the latter alternative there must be no reservation of special rights in respect of schools and other social privileges. The United States in her schools sternly imposes the English language on all her immigrants. Because the conquerors of old time did their work ruthlessly, countries like France and England are to-day homogeneous and free from that mixture of faces which has made the Near East a plague to humanity. Why should we not use our modern powers of transport and organization to achieve the same happy condition of affairs—justly and generously? The reasons for doing so in this particular instance are far-reaching: a Polish Posen would bite a very threatening bay into the eastern frontier of Germany, and a German East Prussia would be a stepping-stone for German penetration into Russia.[1]

Next among our "border" peoples are the Czechs and Slovaks, until recently severed by the line dividing Austria from Hungary, as the Poles were severed by the frontiers between Russia, Prussia, and Austria. The Czechs and Slovaks together number perhaps nine millions; they will make one of the most virile little peoples in Europe, and they are equipped with a remarkable country, offering coal, metals, timber, water-power, corn, and wine, and centered on the main line of rail-

[1] To meet the obvious *argumentum ad hominem*, let me say that I see no really comparable strategical necessities in the case of Ireland!

way from the Baltic and Warsaw to Vienna and the Adriatic.

Then we come to the South Slavs—Jugo means South —in their three tribes of Slovenes, Croatians, and Serbs. They number about twelve millions. They also have been sundered by the line between Austria and Hungary; moreover, they are of the rival Latin and Greek Churches. For anyone who knows the Balkans, it is eloquent testimony indeed to the effect of Austro-Hungarian tyranny that the Roman Catholic Slovenes and Croatians should have made the pact of Corfu with the Greek Orthodox Serbs. The South Slavs will have access to Dalmatian ports on the Adriatic, and one of the trunk railways of the world will run down the Save Valley to Belgrade, and then through the Morava and Maritza "Corridor" to Constantinople.

Rumania is the next state of this middle east of Europe. The natural focus of Rumania is the great Transylvanian bastion of the Carpathians, with fruitful valleys, metalliferous mountains, oil wells, and splendid forests. The Transylvanian peasantry is Rumanian, but a "privileged" minority of Magyars and "Saxons" have been the rulers. Here again it should be no quite impossible feat of statesmanship to arrange for an equitable exchange of homes, or a full acceptance of Rumanian nationality, though it must be admitted that the hostility between Saxon and Ruman is not so acute as that between Prussian and Pole.

The rest of Rumania, the present kingdom, is the glacis, eastward and southward, of Transylvania, watered by the Transylvanian rivers. This fertile glacis is one of the chief sources in Europe of oil, wheat, and maize; the twelve million Rumanians will be a rich people. At Galatz, Braila, and Constanza they have ports on the Black Sea, and it will be a prime interest of all free peoples that there should be Rumanian ships on that sea, for it is naturally a closed water of the Heartland. The time will never come when the League of Nations will be able to regard the Baltic and Black.Seas without concern, for the Heartland offers the basis of an all-powerful militarism. Civilization consists in the control of nature and of ourselves, and the League of. Nations, as the supreme organ of united humanity, must closely watch the Heartland and its possible organizers, for the same reason that the control of the police in London and Paris is regarded as a national and not merely a municipal concern.

The Greeks were the first of our seven peoples of the Middle Tier to achieve their emancipation from German control in this war for the simple reason that they are outside the Heartland and therefore accessible to sea-power. But in these days of submarines and aeroplanes, the possession of Greece by a great Heartland power would probably carry with it the control of the World-Island; the Macedonian history would be reenacted.

Now as to the Magyars and Bulgarians. The truth is that both of them were exploited by, although not subject to, the Prussians. Everyone who knows Budapest is aware of the deeply alien feeling of the Magyars toward the Germans; the recent alliance was strictly one of convenience and not of hearts. The ruling Magyar caste of about a million people has been oppressive of the other nine millions of its own race no less than of subject races. The alliance with Prussia—for it has in reality been an alliance with Prussia rather than with Austria—has been strictly in return for support of the Magyar oligarchy. No doubt the Magyars have begotten deep feelings of hostility among the Slavs and Rumanians, but if there be no more profit to be made from farming Slavs in the German behalf, a democratic Hungary will sooner or later adapt herself to the new environment. The Bulgarians fought, let us remember, as allies of the Serbs against the Turks, and the difference between Serb and Bulgar, though bitter for the time being, is a family difference. It is a difference of recent growth, and based largely on rival ecclesiastical organizations of recent foundation. The Bulgarians must not be allowed to exploit their treachery in the Second Balkan War, but if an equitable settlement be *dictated* by the Allies, both nations, the Bulgarians and the Serbs, deeply war weary, will probably accept it joyfully. For twenty years only one will, that of the German Czar Ferdinand, has counted in Bulgaria.

The most important point of strategical significance in regard to these middle states of East Europe is that the most civilized of them, Poland and Bohemia, lie in the north, in the position most exposed to Prussian aggression. Securely independent the Polish and Bohemian nations cannot be, unless as the apex of a broad wedge of independence, extending from the Adriatic and Black Seas to the Baltic; but seven independent states, with a total of more than sixty million people, traversed by railways linking them securely with one another, and having access through the Adriatic, Black, and Baltic Seas with the ocean, will together effectively balance the Germans of Prussia and Austria, and nothing less will suffice for that purpose. None the less the League of Nations should have the right under international law of sending war fleets into the Black and Baltic Seas.

.   .   .   .

This great deed of international statesmanship accomplished, there would appear to be no impossibility of realizing the democratic ideal, the League of Nations, whose mirage has haunted our Western peoples from afar over the desert of war. What are the essential conditions which must be fulfilled if you are to have a real and potent League of Nations? Viscount Grey, in his recent pamphlet, laid down two such conditions. The first was that "the Idea must be adopted with earnestness and conviction by the Executive Heads of States." The second was that "the Governments and Peoples of the States willing to found it understand clearly that it will impose some limitation upon the national action of each, and may entail some inconvenient obligation. The stronger nations must forego the right to make their interests prevail against the weaker by force."

These are excellent and very necessary theses, but do they carry us far enough? Before you undertake any general obligation, is it not well to consider what it is likely to mean in concrete terms? Your League will have to reckon with certain realities. There was before the war an incipient League of Nations; its members were the states party to the system of international law. Have we not had to fight the war just because two of the greater states broke the international law, first in regard to one and then another of the smaller states, and have not those two greater states very nearly succeeded in defeating a very powerful League of Nations which intervened in behalf of the law? In the face of such a fact, is it quite adequate to say that stronger nations must "forego" the right to make their interests prevail by force against the weaker? In a word, do not our ideals involve us in a circle unless we reckon with realities?

Is it not plain that if your League is to last there must be no nation strong enough to have any chance against the general will of humanity? Or, to put the matter in another way; there must be no predominant partner or even group of partners in your League. Is there any case of a successful federation with a predominant partner? In the United States you have the great states of New York, Pennsylvania, and Illinois, but no one of them counts for more than a small fraction of the whole Union. In Canada you have Quebec and Ontario balancing one another, so that the smaller provinces of the Dominion are never likely to be bullied by either. In the Commonwealth of Australia you have the approximately equal states of New South Wales and Victoria. In Switzerland not even the large canton of Berne is anything like predominant. Has not German Federation been a pretense because of the dominance of Prussia? Is not the chief difficulty in the way of devolution within the British Isles, even if Irishmen would agree among themselves, the predominance of England? Did not this war originate from the fact that you allowed an almost dominant Germany to arise in Europe? Have not the great wars of the past in Europe come from the fact that one state in the European system, under Napoleon, Louis XIV, or Philip II, had become too powerful? Is it not necessary, if your League of Nations is to have any chance of success, to face this cumulative evidence and not to gloss it over?

Is there not also another reality with which you must reckon, the reality of the Going Concern? If the nations of your League are to settle down to a quiet life, there are two different ways, it seems to me, in which you will have to face the reality of the Going Concern: in respect of the present and of the future. What is meant by this reality in the present will best be conveyed by concrete consideration of the states available as the units to be leagued together.

The British Empire is a Going Concern. You will not persuade a majority of Britons to risk the coherence of the Empire, which has so triumphantly stood the test of this war, for any paper scheme of a Universal League. It follows, therefore, that the governing units of the British Empire can only *grow* by gradual process into their place as units of your League. Yet the relations of six of them are already, in fact, the relations of equality and, under their British League, of independency. Only last year was the last word said in that matter. The Prime Ministers of the Dominions are henceforth to communicate directly with the Prime Minister of the United Kingdom, and no longer through the subordinate Colonial Secretary; the Parliament at Westminster is no longer to be called the Imperial Parliament but only the Parliament of the United Kingdom. It only remains that the King should no longer be called King of the United Kingdom and of the Dominions beyond the Seas, but that the equality of all the Dominions should be recognized by some such title as

King of all the Britains. Even in respect of realities—though in such matters names become realities—have we not now the certainty that the United Kingdom, Canada, and Australia will each have its own fleet and army, to be put under a single strategical command only on the outbreak of war? As regards population, too, is it not now a question of only a few years before Canada and Australia will equal the Motherland in power? We shall then have the three minor Dominions —New Zealand, South Africa, and Newfoundland— counting the more because of the balance between the three major Dominions.

France and Italy are Going Concerns. Are they going to enter a League in which the British Empire is a unit? Fortunately we have achieved the single strategical command in the later stages of the war, so that the name Versailles has now an added historic meaning. No longer merely through their Ambassadors, but in the persons of their Prime Ministers, the United Kingdom, France, and Italy have acquired the habit of taking counsel together. These three countries of West Europe are not unfitted by any decisive inequality of size to be fellow members of a League. Is it not probable that occasions will occur when the Prime Ministers of Canada and Australia may be called into conference with the Prime Ministers of the United Kingdom, France, and Italy? They will be occasions of all the more value if you recognize the Going Concerns of to-day and do not attempt to make merely paper progress. Remember that it required the peril of the German offensive of 1918 to secure the unity of strategical command.[1]

[1] Since this was written the Paris Conference has treated the British Empire as a hybrid—a unit *for some purposes*.

Then what of the United States? There is no good in pretending that the separate American states can be units in your League; the Republic fought the greatest war in history, before this war, in order to weld them together. Yet the United States form something very like a predominant partner as against the separate allied countries of West Europe. The United States must be in your League; and that means that, for healthy working, the six Britains must be held together as a counterbalance. Fortunately three thousand miles of undefended frontier of North America constitute a fact of good omen, though, to be quite frank, it would signify more if the countries which that frontier has separated had been less unequal; the test would have been more severe.

But the need of a reasonable equality of power as between a considerable number of the members of the League, so that in future crises—and they will occur—it may not be exposed to danger from predominance in any quarter, is less urgent in respect of the insular than of the continental members. There are the obvious limitations of sea-power; there are also natural boundaries which define the spread of any one insular, or even peninsular, base of power. The test of the League will be in the Heartland of the Continent. Nature there offers all the prerequisites of ultimate dominance in the world; it must be for man by his foresight and by the taking of solid guarantees to prevent its attainment. Notwithstanding their revolutions the German and Russian peoples are Going Concerns, each with a powerful historical momentum.

Therefore let the idealists who, now that the nations

are locked into a single world system, rightly see in the League of Nations the only alternative to hell on earth, concentrate their attention on the adequate subdivision of East Europe. With a Middle Tier of really independent states between Germany and Russia they will achieve their end, and without it they will not. Any mere trench-line between the German Powers and Russia, such as was contemplated by Naumann in his *Central Europe,* would have left German and Slav still in dual rivalry, and no lasting stability could have ensued. But the Middle Tier, supported by the outer nations of the World League, will accomplish the end of breaking-up East Europe into more than two state-systems. Moreover, the states of that Tier, of approximate equality of power, will themselves be a very acceptable group for the recruitment of the League.

Once thus remove the temptation and opening to world-empire, and who can say what will occur among the German and Russian peoples themselves? There are already indications that Prussia, which, unlike England or France, is a purely artificial structure, will be broken into several federal states. In one region the Prussians belong by history to East Europe and in another to West Europe. Is it not probable that the Russians will fall into a number of states in some sort of loose federation? Germany and Russia have grown into great empires out of opposition to one another; but the peoples of the Middle Tier—Poles, Bohemians, Hungarians, Rumanians, Serbs, Bulgarians, and Greeks—are much too unlike to federate for any purpose except defense, yet they are all so different both from Germans and Russians that they may be trusted to resist any new organization of either great neighbor making towards the empire of East Europe.

There are certain strategical positions in the Heart-land and Arabia which must be treated as of world importance, for their possession may facilitate or prevent a world domination. It does not, however, follow that it would be wise to commit them forthwith to an untried international administration; here, too, it is very necessary to bear in mind the truth of the Going Concern. Condominium has not, as a rule, been a success, for the reason that the agents of the joint protecting Powers almost inevitably take sides with the local nationalities or parties. The most effective method of international control would seem to be that of commissioning some one Power as trustee for humanity—a different Power, of course, in the case of different positions. That was the method experimentally tried when Austria-Hungary was entrusted with the administration of Bosnia and Herzegovina at the Congress of Berlin, and it succeeded so far as the material advancement of the protected provinces was concerned. There is no reason why the new principle and the facts of the Going Concern should not be reconciled in the cases of Panama, Gibraltar, Malta, Suez, Aden, and Singapore, by regarding the American Republic and the British Empire as world trustees for the peace of the ocean and of the straits connecting the basins of the ocean. This, however, would amount merely to a regularization of existing facts. The test of the principle, as of most other world principles, is in connection with the Heartland and Arabia. The islanders of the world cannot be indifferent to the fate either of Copenhagen or of Constantinople, or yet of the Kiel Canal, for a great Power in the Heartland and East Europe could prepare, within the Baltic and Black Seas, for war on the ocean. During the present war it has taken the whole naval strength of the Allies to hold the North Sea and the Eastern Mediterranean. An adequate submarine campaign, based on the Black Sea from the beginning of the war, would probably have given security to an army operating overland against the Suez Canal. It follows, therefore, that Palestine, Syria, and Mesopotamia, the Bosporus and the Dardanelles, and the outlets from the Baltic must be internationalized in some manner. In the case of Palestine, Syria, and Mesopotamia, it has been understood that Britain and France would undertake international trusts. Why should we not solve the problem of Constantinople by making that historic city the Washington of the League of Nations? When the network of railways has covered the World-Island, Constantinople will be one of the most accessible places on the globe by railway, steamer, and aeroplane. From Constantinople the leading nations of the West might radiate light through precisely those regions, oppressed during many past centuries, in which light is most to be desired from the point of view of humanity at large; from Constantinople we might weld together the West and the East, and permanently penetrate the Heartland with oceanic freedom.

The Jewish national seat in Palestine will be one of the most important outcomes of the war. That is a subject on which we can now afford to speak the truth. The Jew, for many centuries shut up in the ghetto, and shut out of most honorable positions in society, developed in an unbalanced manner and became hateful to the average Christian by reason of his excellent, no less than his deficient, qualities. German penetration has been conducted in the great commercial centers of the world in no small measure by Jewish agency, just as German domination in southeastern Europe was achieved through Magyar and Turk, with Jewish assistance. Jews are among the chief of the Bolsheviks of Russia. The homeless, brainful Jew lent himself to such internationalist work, and Christendom has no great right to be surprised by the fact. But you will have no room for these activities in your League of independent, friendly nations. Therefore a national home, at the physical and historical center of the world, should make the Jew "range" himself. Standards of judgment, brought to bear on Jews by Jews, should result, even among those large Jewish communities which will remain as Going Concerns outside Palestine. This, however, will imply the frank acceptance of the position of a nationality, which some Jews seek to forget. There are those who try to distinguish between the Jewish religion and the Hebrew race, but surely the popular view of their broad identity is not far wrong.

In the vast and populous regions of Asia and Africa which lie beyond the girdle of the great deserts and plateaux there are Going Concerns, such as the British Raj in India, which it would be folly indeed to shake down in your hurry to realize a world symmetry for your League of Nations. But it is essential that neither Kiauchau nor East Africa should go back to the Power which took them with a keen strategical eye to the day when armies marching overland should find in each of them a citadel already prepared; which took them, moreover, with the clear intention that the Chinese and the Negroes should be utilized as subsidiary man-power to help in the conquest of the World-Island. What part may ultimately be played by that half of the human race which lives in "The Indies" no man can yet foresee, but it is the plain duty of the insular peoples to protect the Indians and Chinese from Heartland conquest.

German Southwest Africa and the German Australasian colonies must not be returned; the principle of independence within the League implies that, subject to an international trust in the case of a few critically important positions, each nation must be mistress in her own house, and that principle holds in regard to South Africa and Australia. Any other principle would leave the seeds of future quarrels and would impede disarmament.

.   .   .   .

So much in respect of the starting of the League and of the Going Concern in the present. It remains for us to speak of the Going Concern in the future. Viscount Grey has described the state of mind which will be required when we approach this great international enterprise: is there not something more precise to be said in that matter also?

I have expressed my belief that both free trade of the *laissez-faire* type and predatory protection of the German type are principles of empire, and that both make for war. Fortunately the younger Britains refused to accept the free trade of Manchester; they used the fiscal independence granted to them by the Motherland to pursue that economic ideal which was foreshadowed by

the great American statesman, Alexander Hamilton—
the ideal of the truly independent nation, balanced in
all its development. This does not in the least imply
that a great international trade should not be done, but
it should be a trade so controlled that the effect of it
is always tending towards the balance aimed at, and is
not accumulating, beyond hope of recovery, economic
onesidedness.

No stable League of Nations appears to me possible
if any nation is allowed to practice commercial "penetration," for the object of that penetration is to deprive
other nations of their fair share of the more skilled
forms of employment, and it is inevitable that a general
soreness should ensue in so far as it succeeds. Nor, to
speak quite plainly, is there any great difference in result if some nations feel that they are reduced to the
position of hewers and drawers owing to the industrial
specialization of another country under the régime of
unrestricted Cobdenism; wherever an industry is so
developed in one country that it can be content with no
less than a world market for its particular products, the
economic balance of other countries tends to be upset.
No important country, after this war, is going to allow
itself to be deprived either of any "key" or of any "essential" industry.[1] By the time you have exhausted these

[1] The distinction between these two terms is not always observed.
Key industries are those which, although themselves relatively small,
are necessary to other and much greater industries. Thus, for instance,
aniline dyestuffs to the value of two million pounds a year were utilized in Great Britain before the war in textile and paper manufactures
of the annual worth of two hundred millions. The proportion was
something like that of a key to the door which it unlocks. Essential
industries there are which have not this character of a small key; such,
for instance, in this twentieth century is the steel industry. It is well
to preserve the distinction, because different defensive measures may
perhaps be needed in the two cases.

two categories, you will find that you might just as well
have adopted the attractive positive ideal of general economic independence instead of being driven from one
expedient to another in mere defensiveness. If you attempt to maintain a negative Cobdenism *with exceptions,* you will, under the conditions of the world that
are opening before us, very soon build up a large and
clumsy body of merely *ad hoc* machineries. A general
system of low duties and bounties would enable you to
deal quickly and lightly with each difficulty as it develops, because you would have the appropriate machinery of control at your hand. But I am not here going
into the detail of these questions of machinery; I am
dealing with the question of ideal and aim. The Cob-
denite believes that international trade is good in itself, and that specialization as between country and
country, provided that it arises blindly under the guidance of natural causes, should not be thwarted. The
Berliner, on the other hand, has also encouraged economic specialization among the nations, but he operates
scientifically, accumulating in his own country those
industries which give most, and most highly skilled, employment. The result is the same in each case; a going
concern of industry grips the nation and deprives it,
as well as other nations, of true independence. The resulting differences accumulate to the point of quarrel
and collision.

There are three attitudes of mind in regard to the
Going Concern which spell tragedy. There is *laissez-
faire,* which is surrender and fatalism. This attitude
produces a condition comparable with that of a disease brought on by self-neglect; the human body is a

going concern which, becoming unbalanced in its functions, is organically affected, so that in the end no doctor's advice or even surgeon's scalpel can avail, since to stop the disease means the stoppage of life itself. No doubt it seemed, in the warm sunshine of Britain in the middle of the last century, that the wiser political philosophy was to live for the day and to trust in Providence. Fortunately disease had not progressed to a fatal stage when we came to the surgeon's table in August, 1914. But a million men of military age classified as unfit for military service constitute a symptom which almost makes one thank God that the war came when it did.

The second attitude of mind in relation to the Going Concern is that of panic. This has been the attitude of Prussia, though it was hidden by the flattering philosophy of the superman, not less pleasant, while it was credible, than the comforting religion of *laissez-faire*. Nakedly stated, however, Kultur meant that, being obsessed with the idea of competition and natural selection, as finally expressed in Darwinism, and being frightened, the Prussians decided that if, in the end, men must come to man-eating in order to survive, they, at any rate, would be the cannibals! So they assiduously cultivated the strength and efficiency of the prize-fighter. But the monster Going Concern into which they developed their country grew hungrier and hungrier, and at last they had to let it feed. Half the cruel and selfish things which are done in this world are done for reasons of panic.

The third attitude is that of the anarchist and the Bolshevik—they would distinguish no doubt between themselves, but whether you break the Going Concern or take it to pieces makes little practical difference. This attitude means social suicide. It is vital that discipline should be maintained in the Western democracies during the period of reconstruction, whatever Bolshevism may happen in Central as well as East Europe. The Westerners are the victors, and they alone are able to prevent the whole world from having to pass through the cycle so often repeated in the case of individual nations—idealism, disorder, famine, tyranny. Provided that we do not hasten to dismantle running social machinery, but accomplish our ideals by successive acts of social discipline, we shall maintain the steady output of production, the fundamental reality, that is to say, on which now, more than ever before, civilization rests. The disorder of a whole world, let us not forget, implies the absence of any remaining national base as a fulcrum for the restoration of order, and therefore the indefinite prolongation of anarchy and tyranny. It took several centuries to attain again to the stage of civilization which had been reached when the Roman world of antiquity broke down.

But if drifting in the grip of the Going Concern leads to disease in a nation, and if we must not fall into panic because that results in crime, nor yet suffer revolt because that ends in suicide, what course remains open to us? Surely that of control, which in a democracy means self-control. If this war has proved anything, it has proved that these gigantic forces of modern production are capable of control. Beforehand it was assumed by many that a world war would bring so general a financial crash that it would not—could not—be allowed to take place. Yet how easily, when it actually befell, were the British and German systems of credit disengaged by the simple device of using the national credits to carry the roots of individual credit which were pulled out of the enemy soil.

If you once admit control of the Going Concern to be your aim, then the ideal state-unit of your League must be the nation of balanced economic development. Raw materials are unequally distributed over the world, but the primary pursuits of men, other than the growing of the staples of food proper to each region, form in these days but a relatively small part of the total of industry. Minerals must be won in the mines and tropical produce can only be grown within the tropics, but both minerals and tropical produce are now easy of transport, and the higher industries may, therefore, be located at the choice and will of mankind. We are what our occupations make us; every mature man is imprinted with the characteristics of his calling. So is it with the nations, and no self-respecting nation henceforth will allow itself to be deprived of its share of the higher industries. But these industries are so interlocked that they cannot be developed except in balance one with another. It follows, therefore, that each nation will strive for development in each great line of industrial activity, and should be allowed to attain to it.

This is the ideal, I am firmly persuaded, which will make for peace. In ordinary society it is notoriously difficult for people of very unequal fortune to be friends in the true sense; that beautiful relationship is not compatible with patronage and dependence. Civilization, no doubt, consists in the exchange of services, but it should be an equal exchange. Our economics of money have assessed as equal services of very unequal value from the point of view of the quality of the industrial employment which they give. For the contentment of nations we must contrive to secure some equality of opportunity for national development.

Chapter Seven

THE FREEDOM OF MEN

FROM the consideration of the realities presented by the geography of our globe we have come to the conclusion that if the freedom of nations is to be secure, it must rest on a reasonable approach to equality of resources as between a certain number of the larger nations. We have also seen that, given the imperious reality of the Going Concern, it is necessary that the nations should be so controlled in their economic growth that they do not tend to get out of hand and clash. But what have these principles to do with the freedom of men and women? Will free nations in a League be able to give more freedom to their citizens? Certainly the men who have been fighting, the men who have been sailing our ships through danger on the seas, and the mothers and wives who have been working, waiting, and mourning at home, are not looking for the mere defeat of a danger that threatened; they have positive visions of greater happiness in their own lives or in the lives of those dear to them.

Let us analyze from this point of view the successive stages of democratic idealism which were referred to in the opening pages of this book. The American Declaration of Independence claimed for all men the right to pursue happiness. The French Revolution crystallized this phrase into the single word Liberty, and added Equality, which implies control, and Fraternity, which implies self-control. Fraternity is of the essence of successful democracy, the highest but the most difficult of all modes of government, since it demands most of the average citizen. That is the first cycle of democratic thought; it pertains directly and obviously to the freedom of men.

In the middle of the nineteenth century began the second cycle, which has aimed at the freedom of nations. The claim of nationality is to the right of a local group of men to pursue happiness *together,* with their own ways of control to secure equality among them. Fraternal feeling is not easy of attainment unless you have been brought up together; hence the part played by history in the national sentiment. But mere nationalism claims only the right to pursue happiness together; it is not until we come to the League of Nations that we advance to an ideal which has been thought out to a stage equivalent to that of the great trilogy of the French Revolution. Some degree of control by the League is admittedly necessary to secure the equality of nations before the law, and I believe that in the ideal of the balanced development of each nation we have the self-control which is implied in fraternity. Without balanced development nations are sure to acquire special hungers, whether neglectfully or criminally, which can only be satisfied at the expense of other nations. In other words, we can only permanently secure equality among the nations by control from within as well as from without. But this involves the statement that home politics must be conducted with an eye to their effect on foreign politics, a truism in the superficial sense, but carrying deeper implications than are commonly admitted.

It carries, I believe, this implication among others, that, since nations are local societies, their organization *must,* if they are to last, be based dominantly on local communities within them, and not on nation-wide "interests." That is the old English idea of the House of Commons. The word *commons* is, of course, identical with the French word "communes," signifying communities; the House of Communities—shires and burghs—would be the true modern translation. As a fact, the knights and the burgesses of the Middle Ages represented communities of far more complete and balanced life than the artificially equalized constituencies of to-day.

If the real organization of the nation be by classes and interests—and that is the alternative to organization by localities [1]—it is quite inevitable that the corresponding classes in neighboring nations will get themselves together, and that what has been described as the horizontal cleavage of international society will ensue. Fortunately the Tower of Babel was the beginning of certain great Going Concerns known as languages, and these have impeded internationalism. But the development of the modern struggle between capital and labor has led to the use of some international phrases and words which have carried a few key ideas into common currency; they correspond unfortunately to certain social realities which were rapidly gathering importance when this war came upon us. International combines of capital were obtaining such power as to overawe some

[1] As has been pointed out by Mr. H. G. Wells, though he would—wrongly as I think—yield to current tendencies and accept organization by "interests."

of the smaller states of the world, and they were being used by Germany for purposes of penetration, or, in other words, to wreck the economic and social balance of rival nations. Labor could only follow suit, and also try to organize internationally. So came the idea of class warfare between the international proletariat and international capitalism. During the progress of the war we have gone to great trouble to break up the international organization of capital. Is labor now to reverse all that has been achieved in this respect by persisting with an international organization which sprang into existence for the very right purpose of fighting international capital? No less than such a reversal is involved if the momentum of internationally organized labor becomes powerful, for a resuscitation of international capitalism would then be inevitable. The economic war that would ensue could only end either in general Bolshevism or in the victory of one of the parties, and that party would then become the real government of the world, a new empire of organizers. If labor were to win, it would soon be found that labor organizers would not differ from their military and capitalist predecessors in the essential respect that they would cling to power and continue blindly to organize until brought down by a new revolution. So the wheels of history would revolve again with the same recurrent phases of disorder and tyranny, and future students would be taught to recognize one more "age," that of the proletariat, following on the ages of ecclesiasticism, militarism, and capitalism. Become supreme, the labor leaders of the future would no more hesitate to use machine-guns against the mob than any other panic-stricken riders of the whirlwind.

But if it be held that organization based on local communities is essential to the stable and therefore peaceable life of nations, then those local communities must have as complete and balanced a life of their own as is compatible with the life of the nation itself. In no other way can you prevent a "class and interest" organization from crossing powerfully your locality organization. As long as you allow a great metropolis to drain most of the best young brains from the local communities, to cite only one aspect of what goes on, so long must organization center unduly in the metropolis and become inevitably an organization of nation-wide classes and interests. I believe that whether we look at the matter from the point of view of the freedom of men or of nations we shall come to the same conclusion; that the one thing essential is to displace class organization, with its battle-cries and merely palliative remedies, by substituting an organic ideal, that of the balanced life of provinces, and under the provinces of the lesser communities.

.   .   .   .

Let us approach the matter from the other end of the argument, that of the freedom of men. What does the ordinary man want? Mill says that after food and home he wants liberty, but the more modern democrat lays stress not merely on freedom to take opportunity, but on the equality of opportunity itself. It is for opportunity to realize what is in him, to live a life of ideas and of action for the realization of those ideas, that the healthy man—in ever-increasing number—is asking.

His ideas may be of love and of the noble upbringing of his children, or of his craft and delight in his dexterity, or of religion and the saving of souls, or of excellence in sport of some kind, or of the constitution of society and its improvement, or of the appreciation of beauty and of artistic expression; but in one way or another he wishes for the glow of intelligent life, and incidentally for a recognition of his human dignity.

By general elementary education we have begun to teach the art of manipulating ideas to those who in ancient society were slaves. The wholly unlettered man thinks only in concrete terms; therefore it was that the great religious teachers have spoken slowly in parables. The unlettered man is not open either to the pleasures or the dangers of idealism. Undoubtedly our Western communities are passing through a dangerous stage in this generation. Half-educated people are in a very susceptible condition, and the world to-day consists mainly of half-educated people. They are capable of seizing ideas, but they have not attained to the habit of testing them and of suspense of mind in the meantime. In other words, most people to-day are very open to "suggestion," a fact well known to the experienced in elections, who rarely stop to reason with their audiences. Suggestion is the method of the German propagandist.

Now the expression "equality of opportunity" involves two things. In the first place control, because, given average human nature, there cannot be equality without control; and in the second place it implies freedom to do and not merely to think, or, in other words, opportunity to bring ideas to the test of action. Mr. Bernard Shaw says that "He who can, does; he who cannot, teaches." If you interpret the words "can" and "cannot" as implying opportunity and lack of opportunity, then this rather cynical epigram conveys a vital truth.[1] Those who are allowed opportunities of testing their ideas become responsible thinkers, but those who get no such opportunity may continue, for a time, to enjoy ideas, but irresponsibly and, as we say, academically. The latter condition is precisely that of a large part of our intelligent newspaper-reading working classes to-day, and some of them know it and regret it.

What is the bane of our modern industrial life? Surely monotony—monotony of work and of a petty social and communal life. No wonder our men took refuge before the war in betting on football. Most of the responsible decisions are reserved for a few, and those few are not even seen at their work, for they are away in the big centers.

What is it that in the last two or three generations has given such strength to the nationality movement? Nationality had no great hold in the Middle Ages, or indeed in modern times until the nineteenth century. It has arisen as the modern states have not only increased in size, but have also grasped wider functions within the community. Nationalist movements are based on the restlessness of intelligent young men who wish for scope to live the life of ideas and to be among those who "can" because they are allowed to do. In the old Greek and in the medieval world, Society was so loosely knit that there was plenty of scope in any considerable town. Is it not that fact which makes town history so interesting until we come to the eighteenth century and

[1] Bernard Shaw, *Man and Superman*, 12th edition, p. 230.

then so banal? Take up the history of one of our more significant British cities, and see whether that be not true. When you come to the last few generations it becomes mere statistics of material growth; at the best the town becomes specialized in some important way, but it ceases to be a complete organism. All its institutions are second-rate, because its best people have gone away, unless it have some one establishment or industry of more than local fame, and that establishment or industry usually crushes rather than develops real local life.

Why were Athens and Florence the wonderful founts of civilization which have made them the teachers of the world? They were small cities as we now count the size of cities, but they were sovereign cities both in the political and economic sense. The men who shook hands in their streets, and whose families intermarried, were not merely rival masters in the same industry or competing merchants on the same exchange; every principal category of supreme human activity was represented in one intimate circle. Think of the choice of activities open to the able young Florentine, to be practiced, remember, in and for his native town, and with no need to go away to some distant capital. Instead of mayor he might be prime minister; instead of captain of territorials he might be a general leading the town force in actual battle—a small battle no doubt, but enough to give the fullest scope to the activity of his mind; if he were a painter, sculptor, or architect he would be employed on the monuments of his own place instead of seeing them designed by some visiting great man. Of course no one suggests that you should or could return to institutions on the Athenian or Florentine scale, but the fact remains that you have drained your local life of most of its value and interest by the development of nation-wide class organization.

Are you quite sure that the gist of the demand for Home Rule in Ireland, and in a less degree in Scotland, does not come mainly from young men who are agitating, though they do not fully realize it, for equality of opportunity rather than against the assumed wickedness of England? The Bohemians have achieved a very remarkable economic prosperity under the Austrian tyranny, and yet they fight for their Czecho-Slovak nationality. Is there not something of the same human truth in the refractoriness of the shop stewards in our factories against the union executives away in London offices?

It is the principle of *laissez-faire* which has played such havoc with our local life. For a hundred years we have bowed down before the Going Concern as though it were an irresistible god. Undoubtedly it is a reality, but it can be bent to your service if you have a policy inspired by an ideal. *Laissez-faire* was no such policy; it was mere surrender to fate. You tell me that centralization is the "tendency" of the age: I reply to you that it is the blind tendency of every age—was it not said nineteen hundred years ago that "to him that hath shall be given"?

Consider the growth of London. A population of a million a century ago has risen to be more than seven millions to-day; or, to state the fact with more essential point, the London of a century ago contained a sixteenth of the population of England and now it has a fifth. How has it come about? When Parliament was originally set up, you had not only to pay the members to get them to attend, so busy were they with their absorbing local life, but before long you had also to fine the communities which failed to elect their representatives. That was the right condition of things, a federalization against strong local magnetisms. When macadamized roads were introduced a star of them was made, radiating from London; they brought the life of the country up to London, sapping it for the growth of London. When the railways were constructed the main lines formed a star from London, and the expresses run up and down, feeding London, milking the country. Presently the state also must needs step in to accentuate the centralizing tendency by establishing such services as the parcel post. Thus it has come about that the market towns for a hundred miles around are degraded in respect of the variety of their life.

Not in four out of five cases does the Londoner profit in any true sense from the change. He lives in a suburb; he is shot through a tube to an office room in the City, and then shot back to his bedroom in the suburb; only on Saturdays and Sundays has he time for communal life, and then he amuses himself with neighbors who are tied to him by nothing essential. In the great majority of cases he never comes into living contact with a large and trained mind except through the printed page: for him, as for the industrial worker in the country, his life of ideas is detached from his responsible life, and both suffer infinitely in consequence.

Centralization, however, is only one form of a more general process which I would call the segregation of social and economic functions owing to the national fatalism in the presence of the Going Concern. You have allowed industrial life to crowd certain districts and to leave other districts poor. I grant that in the past that was inevitable to some extent owing to the need of generating power near the collieries, but not to the extent that has occurred. By proper control you could have substituted a "village region," with a community dependent on each factory or group of small factories, wherein rich and poor, masters and men, might have been held together in a neighborly responsible relationship; but you have allowed instead the East and West Ends to grow up in your great cities. Surely the essential characteristic of true statesmanship is foresight, the prevention of social disease; but our method for a century past has been to drift, and when things became bad we applied palliative remedies—factory legislation, housing legislation, and so forth. As things stand to-day, the only organic remedy is at any cost to loosen out the town.

These ideas apply not only to industry but also to our educational institutions and the learned professions. Our English system is to buy—we must use plain words, for the element of competition among the colleges exists—the best young brains by means of scholarships open to national competition. In the middle of last century we, in large measure, abolished the system of close scholarships, which tied particular schools to particular colleges; that was, in my opinion, by far the healthier system. By social custom you add to your scholars a number of other fortunate boys from well-to-do homes scattered over the country. So you recruit your public schools and your Oxford and Cambridge;

from the beginning you lift your lads out of their local environment. From the universities many of them pass into a centralized civil service, a centralized legal profession, and even a centralized medical profession. In London they wait, eating out their hearts during their best years. A few of them come through and shine in a great but unnaturally segregated competition of wits, and you complain of your government by lawyers! The whole system results from historical momentum; when the Midlands, the East, and the South of England were all of England that counted, Oxford and Cambridge were local universities, and London was the natural market center of a single countryside. But in the past century the roads and the railways have enabled the metropolis to attract to itself the careers that were destined for the inspiration of other countrysides. The natural place of an exceptional man is to be leading his own people and helping them to bear their burdens. Your exceptional brain is serving the nation best if it remains racy of its own particular soil.[1]

One of the most serious difficulties in the way of the realization of the balanced local community lies in the difference of dialect spoken by the common people and the upper classes. In England after the Norman Conquest our peasants talked English, but our knights French, and our priests Latin, with the result that a knight felt himself more at home with a knight from France than with his own people, and so was it also with the priests. To-day there is a curious difference,

[1] As a loyal son of Oxford who gratefully recognizes what he owes to his Alma Mater, I would not have her flourish less, but more in changing some of her lower functions for higher.

it seems to me, in this respect, between the Scottish and English peoples. In England the upper professional classes go to the same schools and universities as the landed classes, and the merchants and captains of industry also send their sons to those schools. Therefore the line of social cleavage, as shown by speech and bearing, is between the upper and the lower middle classes. In Scotland, on the other hand, the people of the highest tier of society send their sons for the most part to the English public schools and the English universities, whereas the ministers of the Scottish churches, the advocates in the Scottish law courts, and the doctors and schoolmasters are trained in the main in the local universities, which are frequented by the sons of the shop-keepers and artisans to a greater extent than in England. The result, as I believe, is that the Scottish aristocracy has been, to a greater degree than in England, detached from the people. I do not blame them, for they have merely drifted in the grip of fate. It is said that a certain Scottish baronet, who had eight beautiful daughters approaching, some of them, to the age of marriage, put them all on a coach and drove them away from Edinburgh to London, because all the young Scotsmen of his acquaintance who had money, or the wits to make money, had already gone thither! In the end of the eighteenth century, and the beginning of the nineteenth, Edinburgh was one of the lamps of Europe, with its own particular tinge of flame. To-day it is one more instance of the futility of trying to separate the economic from the other aspects of the life either of a nation or a province.

•   •   •   •   •   •   •

Whether we reason downward from the freedom of nations, or upward from the freedom of men, we come to the same conclusion. The nation which is to be fraternal towards other nations, must be independent in an economic as in every other sense; it must have and keep a complete and balanced life. But it cannot be independent if it is broken into classes and interests which are for ever seeking to range themselves for fighting purposes with the equivalent classes and interests of other nations. Therefore you must base national organization on provincial communities. But if your province is to have any sufficient power of satisfying local aspirations it must, except for the federal reservations, have its own complete and balanced life. That is precisely what the real freedom of men requires— scope for a full life in their own locality. The organization by nation-wide classes and interests is the outcome of conflict, but it cannot satisfy, for it removes the larger careers away to the metropolis. Moreover the slums, and most other material afflictions of the people, are the outcome of impotence of local life, for they all result from offenses against the principle of keeping that life complete and balanced.

Provinces of complete life, of course, imply a federal system. It is not a mere decentralization which is contemplated, but decentralization of the different social functions to the same local units. Undoubtedly that is the tendency at the present time, in the Anglo-Saxon world, in regard to the administration of government. The United States, Canada, Australia, and South Africa are all, in greater or less degree, federal, and in Britain we seem to be not very far from becoming so. Only the

Irish question blocks the way, but it is intrinsically a small question, and we ought not to allow the quarrels of four million people to impede permanently the organic remedy of the ills of more than forty millions. A division of England into northern and southern provinces would probably be needed in order to remove the fact of the predominant partner, but from the point of view here taken that division would in itself be a good thing. To achieve the object in view it would not, however, be enough to give to your provinces merely "gas and water" powers; they must be so involved in the economic life of their regions that both masters and men will base their organizations on the provincial areas. If every unit of society—the nation, the province, the locality—were entitled, nay, were desired, to take appropriate steps to maintain the completeness and balance of its life, the need for the widespreading organization of *any* class or interest, save for informative purposes, would gradually cease to be urgent.

Consider the life of trees. In the forests of nature competition is severe, and no tree attains to the full and balanced growth of which it is capable. The trees of the middle forest struggle upward to the light; those of the border spread outward onesidedly; and in the slum depths are all manner of rottenness and parasitism. If, as in Dante's dream, there were spirits imprisoned in the trees, one might imagine a forest league of the foliage against the roots for sending up too many trunks, and a forest league of the roots against the foliage for keeping away the sweet light and air. But they would be futile leagues, because each tree consists of roots and foliage. The landscape gardener of civilization, with his organic remedies, can alone achieve the perfect beauty of trees. He plants them apart, so that they may grow independently, each according to the ideal of its kind; he guides the sapling, prunes the young tree, and cuts away disease from the mature tree. So we enjoy one of the most inspiring sights on earth, a park of noble trees, each complete and balanced in its growth. Only the monkeys and squirrels, which leap from branch to branch, have suffered—the elusive international exploiters and profiteers of the forest.

This parable of the gardener contains also the idea that the functions of growth and control are separate and should be kept separate. When officials of the state become socialistic, and try to initiate instead of merely assuring growth, they become less capable of their own proper function, which is criticism—understanding and sympathetic, but still criticism. The temper of criticism is incompatible with artistic and formative enthusiasm. We have had too little criticism based on steady watchfulness for the signs of unbalance in growth. The British Board of Trade under the régime of *laissez-faire* was so penetrated with the advisability of doing nothing, that it had no appreciable machinery for even watching what the Going Concern was doing. Federal authorities of every description, whether of the League of Nations or of the nations, should consist essentially of defensive and of outlook departments, and the watching or outlook departments should issue warnings, and repeat those warnings, until, thus enlightened, public opinion in the localities concerned intervenes *while there is yet time* to prevent some monstrous outgrowth of the Going Concern from fatally upsetting the equilibrium of the world or of the nation. In the United States the care of agriculture is, I believe, left to the separate states, but the Federal Bureau of Agriculture it is which issues warnings of the need of conserving the natural resources of the country. In Rome we already have an International Agricultural Institute which collects the statistics of the world harvests, and seeks to steady markets and prices by timely warnings; it has rendered considerable service to the Allies during this war.

I have no doubt that I shall be told by practical men that the ideal of complete and balanced economic growth in each locality is contrary to the whole tendency of the age, and is, in fact, archaic. I shall be told that you can only get a great and cheap production by the method of world organization and local specialization. I admit that such is the present tendency, and that it may give you maximum material results for a while. But if you breed animals, does there not come a time when you have gone as far as you can with inbreeding, and must you not then resort again to crossbreeding?

Athens and Florence were great because they saw life whole. If you pursue relentlessly the idols of efficiency and cheapness, you will give us a world in which the young will never see life but only an aspect of life; national and international organizers will alone hold the keys admitting to the observatory of the complete view. Is it in that way that you will get a continuous supply of fruitful brains, and happy, because intellectually active workers? All specialization contains the seeds of death; the most daring army must, at times, wait for the supply columns to come up. In the growth of brains and contentment something far more subtle is involved than any technical education or healthy housing. Is it quite certain that at the end of a century of refusal to get rich as quickly as possible, we should not have been far richer than we are?

I know that in this war you have set your controllers, and your international committees of controllers, to manage vast trades as single concerns, and that they have not let us starve. But in the crisis you have very rightly been using your capital of intellect and experience. Those men are the men that they are because they have built up private businesses with the fear of bankruptcy ever before them; they have grown up with their business lives always in their hands. Great organizations, whether of combines or government services, in that they afford a sheltered life, will not give you unlimited crops of such men.

You urge that credit and insurance must have broad bases, and I agree: their function is to average away local deficiencies due to the varying seasons and the varying success of undertakings. But let us none the less recognize that they present the danger of a financial control of the world. Your League of Nations may have to take them in hand, lest we be ruled by one only of the "interests" of society. There are two courses open to us in regard to them: to control them federally, or to fight them and balance them by the international organization of other "interests." The federal authority, whether of the league or the nation, is constituted of communities of complete growth, and cannot, from its nature, aspire to empire, since it consists everywhere of balanced humanity. But great specialist organizations, guided by experts, will inevitably contend for the upper hand, and the contest must end in the rule of one or other type of expert. That is empire, for it is unbalanced.

.   .   .   .   .   .

Do you realize that we have now made the circuit of the world, and that every system is now a closed system, and that you can now alter nothing without altering the balance of everything, and that there are no more desert shores on which the jetsam of incomplete thought can rest undisturbed? Let us attempt logical, symmetrical thought, but practical, cautious action, because we have to do with a mighty Going Concern. If you stop it, or even slow down its running, it will punish you relentlessly. If you let it run without guidance, it will take you over the cataract again. You cannot guide it by setting up mere fences, and by mending those fences if it breaks them down, because this Going Concern consists of hundreds of millions of human beings who are "pursuing" happiness, and they will swarm over all your fences like an army of ants. You can only guide humanity by the attraction of ideals. That is why Christianity wins on, after nineteen centuries, through all the impediments set up by criticism of its creeds and its miracles.

What we need, in my belief, to guide our reconstruction is a presumption of statesmanship in favor of the balanced nation, and the balanced province, sinning neither with the free-trader nor the protectionist. If we persist for a generation or two, with such an ideal before us, we may gradually change the Going Concern, so that we shall have fraternal nations and fraternal provinces, instead of warring, organized interests ever striving to extend their limits to the international field in order to outflank opposing interests which still lag on the merely national scale. Remember how that curious negative ideal of *laissez-faire* did through a couple of generations gradually assimilate the whole texture of British society, so that it has taken this world war to overthrow the vested interests which grew up.

At present, it seems to me, we are thinking out our reconstruction piecemeal, according to this and that detached ideal of the pre-war philanthropist—housing, temperance, industrial conciliation, and the rest of them. But if you build three hundred thousand new houses, and put them merely where they are "wanted," you may but be drifting again, though with heavier ballast.

In the war we have gradually risen to the conception of the single strategical command, and of the single economic control. Have you the courage for measures of like scope in regard to peace, though more subtle and less executive, because they will deal with growth and not with destruction?

> *"The fault, dear Brutus, is not in our stars*
> *But in ourselves, that we are underlings."*

Chapter Eight

POSTSCRIPT

SINCE the writing of this book I have fought a
Parliamentary election in Scotland, with a
Liberal and a Socialist for my opponents. Of
Liberalism there is nothing just now to be usefully said;
a sturdy individualism will always be one of the elements of character in our British race, whatever the
fate of the political party which was its nineteenth-
century expression. But the ever-recurrent propaganda
of Socialism is at present in a very significant phase.
Mere bureaucratic Socialism has been criticized by
events of late; the more we know of the working of
dominant officialdom during the war, the less likely,
I think, are we to desire it for a permanent master. My
Socialist opponent was out to take away property in
land and to abolish interest on capital; in other words,
he would begin with a confiscatory revolution; but that
was not of the essence of his position. His supporters—
young men with a burning faith in their eyes, though
often without the full power of expressing their argument—were, at almost every meeting, boldly defensive
of the Russian Bolsheviks. There are two sides to Bolshevism; there is the mere violence and tyranny of the
Jacobin, upthrown at a certain stage of most great revolutions; and there is the "syndicalist" idealism. To do
them justice, it is the latter aspect of Bolshevism which
really attracts and holds my young Scottish antagonists.

The Bolsheviks are in revolt against a Parliamentarism based on local communities or, as they would put it, on so many social pyramids each with its capitalist at the top. Their ideal is of a federation of vocational soviets or unions—soviets of workmen, of peasants, and, if you will, of professional men. Therefore the Bolsheviks, both in Petrograd and Berlin, have consistently opposed the meeting of national assemblies for the purpose of framing Parliamentary constitutions on the Western "bourgeois" model. Their revolt is towards an organization by interests rather than localities.[1] For the reasons stated in this book, such an organization would, in my belief, lead inevitably to the Marxian war of international classes, of proletariat against bourgeoisie, and finally of one section of the proletariat against the other sections—already the Russian town-workers are at issue with the Russian peasants. The end could only be world-anarchy or a world-tyranny.

Thus I come back to the quiet of my library with the conviction that what I have written is pertinent to the hot currents of real life in this great crisis of humanity. Our old English conception of the House of Commons or Communities, the American conception of the Federation of States and Provinces, and the new ideal of the League of Nations are all of them opposed to the policies cast in the tyrannical molds of East Europe and the Heartland, whether dynastic or Bolshevik. It may be the case that Bolshevik tyranny is an extreme reaction from dynastic tyranny, but it is none

[1] The vocational soviet of the peasants is only incidentally local; it is not local in the fuller sense of combining various local interests into a community.

the less true that the Russian, Prussian, and Hungarian plains, with their widespread uniformity of social conditions, are favorable alike to the march of militarism and to the propaganda of syndicalism. Against this two-headed eagle of land-power the Westerners and the islanders must struggle. Even in their own peninsulas and islands modern methods of communication are so leveling natural barriers that organization by interests constitutes a real threat. In the Heartland, where physical contrasts are few, it is only with the aid of a conscious ideal, shaping political life in the direction of nationalities, that we shall be able to entrench true freedom. If only as a basis for "penetrating" this dangerous Heartland, the oceanic peoples must strive to root ever more firmly their own organization by localities, each locality with as complete and balanced a life of its own as circumstances may permit of. The effort must go downward through the provinces to the cities. East Ends and West Ends divide our cities into castes; at whatever sacrifice we must tone away such contrasts. The countryside, in which the successful leaders visibly serve the interests of their weaker brethren, must be our ideal.

There was a time when a man addressed his "friends and neighbors." We still have our friends, but too often they are scattered over the land and belong to our own caste in society. Or, if they happen to be near us, is it not because our caste has gathered apart into its own quarter of the town? So was it in the early Middle Ages, when we are told that three men might meet in the market-place, the one obeying the Roman law, another the customs of the Franks, and a third those of the

Goths. So is it to-day in India with Hindu, and Moham-medan, and Christian. So was it not either in four-teenth-century Florence, or Periclean Athens, or Eliza-bethan England.

With too many of us, in our urban and suburban civilization, that grand old word neighbor has fallen almost into desuetude. It is for neighborliness that the world to-day calls aloud, and for a refusal to gad ever about—merely because of modern opportunities for communication. Let us recover possession of ourselves, lest we become the mere slaves of the world's geogra-phy, exploited by materialistic organizers. Neighborli-ness or fraternal duty to those who are our fellow-dwellers, is the only sure foundation of a happy citizen-ship. Its consequences extend upward from the city through the province to the nation, and to the world League of Nations. It is the cure alike of the slumdom of the poor and of the boredom of the rich, and of war between classes and war between nations.

NOTE ON AN INCIDENT AT THE QUAI D'ORSAY 25th JANUARY, 1919

THE representatives of the Allied Nations were assembled in the second plenary session of their Conference at Paris. A resolution was before them to appoint committees for the purpose of reporting on the proposed League of Nations and other matters. The constitution of the committees, giving two members to each of the five Great Powers (United States, British Empire, France, Italy, Japan), and five members to the Smaller Powers collectively, had been settled by the Council of Ten, representing only the Great Powers, and this constitution was now brought up at the plenary session for endorsement. There was not unnaturally discontentment among the Smaller Powers. Sir Robert Borden, on behalf of Canada, asked by whom and on what authority the constitution of the committees had been decided; the question should have been submitted to the Conference. The delegates of Belgium, Brazil, Serbia, Greece, Portugal, Czecho-Slovakia, Rumania, Siam, and China rose in turn to claim special representation for their several countries. Then M. Clemenceau interposed from his presidential chair, where he sat between Mr. Wilson and Mr. Lloyd George. He pointed out that at the cessation of hostilities, the Great Powers had twelve million men on the field of battle; that they might have decided the future of the world on their own initiative; but that, inspired by the new ideals, they had invited the Smaller Powers to co-operate with them. The resolution was passed, *nemine contradicente*, without alteration.

Thus the rule of the world still rests upon force, notwithstanding the juridical assumption of equality between sovereign states, whether great or small. The theme of this book, that we must base our proposed League on realities, if we would have it last, holds good. Let it be remarked, moreover, that the number of the Great Powers—five—is precisely the total of the pre-war Dual Alliance (Triple only with Italy) and Triple Entente, whose hostility caused the war. It follows that we shall be able to maintain our League as long as the five Powers, now allied, continue to agree. Their number is not sufficient to prevent a bid for predominance on the part of one or two of them. No doubt a new Germany and a new Russia will some day increase them to seven. Perhaps the Smaller Powers, taking note of the naked fact which was exposed by this incident, will set about federating among themselves. A Scandinavian group, a group of the Middle Tier of East Europe (Poland to Jugo-Slavia), and a Spanish South American group (if not also including Brazil) may all, perhaps, be attainable. In any case the League should do service in bringing the opinion of mankind to bear for the just revision of obsolescent treaties before they become unbearable misfits. But let us be rid of cant: Democracy must reckon with Reality.

Additional Papers

The following of Mackinder's papers were reprinted from these listed sources:

"The Scope and Methods of Geography," *Proceedings of the Royal Geographical Society,* Vol. 9 (1887), pp. 141-60.

"The Geographical Pivot of History," *Geographical Journal,* Vol. 23 (1904), pp. 421-37.

"The Round World and the Winning of the Peace," *Foreign Affairs,* Vol. 21 (July 1943), pp. 595-605.

ON THE SCOPE AND METHODS OF
GEOGRAPHY[1]

WHAT is geography? This seems a strange question to address to a Geographical Society, yet there are at least two reasons why it should be answered, and answered now. In the first place geographers have been active of late in pressing the claims of their science to a more honoured position in the curriculum of our schools and Universities. The world, and especially the teaching world, replies with the question, "What is geography?" There is a touch of irony in the tone. The educational battle now being fought will turn on the answer which can be given to this question, Can geography be rendered a discipline instead of a mere body of information? This is but a rider on the larger question of the scope and methods of our science.

The other reason for now pressing this matter on your notice comes from within. For half a century several societies, and most of all our own, have been active in promoting the exploration of the world. The natural result is that we are now near the end of the roll of great discoveries. The Polar regions are the only large blanks remaining on our maps. A Stanley can never again reveal a Congo to the delighted world. For a time good work will be done in New Guinea, in Africa, in Central Asia, and along the boundaries of the frozen regions. For a time a Greely will now and again receive the old ringing welcome, and will prove that it is not heroes that are wanting. But as tales of

[1] This and the following papers, including footnotes and maps, are reprinted without alteration.

adventure grow fewer and fewer, as their place is more and more taken by the details of Ordnance Surveys, even Fellows of Geographical Societies will despondently ask, "What is geography?"

It is needless to say that this paper would not be written were it my belief that the Royal Geographical Society must shortly close its history—a corporate Alexander weeping because it has no more worlds to conquer. Our future work is foreshadowed by papers such as those by Mr. Wells on Brazil, Mr. Buchanan on the Oceans, and Mr. Bryce on the Relation of History and Geography. Nevertheless, there will be great advantages in guiding our way into the new groove with our eyes to some extent, at any rate, open. A discussion of the question at the present moment will probably have the further incidental advantage of giving us new weapons in our educational struggle.

The first inquiry to which we must turn our attention is this: Is geography one, or is it several subjects? More precisely, Are physical and political geography two stages of one investigation, or are they separate subjects to be studied by different methods, the one an appendix of geology, the other of history? Great prominence has recently been given to this question by the President of the Geographical Section of the British Association. In his address at Birmingham he took up a very definite position. He said,—

"It is difficult to reconcile the amalgamation of what may be considered 'scientific' geography with history. One is as thoroughly apart from the other as geology is from astronomy."

It is with great reluctance and diffidence that I venture to oppose so justly esteemed an authority as Sir Frederick Goldsmid. I do so only because it is my firm conviction that the position taken up at Birmingham is fatal to the best prospects of geography. I take notice, moreover, of Sir Frederick Goldsmid's declaration that he is quite ready to abandon the conclusion at which he has arrived, before the arguments of sounder reason. In so difficult a discussion it would be extremely presumptuous, were I to assume that *mine* are arguments of sounder reason. I put them forward only because so far as I can see, they have not been met and overthrown in the address in question. Perhaps Sir Frederick Goldsmid has but expressed the vague views of the subject current in most men's minds. This is the more probable, because in his own statement he has used arguments going to support a view opposed to that which he himself formulates.[2]

On the same page as that from which our quotation is taken will be found a paragraph expressing the highest approval of Mr. Bryce's "Geography in its relation to History." The central proposition of Mr. Bryce's lecture is that man is largely "the creature of his environment." The function of political geography is to trace the interaction between man and his environment. Sir Frederick Goldsmid requires of political geography that it shall impart to our future statesmen a "full grasp" of "geographical conditions." So far no exception can be taken to his views. But he seems to imagine that the "full grasp" of which he speaks may be obtained from what remains after "physical and scientific" geography have been eliminated.

Before proceeding further, it will be well to see whether we cannot refine on our definition with advantage. Physiology would answer to the definition of the science which traces the interaction of man and his environment. It is the function of physiology, of physics, and of chemistry to trace the action of forces irrespective for the most part of precise locality. It is especially characteristic of geography that it traces the influence of locality, that is, of environ-

[2] Sir Frederick Goldsmid has written a very courteous answer to this paragraph. From it I gather that I have not attached the meaning to his words which he intended. For that I am sorry. I leave the paragraph standing, however, as I believe that mine is not an unnatural meaning to attach to the words. They might easily be quoted against the geographers, and with more weight because they come from a known friend of geography.

ment varying locally. So far as it does not do this it is merely physiography, and the essential topographical element has been omitted. I propose therefore to define geography as the science whose main function is to trace the interaction of man in society and so much of his environment as varies locally.[3]

Before the interaction can be considered, the elements which are to interact must be analysed. One of these elements[4] is the varying environment, and the analysis of this is, I hold, the function of physical geography. Thus we are driven to a position in direct antagonism to current notions. We hold that no *rational* political geography can exist which is not built upon and subsequent to physical geography. At the present moment we are suffering under the effects of an irrational political geography, one, that is, whose main function is not to trace causal relations, and which must therefore remain a body of isolated data to be committed to memory. Such a geography can never be a discipline, can never, therefore, be honoured by the teacher, and must always fail to attract minds of an amplitude fitting them to be rulers of men.

But it may be retorted—For the purposes of political geography cannot you rest satisfied with a more superficial and more easily learned analysis than that furnished by physical geography? In reply, we take up our lowest position. Such analyses have been tried, and have been found wanting. It is practically easier to learn the profound anal-

[3] For another definition from a rather different standpoint see my speech in opening the discussion ["it is the science of distribution, the science, that is, which traces the arrangement of things in general on the earth's surface"].

[4] The other element is, of course, man in society. The analysis of this will be shorter than that of the environment. It may best be considered on the lines of Bagehot's 'Physics and Politics.' The communities of men should be looked on as units in the struggle for existence, more or less favoured by their several environments. See p. 235 for definition of "community" and "environment."

ysis of science, raising and satisfying as it does at every point the instincts which drive us for ever to ask the question "why?" than to acquire a sufficient amount of information from the name-lists of the old school books or the descriptions of so-called descriptive geography. Topography, which is geography with the "reasons why" eliminated, is almost unanimously rejected both by masters and pupils.

There are other reasons for our position of even higher importance than practical convenience in teaching. I will mention three. The first is this. If you learn what the old geographers term "the physical features" in their causal relations, advance becomes ever easier and easier. New facts fit in an orderly way into the general scheme. They throw a new light on to all previously obtained knowledge, and that knowledge in turn illuminates them from many points. When, however, the method of description has been adopted, and still more that of enumeration, each additional fact adds an ever-increasing amount to the burden to be borne by the memory. It is like throwing another pebble on to a heap of gravel. It is like learning mathematics by trying to remember formulae instead of grasping principles.

Our second reason is shortly this. A superficial analysis is likely to lead into error: on the one hand by failing to go beneath the superficial similarity of things essentially differing; on the other hand by failing to detect the essential similarity of things superficially unlike.

The third reason is this. The mind which has vividly grasped in their true relations the factors of the environment is likely to be fertile in the suggestion of new relations between the environment and man. Even if there be no design of advancing the science, the same conditions will lead to a rapid, a vivid, and therefore a lasting appreciation of the relations which have been detected by others.

It will be well here to pause and to sum up our position in a series of propositions.

(1) It is agreed that the function of political geography is to detect and demonstrate the relations subsisting between man in society and so much of his environment as varies locally.

(2) As a preliminary to this the two factors must be analysed.

(3) It is the function of physical geography to analyse one of these factors, the varying environment.

(4) Nothing else can adequately perform this function. Because—

> No other analysis can exhibit the facts in their causal relations and in their true perspective.

Therefore—

> No other analysis will—
>> firstly, serve the teacher as a discipline;
>> secondly, attract the higher minds among the pupils;
>> thirdly, economise the limited power of memory;
>> fourthly, be equally trustworthy; and
>> fifthly, be equally suggestive.

Here we must expect the observation that, granting the desirability of what we ask, we are none the less asking what is impossible. Our reply will be that it has not been tried. Physical geography has usually been undertaken by those already burdened with geology, political geography by those laden with history. We have yet to see the man who taking up the central, the geographical position, shall look equally on such parts of science and such parts of history as are pertinent to his inquiry. Knowledge is, after all, one, but the extreme specialism of the present day seems to hide the fact from a certain class of minds. The more we specialise the more room and the more necessity is there for students whose constant aim it shall be to bring out the relations of the special subjects. One of the greatest of all gaps lies between the natural sciences and the study of humanity. It is the duty of the geographer to build one bridge over an abyss which in the opinion of many is upsetting the equilibrium of our culture. Lop off either limb of geography and you maim it in its noblest part.

In speaking thus we are not blind to the necessity of specialism within geography itself. If you would do original work in the science you must specialise. But for this purpose either physical or political geography would be as unwieldy as the entire subject. Moreover, your special subject need not fall entirely within the realm of one or other branch; it may lie across the frontier. Geography is like a tree which early divides into two great branches, whose twigs may none the less be inextricably interwoven. You select a few adjacent twigs, but they may spring from different branches. As a subject of education, however, and as a basis for all fruitful specialism within the subject, we insist on the teaching and the grasping of geography as a whole.

This question of possibility leads us naturally into an inquiry as to the relations of geography to its neighbour sciences. We cannot do better than adopt Mr. Bryce's rough classification of the environment. First, we have the influences due to the configuration of the earth's surface; secondly, those belonging to meteorology and climate; and thirdly, the products which a country offers to human industry.

First, then, as to the configuration of the earth's surface. We have here a bone of contention between the geographers and the geologists. The latter hold that the causes which have determined the form of the lithosphere are dealt with by their science, and that there is neither room nor necessity for the physical geographer. The geographer has in consequence damaged his science by refusing to include among his data any but the barest results of geology. The rivalry must be well known to all here present. It has been productive of nothing but evil to geography. Two sciences may have data in part identical, yet there ought to be no bickering in consequence, for the data, though identical, are looked at from different points of view. They are grouped differently. Least of all should the geologist exhibit such weakness. At every step in his own department he is dependent on his scientific brethren. Palaeontology is the key to the relative age of strata, but it is irrational apart from biology. Some of the most difficult problems of physics and chemistry lie within the realm of mineralogy, especially, for instance, the causes and methods of metamorphism. The best attempt to find a common measure of geological and historical time lies in Dr. Croll's astronomical interpretation of recurrent glacial epochs. But enough of this. The true distinction between geology and geography seems to me to lie in this: the geologist looks at the present that he may interpret the past; the geographer looks at the past that he may interpret the present. This line has already been traced for us by one of the greatest of the geologists.

In his 'Text-book of Geology,' Dr. Archibald Geikie gives the following lucid determination of it:[5]

"An investigation of the geological history of a country involves two distinct lines of inquiry. We may first consider the nature and arrangement of the rocks that underlie the surface, with a view to ascertaining from them the successive changes in physical geography and in plant and animal life which they chronicle. But besides the story of the rocks, we may try to trace that of the surface itself, the origin and vicissitudes of the mountains and plains, valleys and ravines, peaks, passes, and lake basins, which have been formed out of the rocks. The two inquiries traced backwards merge into each other, but they become more and

[5] Archibald Geikie, 'Text-book of Geology,' 1882, p. 910.

more distinct as they are pursued towards later times. It is obvious, for instance, that a mass of marine limestone which rises into groups of hills, trenched by river gorges and traversed by valleys, presents two sharply contrasted pictures to the mind. Looked at from the side of its origin, the rock brings before us a sea-bottom over which the relics of generations of a luxuriant marine calcareous fauna accumulated. We may be able to trace every bed, to mark with precision its organic contents, and to establish the zoological succession of which these superimposed sea-bottoms are the records. But we may be quite unable to explain how such sea-formed limestone came to stand as it now does, here towering into hills, and there sinking into valleys. The rocks and their contents form one subject of study, the history of their present scenery another."

The same idea is endorsed by Professor Moseley in his lecture on "The Scientific Aspects of Geographical Education." We quote the following passage[6] from among many others in the same strain:

"Regarding physical geography as a part of geology to be separated from it:—The reason why such a separation should be effected is that there is thus formed and brought together for special treatment a subject which is far more necessary and suitable for general educational purposes than the whole of geology itself, which will attract far more students and act as a lever for promoting the study of other branches of science as special studies, and certainly of geology itself.

"The principal argument that is always brought against the establishment of professorships of physical geography at the Universities is that the subject is already covered by the professors of geology; but Professor Geikie evidently does not take that view, and points out in his letter already referred to, 'Geology is every day increasing in its scope,

6 'R. G. S. Educational Reports,' 1886, p. 228, Professor Moseley.

which is already too vast for the physical powers of even the most indefatigable teacher.' "

In this passage Professor Moseley advocates the establishment of a chair of physical geography. It must not be concluded from this that he is opposed to the unity of geography. This is made clear by other portions of his lecture.

"Possibly, although at the present moment it may not be possible to secure the representation of geography as a whole, because of the apparent vagueness of its bounds and the attacks on all sides to which it is in consequence liable, there may be a chance of success if the attempt be made to press the claims of physical geography."

And again:—"Ought not physical geography to form part of every liberal education as being a subject specially adapted for purposes of general learning, and as the only true basis on which can be founded a knowledge of what is termed political geography?"

Perhaps nowhere is the damage done to geography by the theory which denies its unity better seen than in the case of physical geography. The subject has been abandoned to the geologists, and has in consequence a geological bias. Phenomena such as volcanoes, hot springs, and glaciers, have been grouped into chapters, irrespective of the regions in which they occur. From the geologist's point of view this is sufficient—he is looking at his Rosetta stone; the understanding of the individual hieroglyphics is of great importance, but the meaning of the entire passage, the account of the event recorded, is, for the purpose of interpreting other records, unimportant. But such a science is not really physical geography, and Dr. Archibald Geikie tells us plainly in his 'Elements of Physical Geography'[7] that he is using the words as equivalent to physiography. True physical geography aims at giving us a causal description of the distribution of the features of the earth's surface. The data must

[7] New edition, 1884, p. 3.

be regrouped on a topographical basis. If I may venture to put the matter somewhat abruptly—Physiography asks of a given feature, "Why is it?" Topography, "Where is it?" Physical geography, "Why is it there?" Political geography, "How does it act on man in society, and how does he react on it?" Geology asks, "What riddle of the past does it help to solve?" Physiography is common ground to the geologist and the geographer. The first four subjects are the realm of the geographer. The questions come in sequence. You may stop short of any one of them, but it is my contention that you cannot with advantage answer a later one unless you have answered those which precede it. Geology proper, in its strict sense, is unnecessary to the sequence of the argument.

We will give two illustrations of the inadequacy for geographical purposes of the present (geological) physical geographies even when considered as physiographies.

The first is the undue prominence given to such subjects as volcanoes and glaciers. To this my attention has been several times drawn by your Assistant-Secretary, Mr. Bates. It is perfectly natural in books written by geologists. Volcanoes and glaciers are phenomena which leave most marked and characteristic traces behind them. Therefore, from a geological point of view they are most important, and are worthy of special study. But the result resembles a book on biology written by a palaeontologist. In it we should expect to find the snail's shell, for instance, described in the greatest detail, but to the comparative neglect of the far more important soft parts within.

My other illustration is a practical one, which must appeal to the experience of all thoughtful travellers. Let us say that you go for a trip up the Rhine; you must be strangely wanting in curiosity if you do not ask yourself such questions as the following—Why is it that after passing over many miles of flat land through which the Rhine meanders almost on a level with the surrounding country, we come suddenly to a part of its course in which it passes through a gorge? Why, when we reach Bingen, does that gorge still more suddenly cease, its place taken by a lake-like valley bounded by parallel ranges of mountains? No ordinary physical geography that I have seen adequately answers such questions as these. If you happen to have a special knowledge of the subject, you may know that if you look into the *Journal of the Geological Society*[8] you will find a delightful paper on this subject by Sir Andrew Ramsay. But this implies the time and opportunity for research among original authorities, and even then your reward will be slight. It is only a few isolated regions which have been so treated.

I will close this portion of the subject with a constructive attempt. I shall select a region familiar to all, that your attention may be concentrated on the method rather than the matter. Let us take the south-east of England. The usual method of treating the geography of such a region would be to describe from a physical point of view first the coast and then the surface. The capes and inlets of the one and the hills and valleys of the other would be enumerated in order. You would then have a list of the political divisions, and a further list of the chief towns, stating the rivers on whose banks they stand. In some cases a few interesting but isolated facts would be added, mental pegs on which to hang the names. The political portion of such a work even at best rises no higher than to the rank of a good system of mnemonics. As for the physical portion, all the text-books agree in committing what is, from my point of view, a fundamental error. They separate the descriptions of the coast and the surface. This is fatal to the demonstration in due perspective of the chain of causes and effects. The accidents of the surface and of the coast are alike the results

[8] 1874.

of the interaction of two forces, the varying resistance of
the rock strata and the varying erosive powers of atmosphere and sea. The erosive powers, whether superficial or
marginal, act on one and the same set of rocks. Why should
there be a Flamborough Head? Why should there be a
Yorkshire Wold? They are but two edges of the rim of one
and the same mass of uptilted chalk-strata.

Let us try to construct a geography of South-eastern England which shall exhibit a continuous series of causal
relations. Imagine thrown over the land like a white tablecloth over a table, a great sheet of chalk. Let the sheet be
creased with a few simple folds, like a tablecloth laid by a
careless hand. A line of furrow[9] runs down the Kennet to
Reading, and then follows the Thames out to sea. A line
of ridge passes eastward through Salisbury Plain and then
down the centre of the Weald. A second line of furrow follows the valley of the Frome and its submarine continua-
tions, the Solent and Spithead. Finally, yet a second line of
ridge is carried through the Isle of Purbeck and its now
detached member the Isle of Wight. Imagine these ridges
and furrows untouched by the erosive forces. The curves of
the strata would be parallel with the curves of the surface.
The ridges would be flat-topped and broad. The furrows
would be flat-bottomed and broad. The Kennet-Thames
furrow would be characterised by increasing width as it
advanced eastward. The slopes joining the furrow-bottom
to the ridge-top would vary in steepness. It is not pretended
that the land ever exhibited such a picture. The upheaving
and the erosive forces have always acted simultaneously.
As with the Houses of Parliament, the process of ruin
commenced before the building was complete. The elimina-

[9] Furrow and ridge are here used in the sense of syncline and anticline.
They must be carefully distinguished from valley and hill. The two are
often causally related, as I point out in this paper, but they are far from
identical.

tion of erosion is merely an expedient to show the simple arrangement of the rocks, which simplicity is masked by the apparent confusion of the ruin. Add one more fact, that above and below the hard chalk lie strata of soft clay, and we have drawn on geology for all that we require.

The moulder's work is complete; the chisel must now be applied. The powers of air and sea tear our cloth to tatters. But as though the cloth had been stiffened with starch as it lay creased on the table, the furrows and ridges we have described have not fallen in. Their ruined edges and ends project stiffly as hill ranges and capes. The furrow-bottoms, buried beneath the superincumbent clay, produce lines of valley along the London and Hampshire basins. Into the soft clay the sea has eaten, producing the great inlet of the Thames mouth, and the narrower but more intricate sea-channels which extend from Poole Harbour through the Solent to Spithead, and which ramify into Southampton Water and Portsmouth, Langstone, and Chichester Harbours. The upturned edge of the chalk-sheet produces the long range of hills, which, under the various names of Berkshire Downs, Chiltern, and Gogmagog Hills, and East Anglian Heights, bounds the Kennet-Thames basin to the north-west. The North and South Downs stand up facing each other, the springs of an arch from which the key-stone has been removed. The same arch forms Salisbury Plain, and its eastward prolongation in the chalk uplands of Hampshire; but here the key-stone, though damaged, has not been completely worn through. Beachy Head and the North and South Forelands are but the seaward projection of the Down ranges. The fact that the North Downs end not in a single promontory, like Beachy Head, but in a long line of cliff, the two ends of which are marked by the North and South Forelands, may serve to draw attention to a relation which frequently exists between the slope of the surface and the dip of the strata. A few sentences back, we mentioned the fact, that if our simple ridge and furrow system really obtained, the slopes connecting the ridge-tops and the furrow-bottoms would vary in steepness. By remembering the position of a hill-range in the "restored" ruin, we shall remember not merely its direction, but also the relative steepness of its two faces. One will be produced by the dipping strata, the other will be the escarpment where the strata have been cut short. On the dip of the strata will depend very much whether when we have climbed the escarpment, we see in front of us a sharp descent or an undulating upland. Contrast in this respect the two chalk uplands which form the broad projections of East Anglia and Kent with the narrow ridges, the Chilterns and the Hog's Back. The north-west escarpment of the Chilterns is continuous with the western scarped face of East Anglia. The south-eastern dip-slope of the Chilterns is continuous with the dip-slope which forms the broad uplands of Norfolk. The dip is steep in the case of the Chilterns, slight in that of Norfolk. Similarly the Kentish uplands are a prolongation of the Hog's Back. The southern scarped faces differ but little, whereas the northern dip-slope of the Hog's Back is steep, though its continuation in Kent is only gently inclined. This terminal expansion of the hill-ranges has been of great importance in English history, as will be seen presently. The expansions may be considered as dependent on the eastward widening of the Kennet-Thames basin. It will be noticed that the shores of the Thames estuary are on the whole parallel with the hill-ranges which mark the lips of the basin, the northern shore parallel with the curve traced by the hills from Hunstanton Point to the Chilterns, the southern parallel with the straighter range of the North Downs.

The rivers of the district fall naturally into three classes. First, we have those which flow down the dip-slope of East Anglia. As a consequence, they are numerous and roughly parallel. They do not combine to form one large stream presenting a tree-like appearance on the map. Secondly, we have those which flow down the great furrows, the Kennet and the Thames below Reading on the one hand, the Frome with its submarine prolongation by the Solent and Spithead on the other. The many tributaries of the Thames are obvious, but the tree-like character of the Frome is not obvious unless its submarine continuation be taken into account. Then the Frome, the Stour, the Avon, the Test, the Itchen, and the Medina, would combine to form one great stream, having its mouth east of the Isle of Wight. Such a river may very probably have actually existed. Lastly, there are the streams which pass by ravines right through the chalk ranges, the Thames above Reading, and the various small rivers of the Weald. This circumstance is incomprehensible, unless we suppose that the strata arches were formerly complete. Then these streams would flow down the even slope of the ridge, following the ordinary hydrostatic laws. The only prominent feature of our area which would require a special explanation apart from the flexure of the rocks is the shingle bank which forms Dungeness.[10]

This being the general anatomy of the land, what has been its influence on man? In the midst of forest and marsh three broad uplands stood out in early days, great openings in which man could establish himself with the least resistance from nature. In the language of the Celts they were known as "Gwents," a name corrupted by the Latin conquerors into "Ventae." They were the chalk uplands with which we were familiar, the arch-top of Salisbury Plain and Hampshire and the terminal expansions of the chalk ranges

---

[10] I have omitted in this sketch to account for Leith Hill and the Forest Range of Sussex. They, too, depend on the flexure of the rocks; but to explain their cause would take up too much space in a paper which purports only to indicate methods, and not to exhaust its topic.

in East Anglia and Kent. In East Anglia was Venta Icenorum; in Kent and Canterbury[11] we still have relics of another Gwent. The first syllable of Winchester[12] completes the triplet. In later, but still early times, they were the first nests of the three races which composed the German host. The Angles settled in Norfolk and Suffolk, the Jutes in Kent, the Saxons in Hampshire. In still later England, Winchester, Canterbury, and Norwich were among the chief of mediaeval cities. To this day the isolation of two of these regions at least has left its traces in the marked characteristics of their populations. The Fens cut off Norfolk, the Weald forests shut in Kent. Their people have taken distinct positions in our history. The "men of Norfolk" and the "men of Kent" have been of a remarkably rebellious disposition.

There were four great cities in the east and south; we have mentioned three. The fourth was London. Geographical conditions have determined the greatness of the metropolis. The map will make it clear at once, that the Fens and the Weald would compel the lines of communication from Norfolk and Kent on the one hand, and the rest of England on the other to pass in the general direction of London. Kent lies nearest to the Continent, and hence Watling Street was not merely the Kentish road, but also the road to Flanders. Where the hills narrow the Thames marshes most there is the natural crossing of Watling Street, first a ferry, then a bridge. This point lies between Tower Hill and the heights of Dulwich and Sydenham. Bermondsey, the isle of Bermond, was a dry spot, rising like a stepping-stone from among the surrounding marshes. The existence of solid ground on the immediate banks of the

---

[11] So J. R. Green would have it, 'Making of England,' 1882, p. 9. But Isaac Taylor derives Kent from *Cenn,* a Gadhelic form of the Cymric *Pen*=a head, a projection—'Words and Places,' 1885, p. 148.

[12] Venta Belgarum.

deep water, which is necessary, as the "take-off" for a bridge or ferry, is also necessary for a landing-place. Here then we have a crossing of natural ways on a spot which is a natural halting-place for both, hence a point at which a city is certain to rise. That city will be the more important if one way is by land and the other by water, for it is then a place of transhipment. It will be still more important if it is the necessary meeting-point of river and sea traffic. Even more pregnant with meaning is the position of the Thames mouth relatively to that of the Scheldt. It determines the linked greatness of London and Antwerp, and also much of the Continental policy of England. Thus many causes conspire to maintain the greatness of London. This is a fact to be marked. It is the secret of its persistent growth from the earliest times. The importance of a given geographical feature varies with the degree of man's civilisation. A city which depends on one physical advantage may fall at any moment. A single mechanical discovery may effect the change.[13]

So much for the cities. Lastly as to the political divisions. There are two types of political divisions, natural and arbitrary. The contrast presented by the old division of France into provinces and the revolutionary division into departments will serve to indicate the distinction. The one is the result of an unconscious process, such as the accretion of smaller states to a larger state. The other is the product of conscious legislation. In England we have the two kinds side by side. In the midlands we have arbitrary divisions, counties named after their chief towns, and supposed to have originated from the partition of Mercia.[14] In the east

[13] In this account of the "greatness" of London I have not indicated the full significance of Tower Hill. The "dun" or hill-fort no doubt decided the precise locality of London; but other causes, as given above, have determined its greatness.

[14] Consider J. R. Green, "Conquest of England," 1883, p. 141, note. But compare Isaac Taylor, "Words and Places," 1885, p. 179.

and south, on the other hand, the counties are of natural growth, and bear names indicating their distinct origin. In the case of arbitrary divisions the frontiers are also likely to be arbitrary. The frontiers of natural divisions will usually be natural, and may be of two kinds. Immigrants spread from a centre, either until they meet physical obstacles or until they meet with the opposition of other centrifugal settlements. In the region we are dealing with we see some excellent examples of this last. The inhabitants of Surrey, Kent, and Sussex would establish themselves on the chalk hills and uplands, and then push slowly into the forest until their advanced guards met in the centre. The frontier-lines of those counties are exactly what we should expect under these circumstances. With this we may compare the frontier dividing Berkshire and Hampshire from Surrey and Sussex. It crosses a region of commons, lying largely on the Bagshot sands. Such sterile land would be unworthy of occupation until the better land had been filled up. Take again the region of the Fens. Five counties send tongues into these marshes.

Time forbids our going further into this subject. The broad results are these. From a consideration of the folding of the chalk and of its hardness as compared with the strata above and below it, may be demonstrated the causes of the two great promontories, the two great inlets, and the three great upland openings which have determined the positions, the number, and the importance of the chief cities and divisions of South-eastern England. The same processes of reasoning might be continued to any required degree of detail. The geography of any other region might be treated in a similar way. Further, having once mastered the few simple geological ideas involved, a graphic and precise conception of a land may be conveyed in a few sentences. The effort required to grasp the first application of the method may be greater than that called for by the older methods. Its beauty lies in the fact that every fresh conquest gives increased ease of acquisition.

We will sum up our results bearing on the relation of geology to geography in the form of propositions:—

1. It is essential to know the form of the lithosphere.

2. This can only be accurately and vividly remembered by grasping the causes which have determined it.

3. One of these causes is the relative hardness and arrangement of the rocks.

4. But no geological data or reasoning must be admitted unless it be pertinent to the geographical argument. It must help to answer the question, "Why is a given feature where it is?"

Mr. Bryce's two remaining classes of environment factors call for less remark. The distinction between meteorology and geography must be a practical one. So much of meteorology, and it is much, as deals with weather-forecasting cannot be required by the geographer. Average or recurrent climatic conditions alone come within his ken. Even here he must be content very often to adopt the results of meteorology as data, just as meteorology itself accepts the results of physics. It is a mistake, especially of the Germans, that they include too much in geography. Geography has bearings on many subjects, but it does not bodily include those subjects. Even the great Peschel includes in his 'Physische Erdkunde' [15] a discussion on the barometer and a demonstration of the formulae needed in barometric corrections. Such digressions are the cause of the often repeated charge that geographers are merely dabblers in all the sciences. It is our contention that geography has a separate sphere of work. Its data may overlap those of other sciences, but its function is to point out certain new relations between those data. Geography must be a continuous argument, and the

[15] Vol. ii. pp. 118-127, and ed.

test of whether a given point is to be included or not must be this:—Is it pertinent to the main line of argument? How far digressions with the view of proving data are allowable must of course be a practical question. As a rule they should be excluded if it is the function of any other science to prove them.

Mr. Bryce's last category includes the production of a region. The distribution of minerals is obviously incidental to the rock-structure, and we need refer to it only to give another tap to the nail at which we have been hammering previously. As regards the distribution of animals and plants, we must apply the test to which we referred in the last paragraph:—How far is it pertinent to the main line of geographical argument? So far as the animals and plants in question form an appreciable factor in man's environment, so far their distribution is very pertinent. So far also as that distribution gives evidence of geographical changes, such as the separation of islands from continents or a retirement of the snow-line, so far it is also pertinent. But the study of the distribution of animals and plants in detail and as an aid to the understanding of the evolution of those beings, is in no sense a part of geography. It is a part of zoology or botany, for the proper study of which a preliminary study of geography is necessary.

The truth of the matter is that the bounds of all the sciences must naturally be compromises. Knowledge, as we have said before, is one. Its division into subjects is a concession to human weakness. As a final example of this we will deal with the relation of geography to history. In their elementary stages they must obviously go hand in hand. In their higher stages they diverge. The historian finds full occupation in the critical and comparative study of original documents. He has neither the time nor usually the turn of mind to scan science for himself with a view to selecting the facts and ideas which he requires. It is the function of the geographer to do this for him. On the other hand, the geographer must go to history for the verification of the relations which he suggests. The body of laws governing those relations, which might in time be evolved, would render possible the writing of much "prehistoric" history. John Richard Green's 'Making of England' is largely a deduction from geographical conditions of what must have been the course of history.

It remains that I should set out what I conceive to be the main line of geographical argument. I will do this in two stages. The first will be general, such as might be gathered from the syllabus of a university course of lectures or from the table of contents at the beginning of a text-book. The second will be a special application of this to the solution of a definite problem—the reasons why Delhi and Calcutta should have been respectively the old and the new capitals of India.

We presuppose a knowledge of physiography. We would then start from the idea of a landless globe, and build up a conception of the earth on the analogy of mechanics. First, the laws of Newton are demonstrated in their ideal simplicity on the hypothesis of absolute rigidity. It is not until these are fixed in the mind that the counteracting tendencies of elasticity and friction are introduced. So would we attack the study of geography. Imagine our globe in a landless condition, composed that is of three concentric spheroids—atmosphere, hydrosphere, and lithosphere. Two great world-wide forces would be in action—the sun's heat and the earth's rotation on its axis. Obviously the trade-wind system would have unimpeded sway. Next introduce the third set of world-wide forces—the inclination of the earth's axis to the plane of its orbit and the revolution of the earth round the sun. The result would be an annual march from tropic to tropic of the calm zone separating the trades. The fourth and last of the causes which we have termed world-wide would be the secular variation in the ellipticity of the earth's orbit and in the obliquity of its axis. This would produce similar variations in the annual march and in the intensity of the trade-wind system.

Thus far we have steered clear of longitudinal variations. Given the latitude, the altitude, the season of year, and the year in the secular period, and the climatic conditions are deducible from very few data. Now we abandon our primary hypothesis. Conceive the world as it is, as heated, as cooling, as shrinking, as wrinkling. It was heated, it is cooling, therefore it is shrinking, and the outer more chilled crust is in consequence wrinkling. The lithosphere is no longer concentric with the atmosphere and the hydrosphere. The bed of the ocean is thrown into ridges and furrows. The ridges project into the hydrosphere, and through the hydrosphere into the atmosphere. They act as obstacles in the way of the world-currents. They may be compared to the stones in the bed of a rapid stream on which the currents impinge and are diverted. They either leap over them or are split upon them. This purely mechanical action is well seen in the splitting of the Southern Equatorial Drift on Cape San Roque. Cape San Roque has a distinct influence on the climate of England. The "leaping-over" action is visible in the case of winds rising over mountain-chains, and as a consequence covering their slopes with moisture. But, in addition to the mechanical, there are thermal causes of variation, due mainly to the different specific heats of land and water—hence the monsoons. The lie of the great wrinkles has a special meaning. Were the continents extended east and west instead of in three great bands across the Equator, climate would be approximately indexed by latitude.

Thus may we steadily progress in the analysis of the world's surface. Conceive the world as landless, and you will see the motor-powers of air and water circulation.

Replace your conception by one of a wrinkled world, and you will grasp how by mechanical obstruction and thermal irregularity your simple currents are differentiated into currents of almost infinite but still orderly complexity.

But we must advance a stage further. The form of the lithosphere is not fixed. The shrinkage is still in progress. Old wrinkles are raised and new wrinkles come into existence. As they rise their destruction commences. The currents ever work at the removal of the obstacles which obstruct their course. They tend to achieve the ideal simplicity of circulation. Thus the features of the earth's surface are constantly changing. Their precise form is determined by their past history as well as by their present conditions. Recent changes are the subject of one of the most fascinating chapters in geography. Plains are built by the accumulation of débris. Continents give birth to islands. The evidence is drawn from a hundred sources— from the lines of migration of birds, the distribution of animals, or the depths of the neighbouring seas.

Each successive chapter postulates what has gone before. The sequence of argument is unbroken. From the position of the obstacles and the course of the winds may be deduced the distribution of rain. From the form and distribution of the wrinkle-slopes and from the distribution of the rainfall follows the explanation of the drainage system. The distribution of soils is mainly dependent on the rock-structure, and on a consideration of soil and climate follows the division of the world into natural regions based on vegetation. I am not here referring to the distribution of botanical species, but to that of the broad types of what may be called the vegetable clothing of the world—the polar and tropical deserts, the temperate and tropical forests, and the regions which may be grouped together as grass-plains.

Passing now to the second stage of the investigation, it will be well to make use of two technical terms. "An environment" is a natural region. The smaller the area included the greater tends to be the number of conditions uniform or nearly uniform throughout the area. Thus we have environments of different orders, whose extension and intension, to borrow a logical phrase, vary inversely. So with communities. "A community" is a group of men having certain characteristics in common. The smaller the community, the greater tends to be the number of common characteristics. Communities are of different orders—races, nations, provinces, towns—the last two expressions used in the sense of corporate groups of men. By the use of these two terms precision can be given to such discussions as the effects of exposing two communities to one environment, and one community to two environments. For instance, this—How have geographical conditions differentiated the English race in the three environments, Britain, America, and Australia?

Everywhere political questions will depend on the results of the physical inquiry. Certain conditions of climate and soil are needed for the aggregation of dense populations. A certain density of population seems necessary to the development of civilisation. In the light of such principles would be discussed such problems as the contrast between the ancient upland civilisations of the New World, Peru and Mexico, and the ancient lowland civilisations of the Old World, Egypt and Babylon. Again, comparatively undisturbed strata usually underlie wide plains, and wide plains seem specially favourable to the development of homogeneous races, like the Russians and the Chinese. Yet again, the distribution of animal, vegetable and mineral products has done much to determine the local characteristics of civilisation. Consider in this respect the series presented by the Old World, the New World, and Australia in the matter of comparative wealth in cereals and beasts of burden.

One of the most interesting chapters would deal with the reaction of man on nature. Man alters his environment, and the action of that environment on his posterity is changed in consequence. The relative importance of physical features varies from age to age according to the state of knowledge and of material civilisation. The improvement of artificial lighting has rendered possible the existence of a great community at St. Petersburg. The discovery of the Cape route to India and of the New World led to the fall of Venice. The invention of the steam engine and the electric telegraph have rendered possible the great size of modern states. We might multiply such instances greatly. We might group them into categories, but our object today is merely to indicate the possibilities of the subject. One thing, however, must always be borne in mind. The course of history at a given moment, whether in politics, society, or any other sphere of human activity, is the product not only of environment but also of the momentum acquired in the past. The fact that man is mainly a creature of habit must be recognised. The Englishman, for instance, will put up with many anomalies until they become nuisances of a certain degree of virulence. The influence of this tendency must always be kept in mind in geography. Milford Haven, in the present state of things, offers far greater physical advantages than Liverpool for the American trade; yet it is improbable that Liverpool will have to give way to Milford Haven, at any rate in the immediate future. It is a case of *vis inertiae*.

We propose passing now to the special illustration which we have promised. We will start from the fountain-head. From the sun's heat and the earth's rotation we demonstrate the trade-wind system. From the influence of that heat on the vast mass of Asia we deduce the monsoon variation of the system. Within the monsoon area are collected some seven hundred out of the eight hundred millions of Asia. Right athwart the south-west monsoon extends the Himalaya. The moisture of the Indian Ocean in consequence deluges its southern face. Thus the full importance of the direction of the mountain-chain is brought out. The rains have washed down from the mountains the débris which forms the fertile plain at their base. Hence, along the southern foot of the Himalaya we have a belt of country possessing the conditions of climate and soil needed to sustain a large population. In effect we find two-fifths of the population of the entire peninsula concentrated in the provinces of Bengal, the North-west and the Punjab, although these three provinces have but little more than one-sixth the area. Moreover, the abundant moisture of the monsoon coupled with the height of the Himalaya (the height is a consequence of the comparative newness of the wrinkle) produce an abundant glacial system from above the snowline. One result of this is that the rivers of the plain are perennial, and constantly navigable. Thus we have two conditions favourable to the development of civilisation, density of population, and ease of communication.

A wealthy civilised community is a region tempting to the conqueror. Now conquerors are of two kinds—land-wolves and sea-wolves. How would these respectively gain access to their prey in the Ganges valley? Consider first the landward frontier of India. On the north-east the Himalaya is practically impassable to a host.[16] On the north-west is the Sulaiman range, pierced by many passes. From the Iranian uplands of which this range is the boundary wall have swept down successive waves of conquerors. But within the mountain line is a far more effective obstacle,

[16] Only one exception is recorded by history. A Chinese army once succeeded in reaching Nepaul.

the Thar or great Indian desert, with its continuation the Rann of Katch. This barrier extends parallel to the Sulaiman Mountains from the sea almost to the Himalaya. Between the desert and the foot of the Himalaya the fertile belt is narrowest. Through that gate must pass whoever would gain access to the Ganges valley. Alexander advanced to its entrance. When he swerved to the right and followed the Indus, India was saved. Close to the eastern end of the pass is Delhi. It stands at the head of the Jumna-Ganges navigation, the place of transhipment from land to water carriage. It is therefore a natural centre of commerce. It is also the natural base of operations for the Asiatic conqueror, his left flanked by the mountains, his right by the desert, his line of communications secure to the rear. The strategic importance of the region has not escaped the British. Here is Simla, the summer capital of India. Here also the army cantonments are most thickly sown. Here are the fields of many battles. So much for Delhi. Now for Calcutta. From the sea India is singularly inaccessible. The eastern shore is beaten by a heavy surf. We have had to construct a harbour at Madras at great expense. The western coast has many good harbours, but in its rear rises the steep slope of the Western Ghats. Drenched by the monsoon, they are densely clothed with forests, which to this day are the abode of some of the most savage races of the world. Behind Bombay railways have now been carried over the mountains, but until recently they must have been a most effectual barrier to communication. The Portuguese settled at Goa, and could not advance. The English possession at Bombay was our earliest in India,[17] yet the Presidency of Bombay was the last to grow. The one great natural water-gate is by the mouth of the Ganges. Here, on the Hoogly, the British established them-

[17] Our earliest possession. We had factories at Surat and at Fort St. George somewhat earlier.

selves at Calcutta. It is the place of junction of river and sea shipping, and therefore a commercial centre. It is also the natural basis of operations for the conquerors from over the sea. From it they have extended their influence far and wide. The old presidencies of Bombay and Madras have each been succeeded by a single province, but the Presidency of Bengal has begotten Bengal, the North-west, the Punjab, and the Central Provinces; we might also add Assam and Burma. Thus, to sum up, at the two ends of the fertile belt are the two gates of India—the Khaibar Pass and the Hoogly. Along that belt the great highway is the Jumna-Ganges. At either end of the river navigation stands a strategical and commercial capital, Delhi on the one hand, Calcutta[18] on the other.

Thus we complete our survey of the methods and scope of geography. I believe that on lines such as I have sketched a geography may be worked out which shall satisfy at once the practical requirements of the statesman and the merchant, the theoretical requirements of the historian and the scientist, and the intellectual requirements of the teacher. Its inherent breadth and many-sidedness should be claimed as its chief merit. At the same time we have to recognise that these are the very qualities which will render it "suspect" to an age of specialists. It would be a standing protest against the disintegration of culture with which we are threatened. In the days of our fathers the ancient classics were the common element in the culture of all men, a ground on which the specialists could meet. The world is changing, and it would seem that the classics are also becoming a speciality. Whether we regret the turn which

[18] Calcutta=Kali Katta—the village of the goddess Kali. This suggests the question: Why should this particular village have risen to be a metropolis rather than any other village? I would propose the term "geographical selection" for the process on the analogy of "natural selection."

things have taken or whether we rejoice at it, it is equally our duty to find a substitute. To me it seems that geography combines some of the requisite qualities. To the practical man, whether he aim at distinction in the State or at the amassing of wealth, it is a store of invaluable information; to the student it is a stimulating basis from which to set out along a hundred special lines; to the teacher it would be an implement for the calling out of the powers of the intellect, except indeed to that old-world class of schoolmaster who measure the disciplinary value of a subject by the repugnance with which it inspires the pupil. All this we say on the assumption of the unity of the subject. The alternative is to divide the scientific from the practical. The result of its adoption will be the ruin of both. The practical will be rejected by the teacher, and will be found indigestible in after life. The scientific will be neglected by most men, because it lacks the element of utility in every-day life. The man of the world and the student, the scientist and the historian, will lose their common platform. The world will be the poorer.

THE GEOGRAPHICAL PIVOT OF HISTORY

WHEN historians in the remote future come to look back on the group of centuries through which we are now passing, and see them foreshortened, as we to-day see the Egyptian dynasties, it may well be that they will describe the last 400 years as the Columbian epoch, and will say that it ended soon after the year 1900. Of late it has been a common-place to speak of geographical exploration as nearly over, and it is recognized that geography must be diverted to the purpose of intensive survey and philosophic synthesis. In 400 years the outline of the map of the world has been completed with approximate accuracy, and even in the polar regions the voyages of Nansen and Scott have very narrowly reduced the last possibility of dramatic discoveries. But the opening of the twentieth century is appropriate as the end of a great historic epoch, not merely on account of this achievement, great though it be. The missionary, the conqueror, the farmer, the miner, and, of late, the engineer, have followed so closely in the traveller's footsteps that the world, in its remoter borders, has hardly been revealed before we must chronicle its virtually complete political appropriation. In Europe, North America, South America, Africa, and Australasia there is scarcely a region left for the pegging out of a claim of ownership, unless as the result of a war between civilized or half-civilized powers. Even in Asia we are probably witnessing the last moves of the game first played by the horsemen of Yermak the Cossack and the shipmen of Vasco da Gama. Broadly speaking, we may contrast the Columbian epoch with the age which preceded it, by describing its essential characteristic as the expansion of Europe against almost negligible resistances, whereas mediaeval Christendom was pent into a narrow region and threatened by external barbarism. From the present time forth, in the post-Columbian age, we shall again have to deal with a closed political system, and none the less that it will be one of world-wide scope. Every explosion of social forces, instead of being dissipated in a surrounding circuit of unknown space and barbaric chaos, will be sharply re-echoed from the far side of the globe, and weak elements in the political and economic organism of the world will be shattered in consequence. There is a vast difference of effect in the fall of a shell into an earthwork and its fall amid the closed spaces and rigid structures of a great building or ship. Probably some half-consciousness of this fact is at last diverting much of the attention of statesmen in all parts of the world from territorial expansion to the struggle for relative efficiency.

It appears to me, therefore, that in the present decade we are for the first time in a position to attempt, with some degree of completeness, a correlation between the larger geographical and the larger historical generalizations. For the first time we can perceive something of the real proportion of features and events on the stage of the whole world, and may seek a formula which shall express certain aspects, at any rate, of geographical causation in universal history. If we are fortunate, that formula should have a practical value as setting into perspective some of the competing forces in current international politics. The familiar phrase about the westward march of empire is an empirical and fragmentary attempt of the kind. I propose this evening describing those physical features of the world which I believe to have been most coercive of human action, and presenting some of the chief phases of history as organically connected with them, even in the ages when they were unknown to geography. My aim will not be to discuss the influence of this or that kind of feature, or yet to make a study in regional geography, but rather to exhibit human history as part of the life of the world organism. I recognize that I can only arrive at one aspect of the truth, and I have no wish to stray into excessive materialism. Man and not nature initiates, but nature in large measure controls. My concern is with the general physical control, rather than the causes of universal history. It is obvious that only a first approximation to truth can be hoped for. I shall be humble to my critics.

The late Professor Freeman held that the only history which counts is that of the Mediterranean and European races. In a sense, of course, this is true, for it is among these races that have originated the ideas which have rendered the inheritors of Greece and Rome dominant throughout the world. In another and very important sense, however, such a limitation has a cramping effect upon thought. The ideas which go to form a nation, as opposed to a mere crowd of human animals, have usually been accepted under the pressure of a common tribulation, and under a common necessity of resistance to external force. The idea of England was beaten into the Heptarchy by Danish and Norman conquerors; the idea of France was forced upon competing Franks, Goths, and Romans by the Huns at Chalons, and in the Hundred Years' War with England; the idea of Christendom was born of the Roman persecutions, and matured by the Crusades; the idea of the United States was accepted, and local colonial patriotism sunk, only in the long War of Independence; the idea of the German Empire was reluctantly adopted in South Germany only after a struggle against France in comradeship with North Germany. What I may describe as the literary conception of history, by concentrating attention upon ideas and upon the civilization which is their outcome, is apt to lose sight of the more elemental movements whose pressure is commonly the exciting cause of the efforts in which great ideas are nourished. A repellent personality performs a valuable social function in uniting his enemies, and it was under the pressure of external barbarism that Europe achieved her civilization. I ask you, therefore, for a moment to look upon Europe and European history as subordinate to Asia and Asiatic history, for European civilization is, in a very real sense, the outcome of the secular struggle against Asiatic invasion.

The most remarkable contrast in the political map of modern Europe is that presented by the vast area of Russia occupying half the Continent and the group of smaller territories tenanted by the Western Powers. From a physical point of view, there is, of course, a like contrast between the unbroken lowland of the east and the rich complex of mountains and valleys, islands and peninsulas, which together form the remainder of this part of the world. At first sight it would appear that in these familiar facts we have a correlation between natural environment and political organization so obvious as hardly to be worthy of description, especially when we note that throughout the Russian plain a cold winter is opposed to a hot summer, and the conditions of human existence thus rendered additionally uniform. Yet a series of historical maps, such as that contained in the Oxford Atlas, will reveal the fact that not merely is the rough coincidence of European Russia with the Eastern Plain of Europe a matter of the last hundred years or so, but that in all earlier time there was persistent re-assertion of quite another tendency in the political grouping. Two groups of states usually divided the country into northern and southern political systems. The fact is that the orographical map does not express the particular physical contrast which has until very lately controlled human movement and settlement in Russia. When the screen of

Fig. 1. Eastern Europe before the nineteenth century. (*After Drude in Berghaus' Physical Atlas*)

winter snow fades northward off the vast face of the plain, it is followed by rains whose maximum occurs in May and June beside the Black sea, but near the Baltic and White seas is deferred to July and August. In the south the later summer is a period of drought. As a consequence of this climatic *régime,* the north and north-west were forest broken only by marshes, whereas the south and south-east were a boundless grassy steppe, with trees only along the

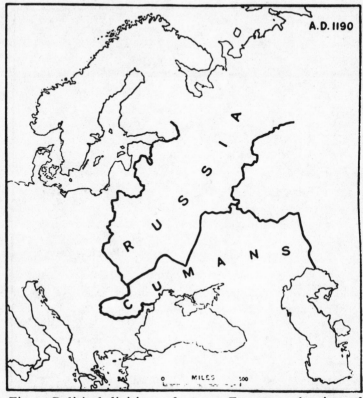

Fig. 2. Political divisions of eastern Europe at the time of the Third Crusade. (*After The Oxford Historical Atlas*)

rivers. The line separating the two regions ran diagonally north-eastward from the northern end of the Carpathians to a point in the Ural range nearer to its southern than to its northern extremity. Moscow lies a little to north of this line, or, in other words, on the forest side of it. Outside Russia the boundary of the great forest ran westward almost exactly through the centre of the European isthmus, which is 800 miles across between the Baltic and the Black seas.

Beyond this, in Peninsular Europe, the woods spread on through the plains of Germany in the north, while the steppe lands in the south turned the great Transylvanian bastion of the Carpathians, and extended up the Danube, through what are now the cornfields of Roumania, to the Iron Gates. A detached area of steppes, known locally as Pusstas, now largely cultivated, occupied the plain of Hungary, ingirt by the forested rim of Carpathian and Alpine mountains. In all the west of Russia, save in the far north, the clearing of the forests, the drainage of the marshes, and the tillage of the steppes have recently averaged the character of the landscape, and in large measure obliterated a distinction which was formerly very coercive of humanity.

The earlier Russia and Poland were established wholly in the glades of the forest. Through the steppe on the other hand there came from the unknown recesses of Asia, by the gateway between the Ural mountains and the Caspian sea, in all the centuries from the fifth to the sixteenth, a remarkable succession of Turanian nomadic peoples— Huns, Avars, Bulgarians, Magyars, Khazars, Patzinaks, Cumans, Mongols, Kalmuks. Under Attila the Huns established themselves in the midst of the Pusstas, in the uttermost Danubian outlier of the steppes, and thence dealt blows northward, westward, and southward against the settled peoples of Europe. A large part of modern history might be written as a commentary upon the changes directly or indirectly ensuing from these raids. The Angles and Saxons, it is quite possible, were then driven to cross the seas to found England in Britain. The Franks, the Goths, and the Roman provincials were compelled, for the first time, to stand shoulder to shoulder on the battlefield of Chalons, making common cause against the Asiatics, who were unconsciously welding together modern France. Venice was founded from the destruction of Aquileia and

Fig. 3. Political divisions of eastern Europe at the accession of Charles V. (*After The Oxford Historical Atlas*)

Padua; and even the Papacy owed a decisive prestige to the successful mediation of Pope Leo with Attila at Milan. Such was the harvest of results produced by a cloud of ruthless and idealess horsemen sweeping over the unimpeded plain—a blow, as it were, from the great Asiatic hammer striking freely through the vacant space. The Huns were followed by the Avars. It was for a marchland against these that Austria was founded, and Vienna fortified, as the result of the campaigns of Charlemagne. The Magyar came next, and by incessant raiding from his steppe base in Hungary increased the significance of the Austrian outpost, so drawing the political focus of Germany eastward to the margin of the realm. The Bulgarian established a ruling caste south of the Danube, and has left his name upon the map, although his language has yielded to that of his Slavonic subjects. Perhaps the longest and most effective occupation of the Russian steppe proper was that of the Khazars, who were contemporaries of the great Saracen movement: the Arab geographers knew the Caspian as the Khazar sea. In the end, however, new hordes arrived from Mongolia, and for two centuries Russia in the northern forest was held tributary to the Mongol Khans of Kipchak, or "the Steppe," and Russian development was thus delayed and biassed at a time when the remainder of Europe was rapidly advancing.

It should be noted that the rivers running from the Forest to the Black and Caspian seas cross the whole breadth of the steppe-land path of the nomads, and that from time to time there were transient movements along their courses at right angles to the movement of the horsemen. Thus the missionaries of Greek Christianity ascended the Dnieper to Kief, just as beforehand the Norse Varangians had descended the same river on their way to Constantinople. Still earlier, the Teutonic Goths appear for a moment upon the Dneister, having crossed Europe from the shores of the Baltic in the same south-eastward direction. But these are passing episodes which do not invalidate the broader generalization. For a thousand years a series of horse-riding peoples emerged from Asia through the broad interval between the Ural mountains and the Caspian sea, rode through the open spaces of southern Russia, and struck home into Hungary in the very heart of the European peninsula, shaping by the necessity of opposing them the history of each of the great peoples around—the Russians, the Germans, the French, the Italians, and the Byzantine Greeks. That they stimulated healthy and powerful reaction, instead of crushing opposition under a widespread despotism, was due to the fact that the mobility of their power was conditioned by the steppes, and necessarily ceased in the surrounding forests and mountains.

A rival mobility of power was that of the Vikings in their boats. Descending from Scandinavia both upon the northern and the southern shores of Europe, they penetrated inland by the river ways. But the scope of their action was limited, for, broadly speaking, their power was effective only in the neighbourhood of the water. Thus the settled peoples of Europe lay gripped between two pressures—that of the Asiatic nomads from the east, and on the other three sides that of the pirates from the sea. From its very nature neither pressure was overwhelming, and both therefore were stimulative. It is noteworthy that the formative influence of the Scandinavians was second only in significance to that of the nomads, for under their attack both England and France made long moves towards unity, while the unity of Italy was broken by them. In earlier times, Rome had mobilized the power of her settled peoples by means of her roads, but the Roman roads had fallen into decay, and were not replaced until the eighteenth century.

It is likely that even the Hunnish invasion was by no means the first of the Asiatic series. The Scythians of the Homeric and Herodotian accounts, drinking the milk of mares, obviously practised the same arts of life, and were probably of the same race as the later inhabitants of the steppe. The Celtic element in the river-names *Don, Donetz, Dneiper, Dneister,* and *Danube* may possibly betoken the passage of peoples of similar habits, though not of identical race, but it is not unlikely that the Celts came merely from the northern forests, like the Goths and Varangians of a later time. The great wedge of population, however, which the anthropologists characterize as Brachy-Cephalic, driven westward from Brachy-Cephalic Asia through Central Europe into France, is apparently intrusive between the northern, western, and southern Dolico-Cephalic populations, and may very probably have been derived from Asia.[1]

The full meaning of Asiatic influence upon Europe is not, however, discernible until we come to the Mongol invasions of the fifteenth century; but before we analyze the essential facts concerning these, it is desirable to shift our geographical view-point from Europe, so that we may consider the Old World in its entirety. It is obvious that, since the rainfall is derived from the sea, the heart of the greatest land-mass is likely to be relatively dry. We are not, therefore, surprised to find that two-thirds of all the world's population is concentrated in relatively small areas along the margins of the great continent—in Europe, beside the Atlantic ocean; in the Indies and China, beside the Indian and Pacific oceans. A vast belt of almost uninhabited, because practically rainless, land extends as the Sahara completely across Northern Africa into Arabia. Central and Southern Africa were almost as completely severed from Europe and Asia throughout the greater part of history as were the Americas and Australia. In fact, the southern boundary of Europe was and is the Sahara rather than the Mediterranean, for it is the desert which divides the black man from the white. The continuous land-mass of Euro-Asia thus included between the ocean and the desert measures 21,000,000 square miles, or half of all the land on the globe, if we exclude from reckoning the deserts of Sahara and Arabia. There are many detached deserts

[1] See 'The Races of Europe,' by Professor W. Z. Ripley (Kegan Paul, 1900).

scattered through Asia, from Syria and Persia north-eastward to Manchuria, but no such continuous vacancy as to be comparable with the Sahara. On the other hand, Euro-Asia is characterized by a very remarkable distribution of river drainage. Throughout an immense portion of the centre and north, the rivers have been practically useless for purposes of human communication with the outer world. The Volga, the Oxus, and the Jaxartes drain into salt lakes; the Obi, the Yenisei, and the Lena into the frozen ocean of the north. These are six of the greatest rivers in the world. There are many smaller but still considerable streams in the same area, such as the Tarim and the Helmund, which similarly fail to reach the ocean. Thus the core of Euro-Asia, although mottled with desert patches, is on the whole a steppe-land supplying a widespread if often scanty pasture, and there are not a few river-fed oases in it, but it is wholly unpenetrated by waterways from the ocean. In other words, we have in this immense area all the conditions for the maintenance of a sparse, but in the aggregate considerable, population of horse-riding and camel-riding nomads. Their realm is limited northward by a broad belt of sub-arctic forest and marsh, wherein the climate is too rigorous, except at the eastern and western extremities, for the development of agricultural settlements. In the east the forests extend southward to the Pacific coast in the Amur land and Manchuria. Similarly in the west, in prehistoric Europe, forest was the predominant vegetation. Thus framed in to the north-east, north, and north-west, the steppes spread continuously for 4000 miles from the Pusstas of Hungary to the Little Gobi of Manchuria, and, except in their western-most extremity, they are untraversed by rivers draining to an accessible ocean, for we may neglect the very recent efforts to trade to the mouths of the Obi and Yenisei. In Europe, Western Siberia, and Western Turkestan the

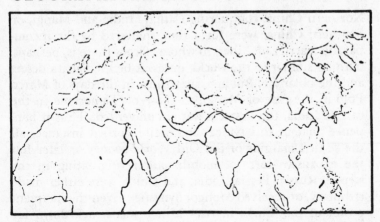

Fig. 4. Continental and Arctic drainage. (*Equal area projection*)

steppe-lands lie low, in some places below the level of the sea. Further to the east, in Mongolia, they extend over plateaux; but the passage from the one level to the other, over the naked, unscarped lower ranges of the arid heartland, presents little difficulty.

The hordes which ultimately fell upon Europe in the middle of the fourteenth century gathered their first force 3000 miles away on the high steppes of Mongolia. The havoc wrought for a few years in Poland, Silesia, Moravia, Hungary, Croatia, and Servia was, however, but the remotest and the most transient result of the great stirring of the nomads of the East associated with the name of Ghenghiz Khan. While the Golden Horde occupied the steppe of Kipchak, from the Sea of Aral, through the interval between the Ural range and the Caspian, to the foot of the Carpathians, another horde, descending south-westward between the Caspian sea and the Hindu Kush into Persia, Mesopotamia, and even into Syria, founded the domain of the Ilkhan. A third subsequently struck into

Northern China, conquering Cathay. India and Mangi, or Southern China, were for a time sheltered by the incomparable barrier of Tibet, to whose efficacy there is, perhaps, nothing similar in the world, unless it be the Sahara desert and the polar ice. But at a later time, in the days of Marco Polo in the case of Mangi, in those of Tamerlane in the case of India, the obstacle was circumvented. Thus it happened that in this typical and well-recorded instance, all the settled margins of the Old World sooner or later felt the expansive force of mobile power originating in the steppe. Russia, Persia, India, and China were either made tributary, or received Mongol dynasties. Even the incipient power of the Turks in Asia Minor was struck down for half a century.

As in the case of Europe, so in other marginal lands of Euro-Asia there are records of earlier invasions. China had more than once to submit to conquest from the north; India several times to conquest from the north-west. In the case of Persia, however, at least one of the earlier descents has a special significance in the history of Western civilization. Three or four centuries before the Mongols, the Seljuk Turks, emerging from Central Asia, overran by this path an immense area of the land, which we may describe as of the five seas—Caspian, Black, Mediterranean, Red, and Persian. They established themselves at Kerman, at Hamadan, and in Asia Minor, and they overthrew the Saracen dominion of Bagdad and Damascus. It was ostensibly to punish their treatment of the Christian pilgrims at Jerusalem that Christendom undertook the great series of campaigns known collectively as the Crusades. Although these failed in their immediate objects, they so stirred and united Europe that we may count them as the beginning of modern history—another striking instance of European advance stimulated by the necessity of reacting against pressure from the heart of Asia.

The conception of Euro-Asia to which we thus attain is that of a continuous land, ice-girt in the north, water-girt elsewhere, measuring twenty-one million square miles, or more than three times the area of North America, whose centre and north, measuring some nine million square miles, or more than twice the area of Europe, have no available water-ways to the ocean, but, on the other hand, except in the subarctic forest, are very generally favourable to the mobility of horsemen and camelmen. To east, south, and west of this heart-land are marginal regions, ranged in a vast crescent, accessible to shipmen. According to physical conformation, these regions are four in number, and it is not a little remarkable that in a general way they respectively coincide with the spheres of the four great religions—Buddhism, Brahminism, Mahometanism, and Christianity. The first two are the monsoon lands, turned the one towards the Pacific, and the other towards the Indian ocean. The fourth is Europe, watered by the Atlantic rains from the west. These three together, measuring less than seven million square miles, have more than 1000 million people, or two-thirds of the world population. The third, coinciding with the land of the Five Seas, or, as it is more often described, the Nearer East, is in large measure deprived of moisture by the proximity of Africa, and, except in the oases, is therefore thinly peopled. In some degree it partakes of the characteristics both of the marginal belt of the central area of Euro-Asia. It is mainly devoid of forest, is patched with desert, and is therefore suitable for the operations of the nomad. Dominantly, however, it is marginal, for sea-gulfs and oceanic rivers lay it open to sea-power, and permit of the exercise of such power from it. As a consequence, periodically throughout history, we have here had empires belonging essentially to the marginal series, based on the agricultural populations of the great oases of Babylonia and Egypt, and in free water-communication with the civilized worlds of the Mediterranean and the Indies. But, as we should expect, these empires have been subject to an unparalleled series of revolutions, some due to Scythian, Turkish, and Mongol raids from Central Asia, others to the effort of the Mediterranean peoples to conquer the overland ways from the western to the eastern ocean. Here is the weakest spot in the girdle of early civilizations, for the isthmus of Suez divided sea-power into Eastern and Western, and the arid wastes of Persia advancing from Central Asia to the Persian gulf gave constant opportunity for nomad-power to strike home to the ocean edge, dividing India and China, on the one hand, from the Mediterranean world on the other. Whenever the Babylonian, the Syrian, and the Egyptian oases were weakly held, the steppe-peoples could treat the open tablelands of Iran and Asia Minor as forward posts whence to strike through the Punjab into India, through Syria into Egypt, and over the broken bridge of the Bosphorus and Dardanelles into Hungary. Vienna stood in the gateway of Inner Europe, withstanding the nomadic raids, both those which came by the direct road through the Russian steppe, and those which came by the loop way to south of the Black and Caspian seas.

Here we have illustrated the essential difference between the Saracen and the Turkish controls of the Nearer East. The Saracens were a branch of the Semitic race, essentially peoples of the Euphrates and Nile and of the smaller oases of Lower Asia. They created a great empire by availing themselves of the two mobilities permitted by their land—that of the horse and camel on the one hand, that of the ship on the other. At different times their fleets controlled both the Mediterranean as far as Spain, and the Indian ocean to the Malay islands. From their strategically central position between the eastern and western oceans, they attempted the conquest of all the marginal lands of the Old World, imitating Alexander and anticipating Napoleon. They could even threaten the steppe-land. Wholly distinct from Arabia as from Europe, India, and China were the Turanian pagans from the closed heart of Asia, the Turks who destroyed the Saracen civilization.

Mobility upon the ocean is the natural rival of horse and camel mobility in the heart of the continent. It was upon navigation of oceanic rivers that was based the Potamic stage of civilization, that of China on the Yangtse, that of India on the Ganges, that of Babylonia on the Euphrates, that of Egypt on the Nile. It was essentially upon the navigation of the Mediterranean that was based what has been described as the Thalassic stage of civilization, that of the Greeks and Romans. The Saracens and the Vikings held sway by navigation of the oceanic coasts.

The all-important result of the discovery of the Cape road to the Indies was to connect the western and eastern coastal navigations of Euro-Asia, even though by a circuitous route, and thus in some measure to neutralize the strategical advantage of the central position of the steppe-nomads by pressing upon them in rear. The revolution commenced by the great mariners of the Columbian generation endowed Christendom with the widest possible mobility of power, short of a winged mobility. The one and continuous ocean enveloping the divided and insular lands is, of course, the geographical condition of ultimate unity in the command of the sea, and of the whole theory of modern naval strategy and policy as expounded by such writers as Captain Mahan and Mr. Spenser Wilkinson. The broad political effect was to reverse the relations of Europe and Asia, for whereas in the Middle Ages Europe was caged between an impassable desert to south, an unknown ocean to west, and icy or forested wastes to north and north-east, and in the east and south-east was constantly threatened by the superior mobility of the horsemen and camelmen, she now emerged upon the world, multiplying more than thirty-fold the sea surface and coastal lands to which she had access, and wrapping her influence round the Euro-Asiatic land-power which had hitherto threatened her very existence. New Europes were created in the vacant lands discovered in the midst of the waters, and what Britain and Scandinavia were to Europe in the earlier time, that have America and Australia, and in some measure even Trans-Saharan Africa, now become to Euro-Asia. Britain, Canada, the United States, South Africa, Australia, and Japan are now a ring of outer and insular bases for sea-power and commerce, inaccessible to the land-power of Euro-Asia.

But the land power still remains, and recent events have again increased its significance. While the maritime peoples of Western Europe have covered the ocean with their fleets, settled the outer continents, and in varying degree made tributary the oceanic margins of Asia, Russia has organized the Cossacks, and, emerging from her northern forests, has policed the steppe by setting her own nomads to meet the Tartar nomads. The Tudor century, which saw the expansion of Western Europe over the sea, also saw Russian power carried from Moscow through Siberia. The eastward swoop of the horsemen across Asia was an event almost as pregnant with political consequences as was the rounding of the Cape, although the two movements long remained apart.

It is probably one of the most striking coincidences of history that the seaward and the landward expansion of Europe should, in a sense, continue the ancient opposition between Roman and Greek. Few great failures have had more far-reaching consequences than the failure of Rome to Latinize the Greek. The Teuton was civilized and Christianized by the Roman, the Slav in the main by the Greek.

It is the Romano-Teuton who in later times embarked upon the ocean; it was the Graeco-Slav who rode over the steppes, conquering the Turanian. Thus the modern land-power differs from the sea-power no less in the source of its ideals than in the material conditions of its mobility.[2]

In the wake of the Cossack, Russia has safely emerged from her former seclusion in the northern forests. Perhaps the change of greatest intrinsic importance which took place in Europe in the last century was the southward migration of the Russian peasants, so that, whereas agricultural settlements formerly ended at the forest boundary, the centre of the population of all European Russia now lies to south of that boundary, in the midst of the wheatfields which have replaced the more western steppes. Odessa has here risen to importance with the rapidity of an American city.

A generation ago steam and the Suez canal appeared to have increased the mobility of sea-power relatively to land-power. Railways acted chiefly as feeders to ocean-going commerce. But trans-continental railways are now transmuting the conditions of land-power, and nowhere can they have such effect as in the closed heart-land of Euro-Asia, in vast areas of which neither timber nor accessible stone was available for road-making. Railways work the greater wonders in the steppe, because they directly replace horse and camel mobility, the road stage of development having here been omitted.

In the matter of commerce it must not be forgotten that ocean-going traffic, however relatively cheap, usually involves the fourfold handling of goods—at the factory of

[2] This statement was criticized in the discussion which followed the reading of the paper. On reconsidering the paragraph, I still think it substantially correct. Even the Byzantine Greek would have been other than he was had Rome completed the subjugation of the ancient Greek. No doubt the ideals spoken of were Byzantine rather than Hellenic, but they were not Roman, which is the point.

origin, at the export wharf, at the import wharf, and at the inland warehouse for retail distribution; whereas the continental railway truck may run direct from the exporting factory into the importing warehouse. Thus marginal ocean-fed commerce tends, other things being equal, to form a zone of penetration round the continents, whose inner limit is roughly marked by the line along which the cost of four handlings, the oceanic freight, and the railway freight from the neighbouring coast, is equivalent to the cost of two handlings and the continental railway freight. English and German coals are said to compete on such terms midway through Lombardy.

The Russian railways have a clear run of 6000 miles from Wirballen in the west to Vladivostok in the east. The Russian army in Manchuria is as significant evidence of mobile land-power as the British army in South Africa was of sea-power. True, that the Trans-Siberian railway is still a single and precarious line of communication, but the century will not be old before all Asia is covered with railways. The spaces within the Russian Empire and Mongolia are so vast, and their potentialities in population, wheat, cotton, fuel, and metals so incalculably great, that it is inevitable that a vast economic world, more or less apart, will there develop inaccessible to oceanic commerce.

As we consider this rapid review of the broader currents of history, does not a certain persistence of geographical relationship become evident? Is not the pivot region of the world's politics that vast area of Euro-Asia which is inaccessible to ships, but in antiquity lay open to the horse-riding nomads, and is to-day about to be covered with a network of railways? There have been and are here the conditions of a mobility of military and economic power of a far-reaching and yet limited character. Russia replaces the Mongol Empire. Her pressure on Finland, on Scandinavia, on Poland, on Turkey, on Persia, on India, and on

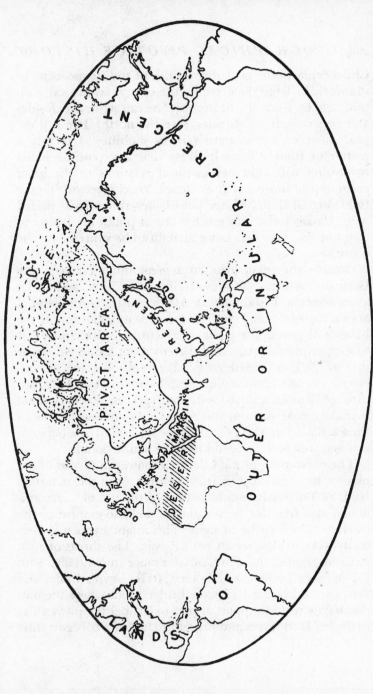

Fig. 5. The Natural Seats of Power. Pivot area: wholly continental; Outer crescent: wholly oceanic; Inner crescent: partly continental, partly oceanic.

China replaces the centrifugal raids of the steppe-men. In the world at large she occupies the central strategical position held by Germany in Europe. She can strike on all sides and be struck from all sides, save the north. The full development of her modern railway mobility is merely a matter of time. Nor is it likely that any possible social revolution will alter her essential relations to the great geographical limits of her existence. Wisely recognizing the fundamental limits of her power, her rulers have parted with Alaska; for it is as much a law of policy for Russia to own nothing over seas as for Britain to be supreme on the ocean.

Outside the pivot area, in a great inner crescent, are Germany, Austria, Turkey, India, and China, and in an outer crescent, Britain, South Africa, Australia, the United States, Canada, and Japan. In the present condition of the balance of power, the pivot state, Russia, is not equivalent to the peripheral states, and there is room for an equipoise in France. The United States has recently become an eastern power, affecting the European balance not directly, but through Russia, and she will construct the Panama canal to make her Mississippi and Atlantic resources available in the Pacific. From this point of view the real divide between east and west is to be found in the Atlantic ocean.

The oversetting of the balance of power in favour of the pivot state, resulting in its expansion over the marginal lands of Euro-Asia, would permit of the use of vast continental resources for fleet-building, and the empire of the world would then be in sight. This might happen if Germany were to ally herself with Russia. The threat of such an event should, therefore, throw France into alliance with the over-sea powers, and France, Italy, Egypt, India, and Korea would become so many bridge heads where the outside navies would support armies to compel the pivot allies to deploy land forces and prevent them from concentrating their whole strength on fleets. On a smaller scale that was what Wellington accomplished from his sea-base at Torres Vedras in the Peninsular War. May not this in the end prove to be the strategical function of India in the British Imperial system? Is not this the idea underlying Mr. Amery's conception that the British military front stretches from the Cape through India to Japan?

The development of the vast potentialities of South America might have a decisive influence upon the system. They might strengthen the United States, or, on the other hand, if Germany were to challenge the Monroe doctrine successfully, they might detach Berlin from what I may perhaps describe as a pivot policy. The particular combinations of power brought into balance are not material; my contention is that from a geographical point of view they are likely to rotate round the pivot state, which is always likely to be great, but with limited mobility as compared with the surrounding marginal and insular powers.

I have spoken as a geographer. The actual balance of political power at any given time is, of course, the product, on the one hand, of geographical conditions, both economic and strategic, and, on the other hand, of the relative number, virility, equipment, and organization of the competing peoples. In proportion as these quantities are accurately estimated are we likely to adjust differences without the crude resort to arms. And the geographical quantities in the calculation are more measurable and more nearly constant than the human. Hence we should expect to find our formula apply equally to past history and to present politics. The social movements of all times have played around essentially the same physical features, for I doubt whether the progressive desiccation of Asia and Africa, even if proved, has in historical times vitally altered the human environment. The westward march of empire appears to me to have been a short rotation of marginal power round the south-western and western edge of the pivotal area. The Nearer, Middle, and Far Eastern questions relate to the unstable equilibrium of inner and outer powers in those parts of the marginal crescent where local power is, at present, more or less negligible.

In conclusion, it may be well expressly to point out that the substitution of some new control of the inland area for that of Russia would not tend to reduce the geographical significance of the pivot position. Were the Chinese, for instance, organized by the Japanese, to overthrow the Russian Empire and conquer its territory, they might constitute the yellow peril to the world's freedom just because they would add an oceanic frontage to the resources of the great continent, an advantage as yet denied to the Russian tenant of the pivot region.

THE ROUND WORLD AND THE
WINNING OF THE PEACE*

I HAVE been asked to carry further some of the themes with which I have dealt in my past writings, in particular to consider whether my strategical concept of a "Heart-land" has lost any of its significance under the conditions of modern warfare. In order to set the concept into its context, I must begin with a short account of how it originally came to take shape.

My earliest memory of public affairs goes back to the day in September 1870 when, as a small boy who had just begun attendance at the local grammar school, I took home the news, which I had learned from a telegram affixed to the post office door, that Napoleon III and his whole army had surrendered to the Prussians at Sedan. This came as a shock to Englishmen, who still moved mentally in the wake of Trafalgar and the retreat from Moscow, but the full effect of it was not realized until some years later. Britain's supremacy on the ocean had not yet been challenged, and the only danger she saw at that time to her overseas empire was in the Asiatic position of Russia. During this period the London newspapers were quick to detect evidence of Russian intrigue in every rumor from Constantinople and in every tribal disturbance along the northwest frontier of India, British sea power and Russian land power held the center of the international stage.

Thirty years later, at the turn of the century, von Tirpitz

* Reprinted by special permission from *Foreign Affairs,* July 1943. Copyright by the Council on Foreign Relations, Inc., New York.

began to build a German high seas fleet. I was busy at this time setting up the teaching of political and historical geography at the universities of Oxford and London, and was noting current events with a teacher's eye for generalization. The German movement meant, I saw, that the nation already possessing the greatest organized land power and occupying the central strategical position in Europe was about to add to itself sea power strong enough to neutralize British sea power. The United States was also rising steadily to the rank of a Great Power. As yet, however, its rise could be measured only in statistical tables; although in my childhood someone had already been impressed with American resourcefulness, for I remember in our schoolroom a picture of the battle between the *Merrimac* and the *Monitor,* the first armored ship and the first turret ship. Thus Germany and the United States came up alongside of Britain and Russia.

The particular events out of which sprang the idea of the Heartland were the British war in South Africa and the Russian war in Manchuria. The South African war ended in 1902, and in the spring of 1904 the Russo-Japanese war was clearly imminent. A paper which I read before the Royal Geographical Society early in the latter year, entitled "The Geographical Pivot of History," was therefore topical, but it had a background of many years of observation and thought.

The contrast presented by the British war against the Boers, fought 6,000 miles away across the ocean, and the war fought by Russia at a comparable distance across the land expanse of Asia, naturally suggested a parallel contrast between Vasco da Gama rounding the Cape of Good Hope on his voyage to the Indies, near the end of the fifteenth century, and the ride of Yermak, the Cossack, at the head of his horsemen, over the Ural range into Siberia early in the sixteenth century. That comparison in turn led to

a review of the long succession of raids made by the nomadic tribes of Central Asia, through classical antiquity
and the Middle Ages, upon the settled populations of the
crescent of subcontinents: peninsular Europe, the Middle
East, the Indies, and China proper. My conclusion was
that,

. . . in the present decade we are for the first time in a position to attempt, with some degree of completeness, a correlation between the larger geographical and the larger historical
generalizations. For the first time we can perceive something of
the real proportion of features and events on the stage of the
whole world, and may seek a formula which shall express certain aspects, at any rate, of geographical causation in universal
history. If we are fortunate, that formula should have a practical value as setting into perspective some of the competing
forces in current international politics.

The word Heartland occurs once in the 1904 paper, but
incidentally and as a descriptive and not a technical term.
The expressions "pivot area" and "pivot state" were used
instead, thus:

The oversetting of balance of power in favor of the pivot
state, resulting in its expansion over the marginal lands of
Euro-Asia, would permit of the use of vast continental resources for fleet-building, and the empire of the world would
then be in sight. This might happen if Germany were to ally
herself with Russia.
In conclusion, it may be well expressly to point out that the
substitution of some new control of the inland area for that
of Russia would not tend to reduce the geographical significance of the pivot position. Were the Chinese, for instance,
organized by the Japanese, to overthrow the Russian Empire
and conquer its territory, they might constitute the yellow
peril to the world's freedom just because they would add an
oceanic frontage to the resources of the great continent.

At the end of the First World War, my book, "Democratic Ideals and Reality," was published in London and New York. Clearly the "pivot" label, which had been appropriate for an academic thesis at the beginning of the century, was no longer adequate to the international situation as it emerged from that first great crisis of our world revolution: hence "Ideals," "Realities" and the "Heartland." But the fact that, even when additional criteria were brought to bear, the thesis of 1904 still sufficed as the background for an estimate of the position fifteen years later, gave confidence that the formula sought had been found.

II

We turn now to the main object of the present article—the drafting of an interim estimate of the value of the Heartland concept in a survey of the world preliminary to the coming settlement. It must be understood that I am dealing with strategy, which, of course, is effective in peacetime no less than in wartime. I do not presume to join in the wide-sweeping debates already in progress which look forward over generations to come; I center my thoughts on the years during which the enemy is to be held down while, in the language of Casablanca, his philosophy of war is being killed.

The Heartland is the northern part and the interior of Euro-Asia. It extends from the Arctic coast down to the central deserts, and has as its western limits the broad isthmus between the Baltic and Black Seas. The concept does not admit of precise definition on the map for the reason that it is based on three separate aspects of physical geography which, while reinforcing one another, are not exactly coincident. First of all, we have in this region by far the widest lowland plain on the face of the globe. Secondly, there flow across that plain some great navigable rivers; certain of them go north to the Arctic Sea and are inaccessible from the ocean because it is cumbered with ice, while others flow into inland waters, such as the Caspian, which have no exit to the ocean. Thirdly, there is here a grassland zone which, until within the last century and a half, presented ideal conditions for the development of high mobility by camel and horse-riding nomads. Of the three features mentioned, the river basins are the easiest to present cartographically; the water divide which delimits the whole group of Arctic and "continental" rivers into a single unit does isolate neatly on the map a vast coherent area which is the Heartland according to that particular criterion. The mere exclusion of sea mobility and sea power, however, is a negative if important differential; it was the plain and the grassland belt which offered the positive conditions conducive to the other type of mobility, that proper to the prairie. As for the grassland, it traverses the whole breadth of the plain but does not cover its entire surface. Notwithstanding these apparent discrepancies, the Heartland provides a sufficient physical basis for strategical thinking. To go further and to simplify geography artificially would be misleading.

For our present purpose it is sufficiently accurate to say that the territory of the U.S.S.R. is equivalent to the Heartland, except in one direction. In order to demarcate that exception—a great one—let us draw a direct line, some 5,500 miles long, westward from Bering Strait to Rumania. Three thousand miles from Bering Strait that line will cross the Yenisei River, flowing northward from the borders of Mongolia to the Arctic Ocean. Eastward of that great river lies a generally rugged country of mountains, plateaux and valleys, covered almost from end to end with coniferous forests; this I shall call Lenaland, from its central feature, the great River Lena. This is not included in Heartland Russia. Lenaland Russia has an area of three and three-quarter million square miles, but a population of only some six millions, of whom almost five millions are settled along the transcontinental railroad from Irkutsk to Vladivostok. In the remainder of this territory there are on the average over three square miles for every inhabitant. The rich natural resources—timber, water power and minerals—are as yet practically untouched.

West of the Yenisei lies what I have described as Heartland Russia, a plain extending 2,500 miles north and south, and 2,500 miles east and west. It contains four and a quarter million square miles and a population of more than 170 millions. The population is increasing at the rate of three millions a year.

The simplest and probably the most effective way of presenting the strategical values of the Russian Heartland is to compare them with those of France. In the case of France, however, the historical background is the First World War while in the case of Russia it is the Second World War.

France, like Russia, is a compact country, as long as it is broad, but not quite so well-rounded as the Heartland and therefore with a rather smaller area in proportion to the length of boundary to be defended. It is encompassed by sea and mountain, except to the northeast. In 1914–18 there were no hostile countries behind the Alps and the Pyrenees, and the fleets of France and her allies dominated the seas. The French and allied armies, deployed across the open northeastern frontier, were therefore well defended on either flank and were secure in the rear. The tragic lowland gateway in the northeast, through which so many armies have surged inward and outward, is 300 miles wide between the Vosges and the North Sea. In 1914, the line of battle, pivoting on the Vosges, wheeled backward to the Marne; and at the end of the war, in 1918, it wheeled forward on the same pivot. Through the four years' interval the elastic front sagged and bent but did not break even in the face of the great German attack in the spring of 1918. Thus, as it proved, there was space within the country sufficient both for defense in depth and for strategical retreat. Unfortunately for France, however, her principal industrial area was in that northeastern sector where the unceasing battle was waged.

Russia repeats in essentials the pattern of France, but on a greater scale and with her open frontier turned westward instead of northeastward. In the present war the Russian army is aligned across that open frontier. In its rear is the vast plain of the Heartland, available for defense in depth and for strategic retreat. Away back, this plain recedes eastward into the natural bulwarks constituted by the "inaccessible" Arctic coast, the Lenaland wilderness behind the Yenisei, and the fringe of mountains from the Altai to the Hindu Kush, backed by the Gobi, Tibetan and Iranian deserts. These three barriers have breadth and substance, and far excel in defensive value the coasts and mountains which engird France.

It is true that the Arctic shore is no longer inaccessible in the absolute sense that held until a few years ago. Convoys of merchant ships, assisted by powerful icebreakers and with airplanes reconnoitring ahead for water lanes through the ice pack, have traded to the Obi and Yenisei Rivers, and even to the Lena River; but a hostile invasion across the vast area of circum-polar ice and over the Tundra mosses and Targa forests of Northern Siberia seems almost impossible in the face of Soviet land-based air defense.

To complete the comparison between France and Russia, let us consider the relative scales of some parallel facts. Heartland Russia has four times the population, four times as wide an open frontier, and twenty times the area of France. That open frontier is not disproportionate to the Russian population; and to equal the breadth of the Soviet deployment Germany has had to eke out her more limited manpower by diluting it with less effective troops drawn from her subject countries. In one important respect, however, Russia began her second war with Germany in no better position than France occupied in 1914; as with France, her most developed agriculture and industries lay directly in the path of the invader. The second Five Year Plan would have remedied that situation had the German aggression been delayed a couple of years. Perhaps that was one of Hitler's reasons for breaking his treaty with Stalin in 1941.

The vast potentialities of the Heartland, however, to say nothing of the natural reserves in Lenaland, are strategically well placed. Industries are growing rapidly in such localities as the southern Urals, in the very pivot of the pivot area, and in the rich Kuznetsk coal basin in the lee of the great natural barriers east of the upper Yenisei River. In 1938 Russia produced more of the following foodstuffs than any other country in the world: wheat, barley, oats, rye and sugar beets. More manganese was produced in Russia than in any other country. It was bracketed with the United States in the first place as regards iron, and it stood second place in production of petroleum. As for coal, Mikhaylov makes the statement that the resources of the Kuznetsk and Krasnoyarsk coal basins are each estimated to be capable of supplying the requirements of the whole world for 300 years.[1] The policy of the Soviet Government was to balance imports and exports during the first Five Year Plan. Except in a very few commodities the country is capable of producing everything which it requires.

All things considered, the conclusion is unavoidable that if the Soviet Union emerges from this war as conqueror of Germany, she must rank as the greatest land Power on the

[1] N. Mikhaylov, "Soviet Geography." London: Methuen, 1937.

globe. Moreover, she will be the Power in the strategically strongest defensive position. The Heartland is the greatest natural fortress on earth. For the first time in history it is manned by a garrison sufficient both in number and quality.

III

I cannot pretend to exhaust the subject of the Heartland, the citadel of land power on the great mainland of the world, in a short article like this. But a few words should be devoted to another concept to balance it.

From Casablanca there came lately the call to destroy the ruling German philosophy. That can be done only by irrigating the German mind with the clean water of a rival philosophy. I assume that for, say, two years from the time the "cease fire" order is given, the Allies will occupy Berlin, try the criminals, fix frontiers on the spot and complete other surgical treatment so that the older generation in Germany which will die impenitent and bitter cannot again misrepresent history to the younger generation. But it would obviously be worse than useless to set alien teachers to work in Germany to inculcate the theory of freedom. Freedom cannot be taught; it can only be given to those who can use it. However, the polluted channel might be swept clear very effectively if it were controlled by strong embankments of power on either hand—land power to the east, in the Heartland, and sea power to the west, in the North Atlantic basin. Face the German mind with an enduring certainty that any war fought by Germany must be a war on two *unshakable* fronts, and the Germans themselves will solve the problem.

For this to happen it will be necessary in the first place that there be effective and lasting coöperation between

America, Britain and France, the first for depth of defense, the second as the moated forward stronghold—a Malta on a grander scale—and the third as the defensible bridgehead. The last is no less essential than the other two, because sea power must in the final resort be amphibious if it is to balance land power. In the second place, it is necessary that those three and the fourth conqueror, Russia, be pledged together to coöperate immediately if any breach of the peace is threatened, so that the devil in Germany can never again get its head up and must die by inanition.

Some persons today seem to dream of a global air power which will "liquidate" both fleets and armies. I am impressed, however, by the broad implications of a recent utterance of a practical airman: "Air power depends absolutely on the efficiency of its ground organization." That is too large a subject to discuss within the limits of this paper. It can only be said that no adequate proof has yet been presented that air fighting will not follow the long history of all kinds of warfare by presenting alternations of offensive and defensive tactical superiority, meanwhile effecting few permanent changes in strategical conditions.

I make no pretense to forecasting the future of humanity. What I am concerned with are the conditions under which we set about winning the peace when victory in the war has been achieved. In regard to the pattern of the postwar world, now being studied by many people for the first time, it is important that a line should be carefully drawn between idealistic blueprints and realistic and scholarly maps presenting concepts—political, economic, strategic, and so forth—based on the recognition of obstinate facts.

With that in mind, attention might be drawn to a great feature of global geography: a girdle, as it were, hung around the north polar regions. It begins as the Sahara desert, is followed as one moves eastward by the Arabian, Iranian, Tibetan and Mongolian deserts, and then extends, by way of the wildernesses of Lenaland, Alaska and the Laurentian shield of Canada, to the sub-arid belt of the western United States. That girdle of deserts and wildernesses is a feature of the first importance in global geography. Within it lie two related features of almost equal significance: the Heartland, and the basin of the Midland Ocean (North Atlantic) with its four subsidiaries (Mediterranean, Baltic, Arctic and Caribbean Seas). Outside the girdle is the Great Ocean (Pacific, Indian and South Atlantic) and the lands which drain to it (Asiatic Monsoon lands, Australia, South America and Africa south of the Sahara).

Archimedes said he could lift the world if he could find a fulcrum on which to rest his lever. All the world cannot be lifted back to prosperity at once. The region between the Missouri and the Yenisei, with its great trunk routes for merchant aircraft between Chicago-New York and London-Moscow, and all that the development of them will stand for, must be the first care, for it must be the fulcrum. Wisely the conquering of Japan waits for a while. In due course China will receive capital on a generous scale as a debt of honor, to help in her romantic adventure of building for a quarter of humanity a new civilization, neither quite Eastern nor quite Western. Then the ordering of the Outer World will be relatively easy, with China, the United States and the United Kingdom leading the way, the last two each followed by its trail of a commonwealth of free nations—for though their histories will have been different the result will be similar. But the first enterprise undertaken in economic rebuilding will surely have to be in the area within the desert girdle, lest a whole civilization should deliquesce into chaos. What a pity the alliance, negotiated after Versailles, between the United States, the United Kingdom and France was not implemented! What trouble and sadness that act might have saved!

IV

And now, to complete my picture of the pattern of the round world, let me add, briefly, three concepts to the two already visualized. For the purposes of what I see described in American writings as "Grand Strategy," it is necessary to build broad generalizations in geography no less than in history and economics.

I have described my concept of the Heartland, which I have no hesitation in saying is more valid and useful today than it was either twenty or forty years ago. I have said how it is set in its girdle of broad natural defenses—ice-clad Polar Sea, forested and rugged Lenaland, and Central Asiatic mountain and arid tableland. The girdle is incomplete, however, because of an open gateway, a thousand miles wide, admitting from Peninsular Europe into the interior plain through the broad isthmus between the Baltic and Black Seas. For the first time in all history there is within this vast natural fortress a garrison adequate to deny entry to the German invader. Given that fact, and the defenses to the flanks and rear which I have described, the sheer breadth of the open gateway is an advantage, for it provides the opportunity of defeating the enemy by compelling him to make a broad deployment of his manpower. And upon and beneath the Heartland there is a store of rich soil for cultivation and of ores and fuels for extraction, the equal—or thereabouts—of all that lies upon and beneath the United States and the Canadian Dominion.

I have suggested that a current of cleansing counter-philosophy, canalized between unbreachable embankments of power, may sweep the German mind clear of its black magic. Surely no one is going to be mad enough to set foreign teachers to exorcize the evil spirits from the soul of the conquered German nation. Nor, after the first inevita-

ble punitory years, do I have sufficient trust that the conquering democracies will maintain garrisons of the necessary spirit and number *stationed in the vanquished lands*;
for there is no use in asking democrats to persist in an attitude contrary to the very spirit and essence of democracy.
The cleansing stream might better be released to flow from
some regenerate and regenerating *German* source, between
the embankments of power I have named, the one within
the Heartland and the other within the territories of the
three amphibious powers, American, British and French.
The two friendly forces facing one another across the flow
of the canal would be of equal power and should always be
equally ready for necessary action. Then Germany would
live continuously under the threat of immediate war on
two fronts should she be guilty of any breach of the treaties
which prohibited either physical preparation for war or the
misleading of youth which is another way of preparation
for war. The democratic garrisons in their home countries
would be, by force of example, the teachers.

On this proposal follows my second geographical concept,
that of the Midland Ocean—the North Atlantic—and its
dependent seas and river basins. Without laboring the details of that concept, let me picture it again in its three elements—a bridgehead in France, a moated aerodrome in
Britain, and a reserve of trained manpower, agriculture
and industries in the eastern United States and Canada. So
far as war-potential goes, both the United States and Canada are Atlantic countries, and since instant land-warfare is
in view, both the bridgehead and the moated aerodrome
are essential to amphibious power.

The three remaining concepts I shall do little more than
sketch, and only for the sake of globular completeness and
balance. Girdling the twin unit just described—Heartland
and the basin of the Midland Ocean—there appears on the
globe the mantle of vacancies, constituting a practically

continuous land-space covering some twelve million square miles—that is, about a quarter of all the land on the globe. Upon this vast area there lives today a total population of less than thirty millions, or, say, one-seventieth of the population of the globe. Airplanes will, of course, fly along many routes over this girdle of wilderness; and through it will be driven trunk motor roads. But for long to come it will break social continuity between the major communities of mankind on the globe.[2]

The fourth of my concepts embraces on either side of the South Atlantic the tropical rain-forests of South America and Africa. If these were subdued to agriculture and inhabited with the present density of tropical Java, they might sustain a thousand million people, always provided that medicine had rendered the tropics as productive of human energy as the temperate zones.

Fifthly, and lastly, a thousand million people of ancient oriental civilization inhabit the Monsoon lands of India and China. They must grow to prosperity in the same years in which Germany and Japan are being tamed to civilization. They will then balance that other thousand million who live between the Missouri and the Yenisei. A balanced globe of human beings. And happy, because balanced and thus free.

[2] Some day, incidentally, when coal and oil are exhausted, the Sahara may become the trap for capturing direct power from the Sun.

Index

Index [1]

Actium, sea-battle of, 39, 58
Administrators, their function, 10
Ægean sea, 33-35
Afghan war, first, in 1839, 136
Air navigation, 64
Alexander, King of Macedonia, 35, 37-38, 51, 91
Alsatians, 126
America (North and South), 64-65
American conceptions opposed to policies of E. Europe, 203
Antony and Caesar, 58
Arabia, 76-77; reconquered by Britain for the Arabs, 109
Arabian tableland, 90
Archipelago, 33
Asia Minor, 105
Asia (Northern), the inaccessible coast, 73
Athenian fleet, 35
Athens and Florence, 198; teachers of the world, reasons cited, 189
Attila, leader of Huns, 97-98
Austria, assassination of Archduke Frank Ferdinand, 152;

German advance of in 18th Century, 130-131
Autocracy a "Going Concern," 146-147

Balkan Corridor, Germans given first steps towards, 137
Balkans, the, Austrian and Russian rivalry in, 132
Baltic, the, 43-44, 164; possibilities of preparing for war within, 173; possibility of closing by land-power, 109
Baltic and Mediterranean, the, seven non-German peoples between, 159-161; Russian bureaucracy recruited from Germans of, 131
Belt inhabited by settled plowmen, 91-92
Berlin, dammed-up flood of German man-power set free, 1914, 144
Berlin and Vienna occupy Slav territory of Middle Ages, 126
Berlin-Bagdad visualized on mental relief map, 21

[1] Refers to chapters 1 through 8 only.

INDEX

INDEX

INDEX

INDEX

THE NORTON LIBRARY